Math 5

Second Edition

bju press®

Greenville, South Carolina

This textbook was written by members of the faculty and staff of Bob Jones University. Standing for the "old-time religion" and the absolute authority of the Bible since 1927, Bob Jones University is the world's leading fundamental Christian university. The staff of the University is devoted to educating Christian men and women to be servants of Jesus Christ in all walks of life.

Providing unparalleled academic excellence, Bob Jones University prepares its students through its offering of over 120 majors, while its fervent spiritual emphasis prepares their minds and hearts for service and devotion to the Lord Jesus Christ.

▶ If you would like more information about the spiritual and academic opportunities available at Bob Jones University, please call *1-800-BJ-AND-ME (1-800-252-6363)*. *www.bju.edu*

Math 5
Second Edition

© 1995, 2009 BJU Press
Greenville, South Carolina 29614

ISBN: 978-1-59166-994-4

15 14 13 12 11 10 9 8 7 6 5 4 3 2 1

Contents

Becoming a Pilot

Man has always wanted to fly. Years and years were spent dreaming, studying the flight of birds, trying various inventions, risking and sometimes losing lives for the cause of human flight.

Now with the invention of airplanes, flight is possible for anyone. Many are not content just to ride in a plane while another flies it—they want to pilot a plane themselves. Are you one of these people? You can become a pilot someday—if you are willing to invest the time and money necessary for your training. The first step is to find a flight instructor to help you work toward a private pilot's license. Airports often offer flight instruction, and so do universities, colleges, and even some high schools. You must be at least sixteen to begin flight training, and seventeen to earn your license.

Pilot training begins with ground school. There you will learn the basic principles of flight, the parts of an airplane, and the controls and instruments in the cockpit. You must also have many hours of actual flight instruction with an official instructor. You will keep a log book of the time you spend in the air. The instructor will teach you how to take off and land safely, how to control the plane in the air, and how to navigate the plane using the instruments. You will always fly with your instructor at first, but after some practice and a medical exam, you will start flying solo flights. After you have completed 40 hours of flight time, you will be eligible to take a flight examination.

The flight exam has two parts: a multiple-choice written test and a checkride with an FAA examiner. If you pass both, you will be allowed to fly yourself and others as long as you do not charge them money for the flight. You will be a licensed private pilot.

CHAPTER

1

Place Value

◀ Before taking off on a cross-country flight, a pilot must locate checkpoints on the map and calculate flying time between them so that he can follow his progress and keep track of where he is throughout the flight.

◀ A flight instructor reviews the planned route of a cross-country solo flight with a student.

Place Value

Get ready to take off with math. As you learn about math this year, you will also be learning about air travel, from the Wright brothers to the Space Age. So, buckle up and sharpen your pencils . . . here we go!

Our place value system allows us to use just ten digits (0, 1, 2, 3, 4, 5, 6, 7, 8, and 9) to make any number. The value of a digit changes according to its place in the number. What is the value of each digit in this number?

Thousands			Ones		
Hundred Thousands	Ten Thousands	One Thousands	Hundreds	Tens	Ones
7	9	2	5	6	4

> The comma separates large numbers into periods.

Standard form shows the number in digits: 792,564

Expanded form shows the value of each digit:

$$700,000 + 90,000 + 2,000 + 500 + 60 + 4$$

Expanded form can be shown with multiplication:

$$(7 \times 100,000) + (9 \times 10,000) + (2 \times 1,000) + (5 \times 100) + (6 \times 10) + (4 \times 1)$$

Word form shows the number in words:

seven hundred ninety-two thousand, five hundred sixty-four

Rounding is a useful skill. Can you think of times you use rounding? This flow chart shows the steps for rounding a number to the nearest thousand.

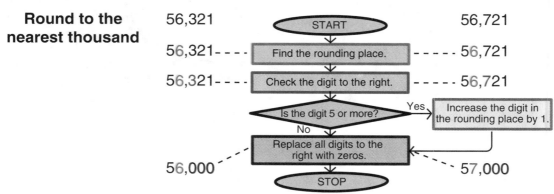

Round to the nearest thousand

Practice

Write the value of the 5 in each number.

Example: 35,893   *5,000*

1. 354,679   **2.** 512,677   **3.** 867,510

Write the place the 7 is in for each number.

Example: 392,723   *hundreds place*

4. 178,432   **5.** 617,058   **6.** 345,679

Write each number in standard form.

7. $400,000 + 30,000 + 2,000 + 5$

8. $(8 \times 100,000) + (4 \times 10,000) + (3 \times 1,000) + (7 \times 100) + (6 \times 1)$

Write each number in word form.

9. 256,110

10. 98,055

Write each number in expanded form.

11. 812,090

12. 52,619

Write each number using multiplication in the expanded form.

13. 21,403

14. 328,078

Round each number to the nearest ten and to the nearest hundred.

15. 5,647

16. 39,852

Round each number to the nearest one thousand, ten thousand, and hundred thousand.

17. 718,058

18. 682,101

Behold, the heaven and the heaven of heavens is the Lord's thy God, the earth also, with all that therein is.
Deuteronomy 10:14

Millions

The busiest airport in the world is Chicago International Airport (O'Hare Field). In one year, a total of 59,852,330 passengers flew into and out of this airport.

Millions			Thousands			Ones		
Hundred Millions	Ten Millions	One Millions	Hundred Thousands	Ten Thousands	One Thousands	Hundreds	Tens	Ones
5	9	8	5	2	3	3	0	

Standard form: 59,852,330

Expanded form:
50,000,000 + 9,000,000 + 800,000 + 50,000 + 2,000 + 300 + 30

Expanded form with multiplication:
$(5 \times 10,000,000) + (9 \times 1,000,000) + (8 \times 100,000) + (5 \times 10,000) +$
$(2 \times 1,000) + (3 \times 100) + (3 \times 10)$

Word form:
Fifty-nine million, eight hundred fifty-two thousand, three hundred thirty

Class Work

Write the number in the form that corresponds with the airport terminal.

Standard Form Terminal

1. 300,000,000 + 70,000,000
+ 500,000 + 6,000 + 40 + 2

Word Form Terminal

2. 321,476,805

Expanded Form Terminal

3. six hundred eighty-one million, five hundred forty thousand, fifty-seven

Expanded Form with Multiplication Terminal

4. 900,000,000 + 80,000,000 + 1,000,000
+ 500,000 + 20,000 + 50 + 7

Practice

962,058,431

Write the digit that is in each of the following places in the number above.

1. one millions
2. ones
3. ten millions

4. hundred millions
5. one thousands
6. hundred thousands

7. tens
8. hundreds
9. ten thousands

Write the value of the underlined digit in each number.

10. 568,<u>2</u>32,008
11. 72<u>1</u>,549,617

12. 340,000,2<u>9</u>9
13. <u>1</u>35,254,975

14. 3<u>4</u>9,926
15. <u>3</u>6,528,400

16. 825,654,90<u>2</u>
17. 4,65<u>9</u>,166

Write each number in the form indicated.

18. There were 48,198,208 passengers at Dallas/Ft. Worth Airport during one year. Write the number of passengers in expanded form.

19. Ten leading airlines carried a combined total of 418,712,000 passengers in one year. Write the number of passengers in word form.

20. A man flew a hot-air balloon to an altitude of 113,740 feet. Write the altitude in expanded form with multiplication.

21. King Khalid International Airport in Saudi Arabia covers fifty-five thousand, forty acres. Write the number of acres in standard form.

There are more than
100,000,000,000
stars in the Milky Way.

The population of
the earth is about
6,000,000,000.

By January 1994, McDonalds
had sold more than
95,000,000,000 hamburgers.

These numbers are so large they do not mean very much to us. Even one billion is hard to imagine. One billion is 1,000 millions. It is a 1 followed by 9 zeros. If you had one billion dollars and spent $1,000.00 an hour, you would spend—

$24,000.00 in one day,
$168,000.00 in one week,
$8,760,000.00 in one year,
$87,600,000.00 in ten years,
$876,000,000.00 in one hundred years, and
$1,007,400,000.00 in one hundred fifteen years.

Is there a "largest number"? We can say that the set of numbers is infinite because there is no end to it. Have you ever heard that God loves you with an infinite love? What does that mean?

Class Work

Write each number in the form indicated.

1. **standard form:** nine hundred sixty-eight billion, four hundred three million, seventy-one thousand, one hundred nine

2. **expanded form with multiplication:** 67,052,415,002

Practice

Billions			Millions			Thousands			Ones		
Hundred Billions	Ten Billions	One Billions	Hundred Millions	Ten Millions	One Millions	Hundred Thousands	Ten Thousands	One Thousands	Hundreds	Tens	Ones
5	7	8,	4	0	6,	0	1	9,	3	2	0

Use the number on the chart to write the value of each digit.

1. 2   2. 9   3. 5

4. 6   5. 1   6. 4

7. 7   8. 8   9. 3

In 1991, the United States government borrowed $268,729,000,000. Write the amount in—

10. expanded form

11. word form

Write four hundred one billion, five hundred twelve million, three hundred fifty-eight in—

12. standard form   13. expanded form with multiplication

Write the place the 4 is in for each number.

14. 807,643,915   15. 476,153,902   16. 1,400,829

Did you know . . .

A 1 followed by 100 zeros is called a *googol*.
A 1 with a googol of zeros after it is called
a *googolplex*. Is a googolplex the largest number
there is? Is a googolplex plus one larger?

Comparing and Ordering Numbers

Steps for Comparing Numbers

1. Compare the number of digits. If they have a different number of digits, the number with more digits is the greater number. If they have the same number of digits, go to Step 2.

2. Compare the digits that have the highest place value. If the digits are different, the number with the digit of greater value is the greater number. If the digits are the same, go to Step 3.

3. Continue comparing the digits for each place value until you come to digits that are different. The number with the digit of greater value is the greater number.

In 1949, Captain James Gallagher flew around the world, taking off from Fort Worth, Texas, and landing there four days later. He traveled 23,452 miles.

In 1986, Richard Rutan and Jeanna Yeager flew around the world in nine days. They took off from and landed at Edwards Air Force Base in California. They traveled 24,986 miles.

Follow the steps to find which was the longer flight.

1. Each number has five digits. Go to Step 2.	23,452	24,986
2. Both digits in the ten thousands place are 2. Go to Step 3.	23,452	24,986
3. 4,000 > 3,000, so 24,986 is greater. Rutan and Yeager's flight was longer.	23,452	24,986

Practice

Complete the number sentences using a >, <, or =.

1. 728 ☐ 549

2. 1,509 ☐ 958

3. 7,862,438 ☐ 988,706

4. 662,138 ☐ 662,138

5. 32,867 ☐ 132,298

6. 258,310,658 ☐ 258,687,212

7. 49,187,629 ☐ 9,329,657

8. 3,982 ☐ 3,988

9. 662,138 ☐ 600,000 + 60,000 +2,000 + 100 + 30 + 8

10. 4,064,291 ☐ four million, sixty-five thousand, two hundred ninety-one

11. 180,476,003 ☐ $(1 \times 100,000,000) + (1 \times 10,000,000) + (4 \times 100,000) + (7 \times 10,000) + (5 \times 1,000) + (3 \times 1)$

Make the greatest possible number using each group of digits.

12. 58421

13. 1852962

14. 408278953

Application

Order the number of airline passengers in each table from least to greatest.

15.

Airline	Passengers in 1991
TransWorld	20,523,000
Midway	4,314,000
Aloha	4,915,000
America West	16,844,000

16.

Airline	Passengers in 1991
Delta	74,125,000
United	61,891,000
Southwest	25,211,000
American	75,892,000

Use both tables to answer the questions.

17. Which of the eight airlines carried the fewest passengers?

18. Which of the eight airlines carried the most passengers?

Roman Numerals

I = 1	V = 5	X = 10	L = 50	C = 100	D = 500	M = 1,000

If I is on the left of V or X, subtract.   IX = 10 – 1 = 9
If I is on the right of V or X, add.   XI = 10 + 1 = 11

If X is on the left of L or C, subtract.   XL = 50 – 10 = 40
If X is on the right of L or C, add.   LX = 50 + 10 = 60

If C is on the left of D or M, subtract.   CM = 1,000 – 100 = 900
If C is on the right of D or M, add.   MC = 1,000 + 100 = 1,100

CMLXVI

$(1,000 - 100) + (50 + 10) + (5 + 1)$

$900 + 60 + 6$

966

Practice

Write the standard number for each of the Roman numerals.

1. DVI
2. XLVII
3. CLXXX
4. MMDCXLV

5. CCCXII
6. MXV
7. XVIII
8. CMXCI

Write the Roman numerals for each standard number.

9. 308
10. 120
11. 1,652
12. 1,987

13. 93
14. 17
15. 529
16. 2,792

Logic

Practice

Follow the steps to solve the problems.

1. Which boy owns each dog?

1. The boys are Andrew, Bob, and Chris.
2. The dogs are Arnold, Butch, and Curly.
3. Each boy's name starts with a different letter than his dog's name.
4. Andrew's dog likes to play with Bob's dog.
5. Bob's dog is Curly.
6. Curly and Arnold fight when they are together.
7. Bob's dog fights with Arnold.
8. Butch is a basset hound.
9. Andrew owns a basset hound.

2. What number am I?

I am a seven-digit number. My one thousands digit is 8. My ones digit is three less than my one thousands digit. The sum of my tens digit and my ones digit is nine. My hundred thousands digit is the difference between my one thousands digit and my ones digit. My one millions digit is the difference between my one thousands digit and my tens digit. My ten thousands digit is the sum of my hundred thousands digit and my one millions digit. The sum of my seven digits is 40.

3. What is the order of the buildings?

The library, fire station, service station, and restaurant are all in a row. The restaurant is not first. The service station is between the library and fire station. The library is between the restaurant and the service station.

Airplane Pilot

Dear Fifth Grade:

I'm excited about this class project! I know you'll find out how important math is to many different careers. I do a lot of cross-country flying. It's quite a feeling, soaring above the fields and houses and rivers. I like to keep an eye on the ground so I don't miss all the beautiful sights I'm passing over. There's an important math concept to keep in mind too. When I leave for a cross-country flight, I need to know how long it will take me to reach my destination or my next fuel station; otherwise, I could get lost or run out of fuel! I pick out particular landmarks, or checkpoints, along the way and have the flight computer figure out how long it will take me to get from point to point.

Let's say the computer tells me that it should take about twenty minutes to get to my first checkpoint, the county water tower, at an air speed of 120 miles per hour. If I'm early or just a few minutes late, I know I'm doing fine. But if fifteen minutes pass from the time I should have arrived at the checkpoint, it's time to get concerned. I might have gotten off course and be heading in the wrong direction!

I keep a log of the times I am scheduled to reach each checkpoint and the times that I actually reach them. When I've completed my flight, I add up all my actual arrivals at each checkpoint to figure out the total duration of the flight.

Sincerely,

Chris Hernandez

Chris Hernandez

Buckeye
Aviation
1155 Gwendolynn Drive · Battle Creek, MI 49016

Moore Christian School
334 Tara Lane
Mariposa, CA 95338

USA 22

Write each number in standard form.

1. 900,000,000,000 + 70,000,000,000 + 8,000,000,000 + 60,000,000 + 4,000,000 + 600,000 + 80,000 + 2,000 + 400 + 9

2. three hundred eighteen billion, forty-two million, nine hundred nine thousand, three hundred seventy-five

Write each number in expanded form.

3. 429,628,018

4. three hundred twenty thousand, forty

Write each number using multiplication in the expanded form.

5. 923,253,067

6. seven hundred eighty-nine thousand, six hundred forty-one

Write each number in word form.

7. 600,000,000,000 + 500,000,000 + 2,000,000 + 30,000 + 8,000 + 900 + 20 + 8

8. 3,689,015

Write the place the 8 is in for each number.

9. 768,309   10. 804,765,392   11. 761,384,026,511

Write the value of the 4 in each number.

12. 628,451,612,009

13. 487,029,558,712

14. 72,429

Round each number to the nearest ten and to the nearest hundred.

15. 72,131

16. 63,475

Round each number to the nearest one thousand, ten thousand, and hundred thousand.

17. 76,543,576

18. 319,567,281

Complete the number sentences using a >, <, or =.

19. 15,435 ☐ 150,435

20. 408,628,421 ☐ 406,958,502

21. 7,640,510 ☐ seven million, six hundred forty thousand, five hundred ten

22. 965,201 ☐ 900,000 + 60,000 + 6,000 + 20 + 1

23. 205,006,349 ☐ (2 × 100,000,000) + (5 × 100,000) + (3 × 1,000) + (6 × 100) + (4 × 10) + (9 × 1)

Order the numbers from least to greatest.

24. 4,000,050   67,432,108   4,000,005   68,529,258

25. 72,456,805   72,456   9,989   372,456,628

Use the chart to answer the problems.

26. Write the population of China in expanded form.

27. Write the population of Poland in word form.

28. Order the populations from least to greatest.

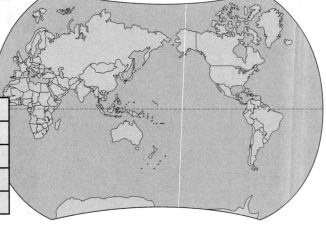

Projected Populations (year 2000)

Country	Population
China	1,303,342,000
India	1,018,092,000
Poland	38,889,000
United States	268,266,000

Write the letter of the correct answer.

1. What is the standard form for $(6 \times 100{,}000) + (3 \times 1{,}000) + (8 \times 100)$?

   a. 603,008   c. 603,080
   b. 603,800   d. 630,008

2. Round 5,465,389 to the nearest ten thousand.

   a. 5,460,000   c. 5,470,000
   b. 5,500,000   d. not given

3. Which sign will make the sentence true?
   6,803,431 ◯ 6,803,613

   a. >   c. =
   b. <   d. not given

4. What is the word form for $(8 \times 100{,}000) + (7 \times 10)$?

   a. eight hundred thousand, seventy
   b. eight hundred thousand, seven
   c. eight hundred seventy thousand
   d. not given

5. What is the value of the 3 in 738,167,421?

   a. 3,000
   b. 3,000,000
   c. 30,000,000
   d. 300,000,000

6. The numbers in the box are ordered least to greatest. Which number is missing?

   a. 7,459,273
   b. 7,582,731
   c. 9,507,302
   d. 9,587,375

   | 7,381,460 |
   | 7,592,731 |
   | ▬ |
   | 9,577,730 |

7. What is the expanded form for three hundred thousand, sixty-one?

   a. $300{,}000 + 600 + 1$
   b. $3{,}000{,}000 + 60 + 1$
   c. $300{,}000{,}000 + 60 + 1$
   d. not given

8. Which of the forms below represents the number 72,302,080?

   a. $70{,}000{,}000 + 2{,}000{,}000 + 300{,}000 + 2{,}000 + 80$
   b. seventy-two million, three hundred two thousand, eighty
   c. $(7 \times 10{,}000{,}000) + (2 \times 1{,}000{,}000) + (3 \times 100{,}000) + (2 \times 1{,}000) + (8 \times 10)$
   d. all of the above

Cloud Types and Turbulence

Clouds are the beauty of the daytime sky, yet they can be a pilot's worst enemy. Clouds fall into three categories based on their appearance. Cumulus clouds are the fluffy white heap clouds that are often present during clear weather. Cirrus clouds are thin and feathery, and they are made up of ice crystals. Stratus clouds collect in layers and are dull gray and thin like a sheet stretched across the sky. Rain clouds are called nimbus clouds. They usually have ragged edges or streaks extending downward that mean rain or snow is falling from them.

The name for a type of cloud is based not only on its appearance but also on its position in the sky. Clouds at the highest levels are cirrus, cirrocumulus, and cirrostratus. In the middle levels are altocumulus and altostratus. And at the lowest levels are stratus, stratocumulus, and nimbostratus. Cumulus and cumulonimbus clouds are often very tall and stretch over several different levels.

Clouds are an indication of air turbulence for pilots. The worst of the "rough air" is found inside the clouds and can be avoided by flying above or around them. Even cumulus clouds, although they look harmless, carry dangerous updrafts and downdrafts that can push a plane in all directions. As part of their training, pilots study the clouds so they will be able to know what to expect from them.

Addition and Subtraction

An RF-101C Voodoo reconnaissance aircraft flies high above scattered cumulus clouds. Clouds like these indicate light-to-moderate turbulence for the pilot flying in or around them.

Addition Properties

You know that addition is used to find the total number when two or more sets are joined together. What are the numbers representing the sets that are joined called? What is the resulting set called?

$$4 \quad + \quad 9 \quad + \quad 5 \quad = \quad 18$$

addend   addend   addend   sum

We use properties (principles) to help us solve problems.

Commutative Property of Addition (Order Principle)
The order of addends can be changed without changing the sum.

4 + 6 = 10   6 + 4 = 10

Associative Property of Addition (Grouping Principle)
The grouping of addends can be changed without changing the sum.

(3 + 5) + 5   3 + (5 + 5)

8 + 5 = 13   3 + 10 = 13

Identity Property of Addition (Zero Principle)
When 0 is an addend, the sum is the other addend.

7 + 0 = 7

Practice

Write only the answer for each fact.

1. $4 + 5 =$ 2. $7 + 6 =$ 3. $9 + 5 =$ 4. $8 + 2 =$ 5. $5 + 7 =$

6. $4 + 3 =$ 7. $9 + 7 =$ 8. $6 + 3 =$ 9. $5 + 8 =$ 10. $3 + 2 =$

11. $0 + 7 =$ 12. $2 + 9 =$ 13. $6 + 8 =$ 14. $4 + 7 =$ 15. $8 + 9 =$

Write another equation using the Commutative Property. Solve.

Example: $3 + 7 =$ $7 + 3 = 10$

16. $3 + 8 =$ 17. $4 + 0 =$ 18. $5 + 2 =$ 19. $6 + 8 =$

Write another equation using the Associative Property. Solve.

Example: $5 + (3 + 4) =$ $(5 + 3) + 4 = 12$

20. $(3 + 6) + 7 =$ 21. $4 + (8 + 2) =$ 22. $5 + (3 + 9) =$ 23. $(6 + 2) + 9 =$

Write Commutative, Associative, or Identity for each equation.

24. $3 + 4 = 4 + 3$ 25. $0 + 9 = 9$ 26. $(3 + 2) + 5 = 3 + (2 + 5)$

27. $2 + (8 + 1) = (2 + 8) + 1$ 28. $3 + 9 = 9 + 3$ 29. $5 + 0 = 5$

Mental Math: Write only the answer for each problem.

30.	31.	32.	33.	34.
6	7	9	3	8
5	2	7	1	8
$+\,5$	$+\,6$	$+\,3$	5	2
			$+\,6$	$+\,5$

Application

Write an equation for the word problem. Solve and label.

35. Derek read Psalms 11, 12, and 13. Psalm 11 has 7 verses, Psalm 12 has 8 verses, and Psalm 13 has 6 verses. How many verses did Derek read altogether?

Write a word problem for the equation. Solve and label. 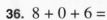 Idea: dogs, fish, flowers

36. $8 + 0 + 6 =$

Subtraction

We use subtraction in four different situations. What are the numbers in a subtraction problem called?

$$17 \quad - \quad 8 \quad = \quad 9$$

minuend   subtrahend   difference

Take Away
You want to find out how much is left after some have been removed from a set.

Joseph had 17 model airplanes. His little brother broke 8 of the airplanes. How many airplanes does Joseph have now?

$17 - 8 = 9$ airplanes

Comparing
You want to find out how many more (or fewer) one set has than another set.

Joseph has 17 model airplanes. Joshua has 8. How many more does Joseph have than Joshua?

$17 - 8 = 9$ airplanes

Missing Addend
You want to find out how many are needed.

Joshua needs 17 model airplanes to complete his collection. He has 8 airplanes. How many more airplanes does he need?

$8 + n = 17$ $17 - 8 = 9$ airplanes

Unknown Part
You want to find the other part of a set that has been separated into two parts.

Joseph has 17 model airplanes. He has 8 models of commercial airplanes. The rest are military airplanes. How many military airplanes does Joseph have?

$17 - 8 = 9$ military airplanes

Practice

Write only the answer for each fact.

1. $9 - 0 =$ 2. $5 - 4 =$ 3. $18 - 9 =$ 4. $16 - 9 =$ 5. $14 - 8 =$

6. $\begin{array}{r} 10 \\ -\ 7 \\ \hline \end{array}$ 7. $\begin{array}{r} 7 \\ -\ 7 \\ \hline \end{array}$ 8. $\begin{array}{r} 8 \\ -\ 5 \\ \hline \end{array}$ 9. $\begin{array}{r} 11 \\ -\ 7 \\ \hline \end{array}$ 10. $\begin{array}{r} 6 \\ -\ 4 \\ \hline \end{array}$

Application

Write *take away, comparing, missing addend,* or *unknown part* for each word problem. Write an equation for the word problem. Solve and label.

11. Margie needs $15.00 for a gift for her mother. She has saved $6.00. How much more money does Margie need to save?

12. Emilio sold 14 boxes of candy for the school fund raiser. Maryann sold 8 boxes. How many more boxes did Emilio sell than Maryann?

13. Mrs. Johnson has 15 grandchildren. She has 7 granddaughters. How many grandsons does she have?

14. Sue Ellen had 13 stuffed animals. She donated 4 of them to her mother's yard sale. How many stuffed animals does she have now?

Using the equation 12 – 7 = ?, write a different word problem for each type of subtraction.

 Ideas: vacations, suitcases, food

15. take away

16. comparing

17. missing addend

18. unknown part

Fact Families

You have used addition/subtraction fact families before. The fact family shows a relationship between addition and subtraction. Usually 4 equations can be made from each family, but some fact families have only two equations.

Four equations can be made from the fact family $\boxed{4 \ 6 \ 10}$.

two addition equations	two subtraction equations
$4 + 6 = 10$	$10 - 6 = 4$
$6 + 4 = 10$	$10 - 4 = 6$

Two equations can be made from the fact family $\boxed{4 \ 4 \ 8}$.

one addition equation	one subtraction equation
$4 + 4 = 8$	$8 - 4 = 4$

Finding the Missing Number

1. For a *missing addend,* subtract.
   Anna has made 5 pies. She needs to make 11 pies in all. How many more pies does Anna need to make?

   $5 + n = 11$
   $n = 11 - 5$
   $n = 6$ pies

2. For a *missing subtrahend,* subtract.
   Anna made 14 cookies. Her cousin Scott ate some of the cookies. There are 9 cookies left. How many cookies did Scott eat?

   $14 - n = 9$
   $n = 14 - 9$
   $n = 5$ cookies

3. For a *missing minuend,* add.
   Mrs. Newton made some cinnamon rolls. Eight were eaten and 9 are left. How many rolls did she make in all?

   $n - 8 = 9$
   $n = 9 + 8$
   $n = 17$ rolls

Practice

Write the addition and subtraction facts for each fact family.

1. 5 7 12   **2.** 3 6 9   **3.** 5 5 10

Copy each equation. Write another equation to find the missing number. Solve for _n_.

4. $4 + n = 11$ **5.** $8 - n = 3$ **6.** $12 - n = 7$

7. $n - 9 = 3$ **8.** $n + 5 = 9$ **9.** $n - 9 = 8$

Application

Write an equation showing the missing number as _n_ for each word problem.
Write another equation to find the missing number. Solve for _n_. Label the answer.

10. Mandy has flown 5 hours this week. She needs to log a total of 9 hours for the week. How many more hours does she need to fly?

11. Janice had 14 dolls. She gave some of them to her younger sister. She has 8 dolls left. How many did she give away?

12. Cynthia broke 7 of her colored pencils. She has 8 pencils left unbroken. How many pencils did she have before any were broken?

13. Mom had 17 cookies. John ate some of them. There are 9 left. How many cookies did John eat?

Language Link

14. Explain why some fact families have only two equations. Include an example in your explanation.

Estimating

We use estimating to find an *approximate* answer. You have learned two types of estimation: *rounding* and *front-end*.

Steps for Estimating the Sum of an Addition Problem by Rounding

1. Find the rounding place.
2. Look at the digit to the right of the rounding place. If the digit to the right is 5 or greater, increase the rounding place by 1. If the digit to the right is less than 5, the rounding place does not change.

	Estimate	Solve
437 ⟶	400	1 1
+264 ⟶	+300	437
	700 ⟷	+264
		701

Steps for Estimating the Sum of an Addition Problem by Front-end Estimation with Adjustment

1. Add the front digits.
2. For a more accurate estimate, add the digits in the next place; rename if necessary.
3. Annex the zeros.

Step 1	Step 2	Step 3	Solve
437	4 37	437	1 1
+ 264	+2 64	+264	437
6	69	690 ⟷	+264
			701

			1 1
586	5 86	586	586
+ 277	+2 77	+277	+277
7	7	850 ⟷	863
	85		

Class Work

Use front-end (with adjustment) or rounding to estimate. Write only the estimate and the type of estimation you used.

1. 324
    +283

2. 462
    +391

3. 704
    +129

4. 656
    +389

Practice

Use rounding to estimate the sums. Solve.

Example: 718
$\underline{+205}$

900 $\overset{1}{7}18$
$\underline{+205}$
923

1. 328
$\underline{+474}$

2. 628
$\underline{+185}$

3. 539
$\underline{+406}$

4. 41
$\underline{+19}$

Use front-end estimation (with adjustment) to estimate the sums. Solve.

Example: 528
$\underline{+396}$

910 $\overset{1\;1}{5}28$
$\underline{+396}$
924

5. 273
$\underline{+426}$

6. 345
$\underline{+678}$

7. 301
$\underline{+459}$

8. 482
$\underline{+263}$

Use front-end estimation (with adjustment) or rounding to estimate the sums. Solve.

9. 643
$\underline{+104}$

10. 725
$\underline{+186}$

11. 29
$\underline{+38}$

12. 486
$\underline{+274}$

Application

Write an addition word problem using any two items from the menu. Write an equation for the word problem. Solve and label.

13.

Menu	
Hamburger	$1.69
French fries	$1.10
Salad	$0.99
Milk	$0.65
Soft drink	$0.95

Language Link

14. Which type of estimation do you like better? Why?

Compensation

Compensation means to "make up for" something. We use compensation in math to make it easier for us to solve addition problems mentally.

> ### Steps for Compensating in an Addition Problem
>
> 1. Add to change one of the addends to a number that is easier to use.
> 2. Add.
> 3. Subtract the same number from the sum that you added to the addend.

Edward rode his bike 37 miles in June and 26 miles in July. How many miles did Edward ride during the two months?

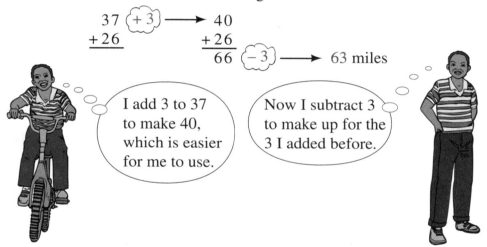

$$37 \, (+3) \longrightarrow 40$$
$$+26 \qquad\qquad +26$$
$$\qquad\qquad\qquad 66 \, (-3) \longrightarrow 63 \text{ miles}$$

I add 3 to 37 to make 40, which is easier for me to use.

Now I subtract 3 to make up for the 3 I added before.

You can change either addend to make the problem easier for you to solve.

$$37 \qquad\qquad 37$$
$$+26 \, (+4) \longrightarrow +30$$
$$\qquad\qquad\qquad 67 \, (-4) \longrightarrow 63 \text{ miles}$$

Class Work

Mental Math: Add using compensation.

1. 497 +256	**2.** $0.34 +0.29	**3.** $1.25 +1.96	**4.** 86 +18	**5.** $3.59 +2.03

Practice

Mental Math: Add using compensation. Write only the answers.

| 1. 48
+15 | 2. 115
+ 76 | 3. $1.99
+1.35 | 4. 463
+198 | 5. $3.97
+2.06 |

Solve.

| 6. 123
492
+321 | 7. $0.99
5.37
+2.03 | 8. 604
59
+217 | 9. 45
69
84
+195 | 10. 73
52
107
+329 |

| 11. 430
219
+ 45 | 12. $0.73
0.14
+3.09 | 13. 50
32
187
+215 | 14. 99
105
33
+587 | 15. $0.16
0.67
0.09
+0.17 |

Language Link

16. Write a letter to a friend describing how compensation works. Include an addition example.

Did you know . . .

As early as 3000 B.C., the Babylonians, the Chinese, and the Egyptians developed written symbols to represent numbers. They also knew simple arithmetic. The great Egyptian pyramids built about 2500 B.C. required careful mathematical measurements.

Adding Larger Numbers

Remember the steps for estimating by rounding. You will use the same steps for larger numbers.

> 1. Find the rounding place.
> 2. Look at the digit to the right of the rounding place. If the digit to the right is 5 or greater, increase the rounding place by 1. If the digit to the right is less than 5, the rounding place does not change.
> 3. Annex zeros.

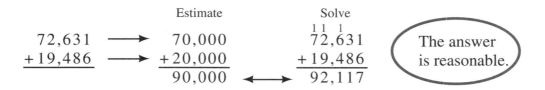

	Estimate	Solve	
72,631	→ 70,000	1 1 1 72,631	The answer
+ 19,486	→ + 20,000	+ 19,486	is reasonable.
	90,000 ↔	92,117	

> **Steps for Estimating the Sum of an Addition Problem by Front-end Estimation with Adjustment**
>
> 1. Find the front digits.
> 2. For a more accurate estimate, add the digits in the next place; rename if necessary.
> 3. Annex zeros.

Step 1	Step 2	Step 3	Solve	
7 2,631	72 ,631	72,631	1 1 1 72,631	The answer
+ 1 9,486	+ 19 ,486	+ 19,486	+ 19,486	is reasonable.
8	8 91	91,000	92,117	

Class Work

Use front-end estimation (with adjustment) or rounding to estimate the sums.

1. 437,821
   + 208,911

2. 77,326
   + 15,701

3. 146,218
   + 350,913

Practice

Estimate the sums. Write only the estimate and the type of estimation you used.

1. 165,294
    + 387,275

2. 4,029
    + 3,651

3. 245
    + 462

4. 77,884
    + 11,968

Estimate the combined population of these cities. Write the type of estimation you used. Solve. Is your answer reasonable?

5. Hemet, California—36,094
    Wahiawa, Hawaii—17,386

6. Brunswick, Ohio—28,230
    Chesterfield, Missouri—37,990

Solve.

7. 387,591
    + 291,862

8. 706,334
    + 159,782

9. 221,486
    + 649,071

10. 18,005
    + 12,986

11. 406,309
    + 271,564

12. 348,671
    + 129,763

13. 846,721
    + 52,065

14. 76,240
    + 58,030

Savers Mart Spring Sale!

lawn mower	$128.50	boys' pants	$12.75
vacuum cleaner	$219.35	girls' skirts	$9.48
portable dishwasher	$386.20	pajamas	$7.30
electric mixer	$29.80	hair bows	$4.29

Application

Write a word problem using the information on the sign. Write an equation for the word problem. Solve and label.

15. Use two of the items on the sign.

16. Use three of the items on the sign.

Estimation and Compensation

Steps for Estimating the Difference in a Subtraction Problem by Rounding

1. Find the rounding place.
2. Look at the digit to the right of the rounding place. If the digit to the right is 5 or more, increase the rounding place by 1. If the digit to the right is less than 5, the rounding place stays the same.
3. Annex zeros.

$$
\begin{array}{r} 4\widehat{2}3 \\ -\,2\widehat{8}6 \\ \hline \end{array}
\longrightarrow
\begin{array}{r} 400 \\ -\,300 \\ \hline 100 \end{array}
$$

Solve
$$
\begin{array}{r} {\scriptstyle 3\ \overset{11}{\cancel{1}}\ 13} \\ \cancel{423} \\ -\,286 \\ \hline 137 \end{array}
$$

The answer is reasonable.

Steps for Estimating the Difference in a Subtraction Problem by Front-end Estimation with Adjustment

1. Subtract the front digits.
2. For a more accurate estimate, subtract the digits in the next place; rename if necessary.
3. Annex zeros.

Step 1	Step 2	Step 3	Solve
$\begin{array}{r}726\\-374\\\hline 4\end{array}$	$\begin{array}{r}726\\-374\\\hline \cancel{4}\\35\end{array}$	$\begin{array}{r}726\\-374\\\hline 350\end{array}$	$\begin{array}{r}{\scriptstyle 6\ 12}\\ \cancel{726}\\-374\\\hline 352\end{array}$

The answer is reasonable.

Remember that compensation means to make up for something. We can use compensation to make subtraction problems easier to solve mentally.

Steps for Compensating in a Subtraction Problem

1. Add to change the subtrahend (second number) to a number that is easier to use.
2. Add the same amount to the minuend (first number).
3. Subtract.

Follow the steps to subtract using compensation.

Step 1
$$
\begin{array}{r} 64 \\ -27\ \ (+3) \\ \hline \end{array}
$$

Step 2
$$
\begin{array}{r} 64\ \ (+3) \\ -30 \\ \hline \end{array}
$$

Step 3
$$
\begin{array}{r} 67 \\ -30 \\ \hline 37 \end{array}
$$

Practice

Use rounding to estimate the differences. Solve.

1.
$$
\begin{array}{r}
374 \\
-226 \\
\hline
\end{array}
$$

2.
$$
\begin{array}{r}
407 \\
-381 \\
\hline
\end{array}
$$

3.
$$
\begin{array}{r}
\$8.78 \\
-4.35 \\
\hline
\end{array}
$$

Use front-end estimation (with adjustment) to estimate the differences. Solve.

4.
$$
\begin{array}{r}
682 \\
-518 \\
\hline
\end{array}
$$

5.
$$
\begin{array}{r}
739 \\
-266 \\
\hline
\end{array}
$$

6.
$$
\begin{array}{r}
403 \\
-215 \\
\hline
\end{array}
$$

Use rounding or front-end estimation to estimate the differences. Solve.

7.
$$
\begin{array}{r}
313 \\
-227 \\
\hline
\end{array}
$$

8.
$$
\begin{array}{r}
\$4.58 \\
-3.97 \\
\hline
\end{array}
$$

9.
$$
\begin{array}{r}
181 \\
-165 \\
\hline
\end{array}
$$

Mental Math: Subtract using compensation. Write only the answers.

10.
$$
\begin{array}{r}
86 \\
-47 \\
\hline
\end{array}
$$

11.
$$
\begin{array}{r}
72 \\
-16 \\
\hline
\end{array}
$$

12.
$$
\begin{array}{r}
84 \\
-29 \\
\hline
\end{array}
$$

13.
$$
\begin{array}{r}
62 \\
-36 \\
\hline
\end{array}
$$

Application

Write an equation for each word problem. Solve and label.

14. The Smiths are missionaries on deputation. They traveled 321 miles the first week and 275 miles the second week. How many miles did they travel during those two weeks?

15. How many more miles did the Smiths travel the first week than the second week?

16. Robert wants to make a list of chapters in the New Testament to keep track of his reading. He found that there are 260 chapters in the New Testament. Eighty-nine of them are in the Gospels. How many are in the rest of the New Testament?

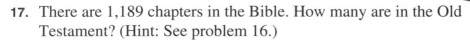

17. There are 1,189 chapters in the Bible. How many are in the Old Testament? (Hint: See problem 16.)

Subtracting with Larger Numbers

Remember: Subtraction is used in four different situations.

Take Away

You want to find out how much is left after some have been removed from a set.

Comparing

You want to find out how many more (or fewer) one set has than another.

Missing Addend

You want to find out how many are needed.

Unknown Part

You want to find the other part of a set that has been separated into two parts.

Class Work

Write *take away, comparing, missing addend,* or *unknown part* for each word problem. Write an equation for each word problem. Solve and label.

1. Maria Lyle has saved $235.79 from her part-time job to take on vacation. She has put $123.84 in a savings account. The rest of the money is in a checking account. How much is in the checking account?

2. A trip to London, England, for 5 days would cost $6,932.37 with hotel accommodations in London. If the family stays at a bed and breakfast inn outside of London, the cost will be $5,331.97. How much will Dr. Lyle save if they stay at the inn rather than at the hotel?

3. Corey Lyle wants the family to travel around Europe. Airplane tickets, hotel accommodations, food, and train passes will cost $9,875.00 for a 2-week vacation. Dr. Lyle has saved $5,769.00 for the vacation. How much more money does he need to save before he can afford the trip?

4. Dr. Lyle purchased 4 airplane tickets for $3,407.00. How much money does Dr. Lyle have left from the $9,875 he planned for the airplane tickets, hotel accommodations, food, and train passes?

Practice

Use rounding or front-end estimation to estimate the difference. Write the type of estimation you used. Solve.

1. 3,967
  − 2,041

2. 73,658
  − 37,210

3. 479,631
  − 158,024

4. 38,609
  − 13,897

5. 47,681
  − 29,384

6. 9,645
  − 7,201

7. 17,554
  − 9,381

8. 63,429
  − 56,242

Application

Write *take away, comparing, missing addend,* or *unknown part* for each word problem. Write an equation for each word problem. Solve and label.

9. Mount McKinley's height is 20,320 feet. Mount Rainier is 14,410 feet high. How much higher is Mount McKinley than Mount Rainier?

10. Mark would like to have 150 customers on his paper route. He currently has 112 customers. How many more customers does Mark need to meet his goal?

11. Lorraine had $735.92 in a savings account. She withdrew $250.00 to buy savings bonds. How much is left in Lorraine's account?

12. At Centerville Christian School, there are 427 elementary students. Two hundred eighty-five of the students are boys. How many students are girls?

13. Theresa has saved $112.78 for summer camp. She needs to save $150.50 in all. How much more does she need to save?

Mount McKinley in central Alaska

Subtracting with Zeros

10,000 − 3,267 =   You must rename 10,000 to subtract. Follow the steps on the abacuses.

1. Put on the minuend (first number).

2. Rename 10,000 as 9 thousands, 10 hundreds.

3. Rename 10 hundreds as 9 hundreds, 10 tens.

4. Rename 10 tens as 9 tens, 10 ones.

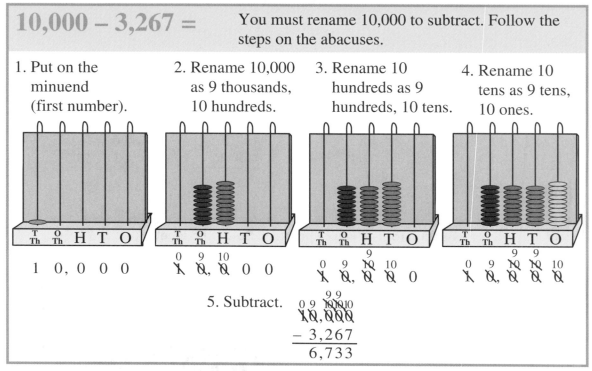

1 0, 0 0 0

5. Subtract.
$$\begin{array}{r} 10,000 \\ -\ 3,267 \\ \hline 6,733 \end{array}$$

Finding the Missing Number

1. For a *missing addend,* subtract.
   Mr. Hunter's class wants to collect 1,274 cans by the end of the semester. They collected 396 cans during October. How many more cans do they need to collect to reach their goal?

$$396 + n = 1,274$$
$$n = 1,274 - 396$$
$$n = 878 \text{ cans}$$

2. For a *missing subtrahend,* subtract.
   Calvary Church had a balance of $20,469.00 in the savings account. It now has a balance of $13,374.00. How much was withdrawn from the savings account?

$$\$20,469 - n = \$13,374$$
$$n = \$20,469 - \$13,374$$
$$n = \$7,095$$

3. For a *missing minuend,* add.
   When the mill closed, 876 people moved out of Brownville. There is a population now of 1,320. What was the population of Brownville before the mill closed?

$$n - 876 = 1,320$$
$$n = 1,320 + 876$$
$$n = 2,196 \text{ people}$$

Practice

Solve.

1. $\begin{array}{r} 12{,}700 \\ -\ 9{,}623 \\ \hline \end{array}$
2. $\begin{array}{r} 5{,}000 \\ -2{,}851 \\ \hline \end{array}$
3. $\begin{array}{r} 9{,}000 \\ -4{,}628 \\ \hline \end{array}$
4. $\begin{array}{r} 7{,}004 \\ -2{,}813 \\ \hline \end{array}$

5. $\begin{array}{r} 36{,}000 \\ -15{,}277 \\ \hline \end{array}$
6. $\begin{array}{r} 50{,}006 \\ -27{,}150 \\ \hline \end{array}$
7. $\begin{array}{r} 200{,}000 \\ -198{,}764 \\ \hline \end{array}$
8. $\begin{array}{r} 401{,}803 \\ -276{,}495 \\ \hline \end{array}$

Copy each equation. Write another equation to find the missing number. Solve for *n*.

9. $n + 19 = 47$
10. $132 + n = 421$
11. $n - 501 = 1{,}276$

12. $4{,}731 - n = 2{,}001$
13. $n - 87 = 246$
14. $292 - n = 75$

Application

Write an equation showing the missing number as *n* for each word problem. Write another equation to find the missing number. Solve for *n*. Label the answer.

15. Kirsten had some books. She gave 39 of the books to her little brother. She has 25 books left. How many did she have at first?

16. Harvest Christian School has 274 students. There are 125 girls. How many of the students are boys?

17. Matthew's family traveled 428 miles. They traveled 284 miles on Wednesday and the rest on Thursday. How many miles did the family travel on Thursday?

18. Erik and his brothers had 214 baseball cards. They sold some of their cards. If they now have 41 cards, how many cards did they sell?

Meet the Challenge!

19. Suzette collected 3,472 pennies. Her sister collected 300 more than twice as many. How many pennies did the girls collect altogether?

Chinese Abacus

The Chinese abacus is an ancient mathematical tool. It has rods indicating each place value. Each rod is divided into two parts. Beads are moved to the horizontal bar to make a number.

When 1 bead is on the Ones rod below the horizontal bar, it equals 1 (1×1). If 1 bead is above the horizontal bar, it is equal to 5 (5×1). When 1 bead is on the Tens row below the horizontal bar, it equals 10 (1×10). If 1 bead is above the horizontal bar, it is equal to 50 (5×10).

This Chinese abacus shows the number 52,378.

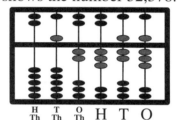

What number is shown on this Chinese abacus?

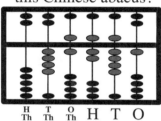

Follow the steps to add using the Chinese abacus.

1. Put on the first addend.   2. Put on the second addend. Rename if necessary.

58 + 61 =   119

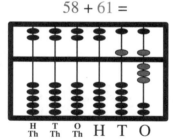   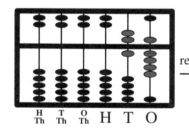   renamed →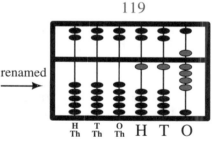

Practice

Use a Chinese abacus to solve each problem.

1. 12 + 5 =   **2.** 57 + 31 =   **3.** 32 + 65 =

4. 35 + 52 =   **5.** 64 + 12 =   **6.** 29 + 40 =

Multistep Word Problems

Problem-Solving Guide

1. Identify the question.
2. Identify the necessary information.
3. Develop a plan to solve the problem.
4. Solve the problem.
5. Decide whether the answer is reasonable.

Practice

Solve.

1. Carla and Nicole made 120 cookies, 62 brownies, and 48 popcorn balls. Michele made 39 cookies, 12 brownies, and 12 popcorn balls. How many more cookies were there than brownies and popcorn balls together?

2. In March, Brandon ran 13 miles the first week, 20 miles the second week, 14 miles the third week, 15 miles the fourth week, and 17 miles the fifth week. His father ran 16 miles the first week, 23 miles the second week, 25 miles the third week, 19 miles the fourth week, and 18 miles the fifth week. How many fewer miles did Brandon run than his father?

3. Marissa, Leanne, Yvette, and Elise went shopping. Marissa bought a book for $4.95 and a calendar for $10.95. Leanne bought a pair of earrings for $6.75 and a matching necklace for $7.00. Yvette bought a skirt that was originally priced at $16.89, but was on sale for $5.00 off the ticket price. Elise bought a pair of shoes that cost $29.99 before the $6.98 discount. How much money in all did the girls spend on their shopping trip?

4. Terrence bought a tape for $11.98 and batteries for $6.25. He gave the cashier $20.00. How much change did he get?

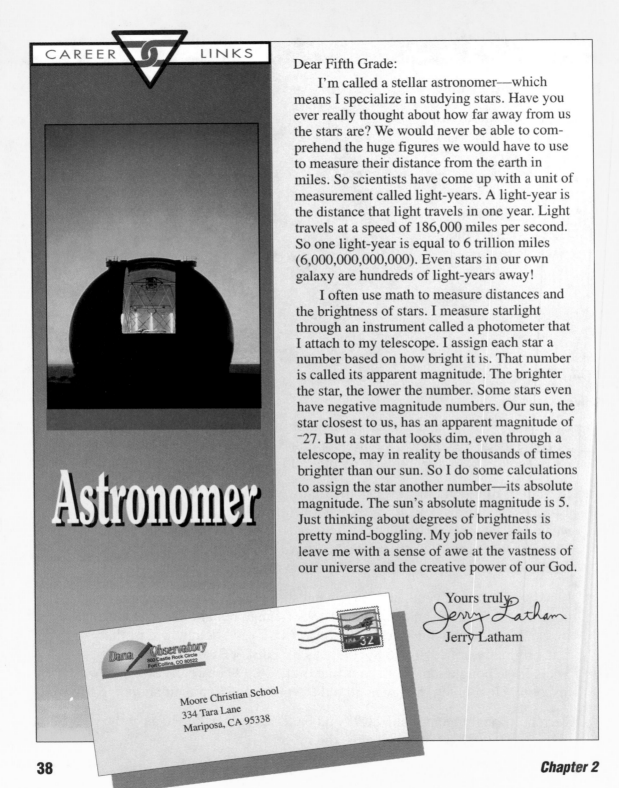

Astronomer

Dear Fifth Grade:

I'm called a stellar astronomer—which means I specialize in studying stars. Have you ever really thought about how far away from us the stars are? We would never be able to comprehend the huge figures we would have to use to measure their distance from the earth in miles. So scientists have come up with a unit of measurement called light-years. A light-year is the distance that light travels in one year. Light travels at a speed of 186,000 miles per second. So one light-year is equal to 6 trillion miles (6,000,000,000,000). Even stars in our own galaxy are hundreds of light-years away!

I often use math to measure distances and the brightness of stars. I measure starlight through an instrument called a photometer that I attach to my telescope. I assign each star a number based on how bright it is. That number is called its apparent magnitude. The brighter the star, the lower the number. Some stars even have negative magnitude numbers. Our sun, the star closest to us, has an apparent magnitude of $^-27$. But a star that looks dim, even through a telescope, may in reality be thousands of times brighter than our sun. So I do some calculations to assign the star another number—its absolute magnitude. The sun's absolute magnitude is 5. Just thinking about degrees of brightness is pretty mind-boggling. My job never fails to leave me with a sense of awe at the vastness of our universe and the creative power of our God.

Yours truly,

Jerry Latham

Jerry Latham

Dana Observatory
800 Castle Rock Circle
Fort Collins, CO 80522

Moore Christian School
334 Tara Lane
Mariposa, CA 95338

Chapter Review

Write *Commutative, Associative,* or *Identity* for each equation.

1. $3 + (9 + 7) = 19$
   $(3 + 9) + 7 = 19$

2. $18 + 0 = 18$

3. $7 + 9 = 16$
   $9 + 7 = 16$

Copy each equation. Write an equation to find the missing number. Solve for *n*.

4. $n + 8 = 17$

5. $9 - n = 5$

6. $n - 8 = 6$

7. $133 - n = 59$

8. $n - 94 = 178$

9. $84 + n = 216$

Use rounding to estimate. Solve.

10. $\begin{array}{r} 12{,}375 \\ +\,27{,}803 \\ \hline \end{array}$

11. $\begin{array}{r} 37{,}056 \\ -\,28{,}311 \\ \hline \end{array}$

12. $\begin{array}{r} 49{,}123 \\ -\,38{,}756 \\ \hline \end{array}$

13. $\begin{array}{r} 8{,}763 \\ +\,4{,}009 \\ \hline \end{array}$

Use front-end estimation with adjustment to estimate. Solve.

14. $\begin{array}{r} 8{,}764 \\ -\,3{,}205 \\ \hline \end{array}$

15. $\begin{array}{r} 7{,}620 \\ +\,5{,}903 \\ \hline \end{array}$

16. $\begin{array}{r} 24{,}618 \\ -\,19{,}247 \\ \hline \end{array}$

17. $\begin{array}{r} 17{,}699 \\ +\,39{,}406 \\ \hline \end{array}$

Solve.

18. $\begin{array}{r} 321 \\ 14{,}687 \\ +\,9{,}210 \\ \hline \end{array}$

19. $\begin{array}{r} 19{,}306 \\ 7{,}879 \\ +\,1{,}354 \\ \hline \end{array}$

20. $\begin{array}{r} 100{,}000 \\ -\,59{,}631 \\ \hline \end{array}$

21. $\begin{array}{r} 462{,}099 \\ +\,321{,}586 \\ \hline \end{array}$

22. $\begin{array}{r} 7{,}845 \\ -\,2{,}104 \\ \hline \end{array}$

23. $\begin{array}{r} 20{,}000 \\ -\,15{,}236 \\ \hline \end{array}$

Write an equation for each word problem. Write *take away, comparing, missing addend,* or *unknown part* for each subtraction word problem. Solve and label.

24. Mr. and Mrs. Eggars have 73 animals on their ranch. Thirty-five of the animals are chickens. How many of the animals are not chickens?

25. The service station sold 92 tires in March and 56 tires in April. How many more tires were sold in March than in April?

26. Orangevale has a population of 26,266. Placerville has a population of 8,355. What is the total population of the 2 cities?

27. In 1850 the population of California was 92,597. In 1869 the population was 379,994. What is the difference in these populations?

28. Calaveras County has a population of 31,998. Kern County's population is 543,477. What is the combined population of the 2 counties?

29. Mother had a collection of 529 buttons. She gave 255 buttons to her daughter. How many buttons does Mother now have?

30. Stacy must save $275.00 to go to forestry camp during the summer. She has saved $195.00. How much more does she need to save to meet her goal?

31. Olga saved $52.69 from odd jobs and allowance. For her birthday, she received $15.50. How much money did she have then?

Cumulative Review

Write the letter of the correct answer.

1. Round 65,372,608 to the nearest hundred thousand.
   - a. 60,000,000
   - b. 65,000,000
   - c. 65,400,000
   - d. 75,400,000

2. What is the standard form for $(9 \times 100,000) + (6 \times 1)$?
   - a. 900,000,001
   - b. 900,000,006
   - c. 900,000,600
   - d. not given

3. Choose the correct type of subtraction.

   Bill has $16.00 from mowing lawns. Jeff has $7.00. How much more does Bill have than Jeff?
   - a. take away
   - b. comparing
   - c. missing addend
   - d. unknown part

4. Choose the correct equation for the word problem.

   Karen has 17 stamps. Kurt borrowed some stamps. There are 8 stamps left. How many stamps did Kurt borrow?
   - a. $17 - n = 8$
   - b. $8 + n = 17$
   - c. $n - 8 = 9$
   - d. not given

5. Use front-end estimation with adjustment to estimate.

   $$\begin{array}{r} 381,585 \\ + 248,062 \\ \hline \end{array}$$
   - a. 500,000
   - b. 520,000
   - c. 600,000
   - d. 620,000

6. Use rounding to estimate.

   $$\begin{array}{r} 671 \\ - 427 \\ \hline \end{array}$$
   - a. 200
   - b. 220
   - c. 290
   - d. not given

7. Which property is represented by $2 + (6 + 3) = (2 + 6) + 3$?
   - a. Commutative
   - b. Associative
   - c. Identity
   - d. not given

8. What place is the 8 in 321,485,137,621?
   - a. ten thousands
   - b. one millions
   - c. ten millions
   - d. not given

9. Which sign will make the sentence true?

   161,405 $\bigcirc$ 16,405
   - a. >
   - b. <
   - c. =
   - d. not given

Principles of Flight

A plane soaring through the sky has become such a common sight that we hardly notice it anymore. But what makes that plane fly? How can a machine that weighs more than air stay up? Why doesn't it crash back down to earth?

Aerodynamics is the scientific name for the principles that govern flight. These principles involve four separate forces: lift, gravity (or weight), thrust, and drag. Each of these forces acts on an aircraft in a different direction.

Lift is the force that pulls the plane upward. It is generated by the flow of air over the curved wing of a plane. Lift is the same force that causes your hand to rise a few inches when you hold it out the window of a moving car. Gravity, or weight, is the force that pulls a plane back down toward the earth, just as it would a ball or a dropped glass. Thrust is the force that pulls a plane

forward, and it is usually created by propellers or jet engines in an aircraft. Drag is the force opposing thrust, pulling the plane backward and slowing it down. While a plane is flying, the flow of air over its wings, fuselage, and tail creates friction, which in turn produces drag. The principles of flight teach us that lift must equal gravity and thrust must equal drag for a plane to stay in flight.

Gliders are a special kind of aircraft. They don't have an engine to produce thrust. Gliders produce their own forward motion by using gravity. As a glider floats downward, the pull of gravity gives it forward momentum at the same time as it forces it down. The speed of a glider can be controlled by the angle of its flight.

CHAPTER 3

Multiplication

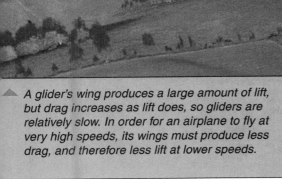

A glider's wing produces a large amount of lift, but drag increases as lift does, so gliders are relatively slow. In order for an airplane to fly at very high speeds, its wings must produce less drag, and therefore less lift at lower speeds.

A bird's wings provide both lift and thrust, like the wings and propeller of an airplane.

43

Multiplication Properties

Multiplication is used to find the total number when equal sets are joined.

$5 \times 7 = 35$

factor factor product

5 sets with 7 in each set = 35

Properties of Multiplication

Zero Property of Multiplication

When 0 is a factor, the product is 0.

$9 \times 0 = 0$ or $0 \times 9 = 0$

Identity Property of Multiplication

When 1 is a factor, the product is the other factor.

$1 \times 5 = 5$ or $5 \times 1 = 5$

Commutative Property of Multiplication (Order Principle)

The order of factors can be changed without changing the product.

$3 \times 4 = 12$ or $4 \times 3 = 12$

Associative Property of Multiplication (Grouping Principle)

The grouping of factors may be changed without changing the product.

$(4 \times 3) \times 5 = 12 \times 5 = 60$
$4 \times (3 \times 5) = 4 \times 15 = 60$
$3 \times (5 \times 4) = 3 \times 20 = 60$

Distributive Property (Multiplication-Addition Principle)

The product of any 2 factors can be found by separating 1 factor into parts, multiplying each part by the other factor, and adding the partial products.

$6 \times 9 =$
$6 \times (4 + 5) =$
$(6 \times 4) + (6 \times 5) =$
$24 + 30 = 54$

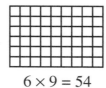

$6 \times 9 = 54$

$(6 \times 4) + (6 \times 5) = 54$

Practice

Write only the answer for each fact.

1. $5 \times 4 =$ 2. $6 \times 8 =$ 3. $7 \times 5 =$ 4. $9 \times 9 =$ 5. $3 \times 6 =$

6. $3 \times 3 =$ 7. $2 \times 5 =$ 8. $8 \times 4 =$ 9. $7 \times 2 =$ 10. $1 \times 8 =$

11. $2 \times 9 =$ 12. $2 \times 3 =$ 13. $4 \times 3 =$ 14. $8 \times 3 =$ 15. $0 \times 6 =$

16. $7 \times 6 =$ 17. $9 \times 4 =$ 18. $8 \times 8 =$ 19. $6 \times 5 =$ 20. $4 \times 7 =$

Identify the property demonstrated by each equation: *Commutative, Associative, Identity, Zero, Distributive.*

21. $9 \times 8 = 8 \times 9$ 22. $6 \times 8 = 6 \times (3 + 5)$ 23. $0 \times 8 = 0$

24. $(3 \times 8) \times 5 = 3 \times (8 \times 5)$ 25. $5 \times 1 = 5$

Application

Write an equation for each word problem. Solve and label. Write the name of the property used.

26. Amberley made cupcakes for her father's birthday. She filled 3 cupcake tins that had 2 rows with 4 cupcakes in each row. How many cupcakes did she make?

27. The ushers collected 4 offering plates. There were 0 visitor cards in each plate. How many visitor cards did they collect altogether?

28. Caleb has 3 banks with 6 quarters in each. Chelsea has 6 banks with 3 quarters in each. How many quarters does each child have?

29. There were 8 tables in the banquet room. Each table needed a candle in the center. How many candles are needed altogether?

Language Link

30. Charis cannot remember what 8×7 equals. Explain how she can find the answer using the Distributive Property. Draw a diagram to illustrate your explanation.

Factors and Multiples

> To find the factors of a number, think of all the pairs of factors whose product is that number.
>
> What are the factors of 7?   What are the factors of 12?
>
> Think: $1 \times 7 = 7$ Think: $1 \times 12 = 12, 2 \times 6 = 12,$ $3 \times 4 = 12$
>
> The factors of a number can be written in order from least to greatest.
>
> 7: 1, 7   12: 1, 2, 3, 4, 6, 12

- All counting numbers except 1 are either prime or composite.

- A prime number has exactly two different factors. These factors are the number itself and 1.

  7 is a prime number. It has exactly two factors, 1 and 7.

- A composite number is a number greater than 1 with more than 2 factors.

  12 is a composite number. It has more than two factors: 1, 2, 3, 4, 6, 12.

> The number 1 is neither prime nor composite.

> A **multiple** is the product of two whole numbers.
> 6 is a multiple of 3 and 2.
> The first 4 multiples of 4 are 0, 4, 8, 12.

Divisibility rules will help you know what numbers are composite. (If a number is divisible by any number other than itself and 1, it is composite.)

- All even numbers are divisible by 2.

  $48 \div 2 = 24$ 2 is a factor of 48.

- All numbers whose digits add up to a multiple of 3 are divisible by 3.

  $69 \rightarrow 6 + 9 = 15$ 15 is divisible by 3; so 69 is divisible by 3.

  $69 \div 3 = 23$ 3 is a factor of 69.

- Numbers with a 5 or a 0 in the Ones place are divisible by 5.

  $75 \div 5 = 15$ 5 is a factor of 75.

  $70 \div 5 = 14$ 5 is a factor of 70.

- Numbers that have a 0 in the Ones place are divisible by 10.

  $90 \div 10 = 9$ 10 is a factor of 90.

Practice

Write the factors of each number in order from least to greatest. Identify each number: *prime* **or** *composite.*

Example: 6   *1, 2, 3, 6   composite*

1. 8   **2.** 18   **3.** 26   **4.** 9   **5.** 11   **6.** 36

List the first 10 multiples of each number.

Example: 2   *0, 2, 4, 6, 8, 10, 12, 14, 16, 18*

7. 3   **8.** 5   **9.** 6   **10.** 7   **11.** 9   **12.** 8

Application

Write a word problem for the equation. Solve and label.

13. $5 \times 7 =$

Ideas: birds, baseball cards, hair bows

Did you know . . .

There are over 9,500 kinds of birds. One of them, the white-throated swift, can fly 200 miles per hour. The ostrich, which cannot fly at all, is the largest bird. It weighs over 300 pounds! The smallest bird, the hummingbird, weighs about 0.06 ounces.

Multiples of 10

To multiply a number times a multiple of 10, multiply the basic fact and annex the same number of zeros that is in the factor that is a multiple of 10.

$3 \times 2 = 6$ (basic fact)

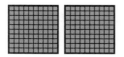 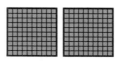 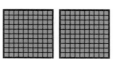

$3 \times 20 = 60$ (Annex 1 zero.)

$3 \times 200 = 600$ (Annex 2 zeros.)

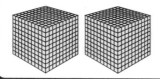 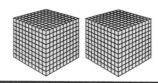 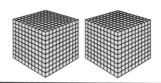

$3 \times 2,000 = 6,000$ (Annex 3 zeros.)

Sometimes both factors are multiples of 10. Multiply the basic fact, then annex the same number of zeros that are in both factors combined.

60×300 Think $6 \times 3 = 18$; annex 3 zeros. $= 18,000$
$400 \times 2,000$ Think $4 \times 2 = 8$; annex 5 zeros. $= 800,000$

Class Work

Mental Math: Write only the answer for each multiplication problem.

1. $4 \times 600 =$

2. $3 \times 7,000 =$

3. $60 \times 90 =$

Write an equation for each word problem. Solve and label.

4. Mrs. Whitaker bought 4 boxes of pencils. Each box has 40 pencils. How many pencils does she have?

5. Mrs. Crowther has 85 stickers. She gave 24 stickers to her class. How many stickers does she have left?

Practice

Mental Math: Write the letter of the correct answer.

1. $500 \times 10 =$ a. 50   b. 500   c. 5,000   d. 50,000
2. $700 \times 50 =$ a. 350   b. 3,500   c. 35,000   d. 350,000
3. $60 \times 40 =$ a. 240   b. 2,400   c. 24,000   d. 240,000

Mental Math: Write only the answer for each multiplication equation.

4. $1,000 \times 9 =$ **5.** $50 \times 300 =$

6. $600 \times 10 =$ **7.** $80 \times 700 =$

8. $4,000 \times 20 =$ **9.** $70 \times 700 =$

10. $40 \times 8,000 =$ **11.** $6,000 \times 50 =$

12. $8 \times 50 =$ **13.** $6 \times 600 =$

14. $900 \times 40 =$ **15.** $30 \times 400 =$

Application

Use the table to write an equation for each word problem. Solve and label.

16. How much longer did Adam live than Enoch?

17. How many years did Jared and Lamech live combined?

18. How much longer did the oldest man live than the youngest of these?

Bible Ages

Name	Age
Adam	930
Jared	962
Enoch	365
Methuselah	969
Lamech	777

Meet the Challenge!

19. Read Genesis 5:25-29. How old was Methuselah when his grandson Noah was born?

One-Digit Multipliers

$$4 \times 27 =$$
$$4 \times (20 + 7) =$$
$$(4 \times 20) + (4 \times 7) =$$

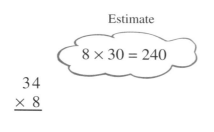

Step 1
Multiply the ones;
rename if necessary.

$$\overset{2}{2}7$$
$$\underline{\times\ 4}$$
$$8$$

Step 2
Multiply the tens;
add any renamed tens.

$$\overset{\cancel{2}}{2}7$$
$$\underline{\times\ 4}$$
$$108$$

Use rounding to estimate before solving. Round the two-digit factor to the
nearest ten. Do not round the one-digit factor.

> On November 15, 8 library assistants repaired 34 books each. How
> many books were repaired altogether?

Estimate

$$8 \times 30 = 240$$

$$34$$
$$\underline{\times\ 8}$$

Step 1
Multiply the ones;
rename if necessary.

$$\overset{3}{3}4$$
$$\underline{\times\ 8}$$
$$2$$

Step 2
Multiply the tens;
add any renamed tens.

$$\overset{\cancel{3}}{3}4$$
$$\underline{\times\ 8}$$
$$272$$

$$8 \times 34 = 272 \text{ books}$$

Class Work

Use rounding to estimate each product. Solve.

1.
$$43$$
$$\underline{\times\ 6}$$

2.
$$\$0.35$$
$$\underline{\times\ \ \ \ 8}$$

3.
$$19$$
$$\underline{\times\ 5}$$

4.
$$22$$
$$\underline{\times\ 3}$$

Practice

Use rounding to determine whether the product shown is sensible. Write *yes* or *no*.

1. $\begin{array}{r} 71 \\ \times\ 6 \\ \hline 4{,}206 \end{array}$	**2.** $\begin{array}{r} 26 \\ \times\ 4 \\ \hline 160 \end{array}$	**3.** $\begin{array}{r} 34 \\ \times\ 9 \\ \hline 306 \end{array}$	**4.** $\begin{array}{r} 96 \\ \times\ 6 \\ \hline 5{,}436 \end{array}$	**5.** $\begin{array}{r} 47 \\ \times\ 7 \\ \hline 159 \end{array}$

Use rounding to estimate the product. Solve.

6. $\begin{array}{r} 48 \\ \times\ 3 \\ \hline \end{array}$	**7.** $\begin{array}{r} 95 \\ \times\ 5 \\ \hline \end{array}$	**8.** $\begin{array}{r} 43 \\ \times\ 9 \\ \hline \end{array}$	**9.** $\begin{array}{r} 82 \\ \times\ 5 \\ \hline \end{array}$	**10.** $\begin{array}{r} 56 \\ \times\ 7 \\ \hline \end{array}$
11. $\begin{array}{r} 32 \\ \times\ 3 \\ \hline \end{array}$	**12.** $\begin{array}{r} 58 \\ \times\ 2 \\ \hline \end{array}$	**13.** $\begin{array}{r} 77 \\ \times\ 5 \\ \hline \end{array}$	**14.** $\begin{array}{r} 16 \\ \times\ 7 \\ \hline \end{array}$	**15.** $\begin{array}{r} 49 \\ \times\ 6 \\ \hline \end{array}$

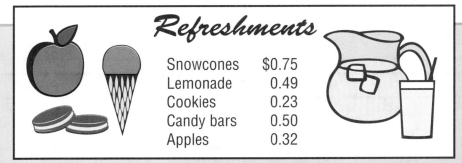

Refreshments

Snowcones	$0.75
Lemonade	0.49
Cookies	0.23
Candy bars	0.50
Apples	0.32

Application

Refer to the refreshment stand sign to write an equation for each word problem. Solve and label.

16. Lenny bought 1 snowcone, 1 candy bar, and 1 apple. How much money did he spend?

17. Mrs. Roberts bought 1 snowcone for each of her 6 children. How much money did she spend?

18. Shelly bought 2 apples, 4 snowcones, and 6 cookies. How much money did she spend altogether?

19. Maria bought 4 candy bars. Maurice bought 9 cookies. Who spent more money? How much more?

More One-Digit Multipliers

Use rounding to estimate before solving the problem. Round three-digit factors to the nearest hundred and four-digit factors to the nearest thousand. Do not round the one-digit factor.

Three-Digit Factor

Round to the nearest hundred.	3×642	$3 \times 600 = 1,800$

$$3 \times 642 =$$
$$3 \times (600 + 40 + 2) =$$
$$(3 \times 600) + (3 \times 40) + (3 \times 2) =$$

Step 1
Multiply the ones. Rename if necessary.

Step 2
Multiply the tens; add any renamed tens. Rename if necessary.

Step 3
Multiply the hundreds; add any renamed hundreds.

$$\begin{array}{r} 642 \\ \times\ \ \ 3 \\ \hline 6 \end{array} \qquad \begin{array}{r} \overset{1}{6}42 \\ \times\ \ \ 3 \\ \hline 26 \end{array} \qquad \begin{array}{r} \overset{1}{6}42 \\ \times\ \ \ 3 \\ \hline 1,926 \end{array}$$

Four-Digit Factor

Round to the nearest thousand.	$5 \times 4,786$	$5 \times 5,000 = 25,000$

$$5 \times 4,786 =$$
$$5 \times (4,000 + 700 + 80 + 6) =$$
$$(5 \times 4,000) + (5 \times 700) + (5 \times 80) + (5 \times 6) =$$

Step 1
Multiply the ones. Rename if necessary.

Step 2
Multiply the tens; add any renamed tens. Rename if necessary.

Step 3
Multiply the hundreds; add any renamed hundreds. Rename if necessary.

Step 4
Multiply the thousands; add any renamed thousands.

$$\begin{array}{r} \overset{3}{4},786 \\ \times\ \ \ 5 \\ \hline 0 \end{array} \qquad \begin{array}{r} \overset{4}{4},\overset{3}{7}86 \\ \times\ \ \ 5 \\ \hline 30 \end{array} \qquad \begin{array}{r} \overset{3}{4},\overset{4}{7}\overset{3}{8}6 \\ \times\ \ \ 5 \\ \hline 930 \end{array} \qquad \begin{array}{r} \overset{3}{4},\overset{4}{7}\overset{3}{8}6 \\ \times\ \ \ 5 \\ \hline 23,930 \end{array}$$

Practice

Write an equation to find the cost for each group of tools. Solve.

1. 5 hammers

2. 9 wrenches

3. 8 screwdrivers

4. 4 saws

$7.67 $3.48 $2.19 $25.36

Use rounding to estimate. Solve.

5. 423×3

6. 671×5

7. 798×4

8. 278×8

9. $3{,}568 \times 2$

10. $4{,}108 \times 6$

11. $7{,}612 \times 4$

12. $9{,}268 \times 9$

Application

13. Write a multiplication problem about the picture. Solve and label.

Two-Digit Multipliers

$26 \times 58 =$
$(20 + 6) \times 58 =$
$(20 \times 58) + (6 \times 58) =$

1. Multiply by the ones.

$$\begin{array}{r} \overset{4}{5}8 \\ \times\ \ 6 \\ \hline 348 \end{array}$$

2. Multiply by the tens.

$$\begin{array}{r} \overset{1}{5}8 \\ \times 20 \\ \hline 1,160 \end{array}$$

3. Add the partial products.

$$\begin{array}{r} 348 \\ +1,160 \\ \hline 1,508 \end{array}$$

Jerry and Jan help their father in the snack shop at camp. They put 24 soft drink cans into each of 38 cases. How many cans were put into cases?

Estimate before solving.
1. Round each factor to the nearest ten.
2. Think of the basic fact.
3. Annex the zeros.

$$\begin{array}{r} 24 \\ \times 38 \end{array}$$

$40 \times 20 = 800$

Solve

$$\begin{array}{r} \overset{1}{\underset{3}{2}}4 \\ \times 38 \\ \hline 192 \\ +720 \\ \hline 912 \end{array}$$

→ Multiply by the ones.

→ Multiply by the tens.
(There are no ones. Write a zero in the Ones place.)

→ Add the partial products.

$38 \times 24 = 912$ cans

Practice

Use rounding to determine whether the product is reasonable. Write *yes* or *no*.

1. $34 \times 58 = 1,972$

2. $62 \times 81 = 558$

3. $62 \times 39 = 248$

4. $82 \times 47 = 3,854$

5. $89 \times 89 = 1,513$

6. $35 \times 71 = 2,485$

Use rounding to estimate the product. Solve.

7. $\begin{array}{r} 65 \\ \times 32 \\ \hline \end{array}$

8. $\begin{array}{r} 43 \\ \times 28 \\ \hline \end{array}$

9. $\begin{array}{r} 42 \\ \times 71 \\ \hline \end{array}$

10. $\begin{array}{r} 12 \\ \times 88 \\ \hline \end{array}$

11. $\begin{array}{r} 56 \\ \times 69 \\ \hline \end{array}$

12. $\begin{array}{r} 77 \\ \times 38 \\ \hline \end{array}$

13. $\begin{array}{r} 63 \\ \times 95 \\ \hline \end{array}$

14. $\begin{array}{r} 51 \\ \times 53 \\ \hline \end{array}$

15. $\begin{array}{r} 82 \\ \times 14 \\ \hline \end{array}$

16. $\begin{array}{r} 32 \\ \times 46 \\ \hline \end{array}$

Application

Write an equation for each word problem. Solve and label.

17. Shelly averaged 18 points per game for the girls' basketball team. How many points did she score in a 12-game season?

18. The Matthews family gives a tithe of $232.50 every month to the church. They also give $50.00 to missionaries and $33.75 to help a young man go to college. What is the total amount of these monthly gifts?

Meet the Challenge!

19. Mr. and Mrs. White budget $2.75 per day for food for each member of the family. The Whites have 5 children. How much money will they budget for food in August?

Three-Digit by Two-Digit

The Distributive Property allows us to "distribute" the factors of a multiplication problem.

During each of the 52 weeks of the year, an average of 717 people visited the art museum. How many people visited the art museum during the year?

$$52 \times 717 =$$
$$(50 + 2) \times 717 =$$
$$(50 \times 717) + (2 \times 717) =$$

Step 1 Multiply by the ones.	Step 2 Multiply by the tens.	Step 3 Add the partial products.
$\begin{array}{r} \overset{1}{7}17 \\ \times\ \ \ 2 \\ \hline 1{,}434 \end{array}$	$\begin{array}{r} \overset{3}{7}17 \\ \times\ 50 \\ \hline 35{,}850 \end{array}$	$\begin{array}{r} \overset{1}{1}{,}434 \\ +35{,}850 \\ \hline 37{,}284 \end{array}$

These steps can be combined:

Estimate

1. Round each factor to its highest place value.
2. Think of the basic fact.
3. Annex the zeros.

$$52 \times 717 =$$

$$50 \times 700 = 35{,}000$$

Solve

$$\begin{array}{r} \overset{3}{7}17 \\ \times\ \ 52 \\ \hline 1434 \\ +35850 \\ \hline 37{,}284 \end{array}$$

→ Multiply by the ones.

→ Multiply by the tens.
(There are no ones. Write a zero in the Ones place.)

→ Add the partial products.

$$52 \times 717 = 37{,}284 \text{ people}$$

Practice

Use rounding to determine whether the product is reasonable. Write *yes* or *no*.

1. $54 \times 891 = 4,811$
2. $28 \times 566 = 15,848$
3. $82 \times 5,421 = 44,452$

Use rounding to estimate. Solve.

4. $\begin{array}{r} 457 \\ \times\ 32 \\ \hline \end{array}$
5. $\begin{array}{r} 507 \\ \times\ 56 \\ \hline \end{array}$
6. $\begin{array}{r} 616 \\ \times\ 44 \\ \hline \end{array}$
7. $\begin{array}{r} \$7.29 \\ \times\ \ \ 63 \\ \hline \end{array}$
8. $\begin{array}{r} 336 \\ \times\ 45 \\ \hline \end{array}$

9. $\begin{array}{r} 5,432 \\ \times\ \ \ \ 18 \\ \hline \end{array}$
10. $\begin{array}{r} 4,608 \\ \times\ \ \ \ 35 \\ \hline \end{array}$
11. $\begin{array}{r} 6,275 \\ \times\ \ \ \ 78 \\ \hline \end{array}$
12. $\begin{array}{r} \$82.75 \\ \times\ \ \ \ 92 \\ \hline \end{array}$
13. $\begin{array}{r} 4,063 \\ \times\ \ \ \ 27 \\ \hline \end{array}$

Application

Use the information in the record book to answer each question. Write the equations you use. Label the answers.

> My Newspaper Delivery Record
>   February, 1999
> Subscriptions: $9.57 per month
> Number of customers: 89
> My costs: $ 0.17 for each daily paper (Monday through Saturday)
> $ 0.73 for each Sunday paper
> $15.00 per month for rubber bands and plastic bags
> NOTE: Always buy 2 extra papers to carry each day, just in case!
> This month: 4 Sundays, 24 other days

14. How much money does Bruce collect monthly from each customer?

15. How many papers does Bruce buy each day?

16. What is Bruce's total cost for newspapers on Sunday?

17. What is Bruce's total cost for newspapers on Monday?

18. What is the total cost of the papers for this month?

19. What is Bruce's expected profit for the month? (Hint: *profit* is the amount of money Bruce has left after buying all his papers and supplies.)

Three-Digit Multipliers

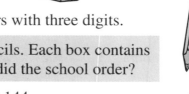

Use the Distributive Property to multiply numbers with three digits.

The school district ordered 158 boxes of pencils. Each box contains 1 gross (144) pencils. How many pencils did the school order?

$$158 \times 144 =$$
$$(100 + 50 + 8) \times 144 =$$
$$(100 \times 144) + (50 \times 144) + (8 \times 144) =$$

Step 1	Step 2	Step 3	Step 4
Multiply by the ones.	Multiply by the tens.	Multiply by the hundreds.	Add the partial products.

Step 1
$$\begin{array}{r} \overset{3\ 3}{144} \\ \times\ \ \ 8 \\ \hline 1{,}152 \end{array}$$

Step 2
$$\begin{array}{r} \overset{2\ 2}{144} \\ \times\ 50 \\ \hline 7{,}200 \end{array}$$

Step 3
$$\begin{array}{r} 144 \\ \times 100 \\ \hline 14{,}400 \end{array}$$

Step 4
$$\begin{array}{r} 1{,}152 \\ 7{,}200 \\ +14{,}400 \\ \hline 22{,}752 \end{array}$$

$$158 \times 144 = 22{,}752 \text{ pencils}$$

These steps can be combined:

Solve
$$\begin{array}{r} 144 \\ \times 158 \\ \hline 1{,}152 \\ 7{,}200 \\ +14{,}400 \\ \hline 22{,}752 \end{array}$$

1,152 → Multiply by the ones.

7,200 → Multiply by the tens. (There are no ones.)

+14,400 → Multiply by the hundreds. (There are no ones or tens.)

22,752 → Add the partial products.

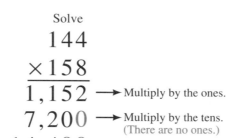

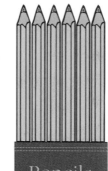

Pencils

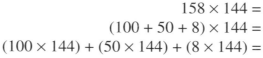

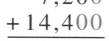

Practice

Solve.

1. 429
   ×315

2. 928
   ×411

3. $6.17
   × 456

4. 1,528
   × 156

5. 5,987
   × 263

6. $25.73
    ×   348

7. 366
   ×149

8. 492
   ×260

9. 628
   ×351

10. 7,682
    × 319

Application

Write a word problem for the equation. Solve and label.

11. 251 × $6.48 =
    Ideas: museum admission, dinners sold, school pictures

Did you know . . .

Most birds have eyes on the sides of their head, rather than in front as people do. The woodcock, which lives in marshy regions of the eastern United States and Canada, has eyes so far back on the sides of its head that it can see all the way around itself!

Zero in the Multiplier

If there is a 0 in the Ones place, skip step 1 (multiplying by the ones).
If there is a 0 in the Tens place, skip step 2 (multiplying by the tens).

> Mr. and Mrs. Vick make a mortgage payment of $748.27 each month for their house. They will pay this amount for 360 months (30 years). How much will they have paid when the house is paid off?

$$
\begin{array}{r}
\$748.27 \\
\times\quad 360 \\
\hline
4489620 \\
+\ 22448100 \\
\hline
\$269{,}377.20
\end{array}
$$

Zero in the Ones place.
There are no ones. → Multiply by the tens.
Multiply by the hundreds.
Add the partial products.

$$360 \times \$748.27 = \$269{,}377.20$$

> The fair is open for 208 days a year. If an average of 4,383 people visited the fair each day, how many people visited the fair during the year?

$$
\begin{array}{r}
4{,}383 \\
\times\quad 208 \\
\hline
35064 \\
+876600 \\
\hline
911{,}664
\end{array}
$$

Zero in the Tens place.
Multiply by the ones.
There are no tens. → Multiply by the hundreds.
Add the partial products.

$$208 \times 4{,}383 = 911{,}664 \text{ people}$$

Did you know . . .

The symbol 0, used to indicate the absence of quantity in a place, was not used in Europe until the 1400s. It is believed that the Mayan people were the first to have a symbol for zero sometime before A.D. 300.

Practice

Solve.

1. 4,381 × 210	**2.** 5,067 × 408	**3.** $26.90 × 912	**4.** 9,561 × 305	**5.** 8,794 × 760
6. 638 ×930	**7.** 708 ×417	**8.** 5,540 × 602	**9.** 9,672 × 130	**10.** 6,342 × 504

Application

Write an equation for each word problem. Solve and label.

11. Mr. Davis is a salesman for Johnson's Athletic Supplies. The company pays him regular wages of $250.00 per week plus a commission on the amount that he sells. For the first week in August, his commission was $175.40. How much did he earn altogether that week?

12. At the end of each month, Mr. Davis reports the number of miles he has traveled in the company car. On August 1, the car's odometer read 35,892, and at the end of August it read 37,256. How far had Mr. Davis driven during August?

13. Mr. Davis sold athletic supplies to 125 schools and teams. The average amount spent by each group was $297.50. What was the total of these sales?

Use the table to write an equation for each word problem. Solve and label.

14. The Director of Parks & Recreation ordered 34 basketballs for summer camps. How much is the bill if he is charged the sale price?

15. How much can a customer save by purchasing five baseballs at the sale price?

Item	Regular Price	Sale Price
badminton set	$13.99	$ 9.99
football	$26.99	$21.99
soccer ball	$24.99	$21.99
basketball	$19.00	$16.99
baseball	$ 2.95	$ 2.50
baseball glove	$26.99	$24.99

Number of Combinations

Sandwiches	Ice cream	Drinks
hamburger	vanilla	cola
grilled cheese	chocolate	milk
chicken salad	strawberry	iced tea
Side orders	**Toppings**	orange juice
french fries	hot fudge	coffee
onion rings	butterscotch	
mozarella sticks	caramel	
garden salad	marshmallow	

Joy ordered one scoop of ice cream and one topping. How many possible combinations could she have?

I can have . . . .

vanilla with hot fudge
vanilla with butterscotch
vanilla with caramel
vanilla with marshmallow

chocolate with hot fudge
chocolate with butterscotch
chocolate with caramel
chocolate with marshmallow

strawberry with hot fudge
strawberry with butterscotch
strawberry with caramel
strawberry with marshmallow

$3 \times 4 = 12$ choices

Class Work

Write an equation for each word problem. Solve.

1. John wanted to order a sandwich and a drink at the Sandwich Shop. How many possible combinations are there? List the combinations.

2. Ted is ordering a drink and a side order for a snack. How many possible combinations are there? List the combinations.

3. Pastor Schmidt will order a sandwich, a side order, and a drink. How many possible combinations are there?

4. Mrs. Schmidt will order a sandwich, a side order, a drink, and ice cream without any toppings. How many choices does she have?

Multistep Word Problems

It is sometimes necessary to complete more than one equation to solve a word problem.

> Mr. Kovatch bought a mountain bike and a ten-speed bike. He also bought 4 all-terrain tires. How much more did he spend on the bikes than the tires?

Step 1: Find the cost of the bicycles: $201.95 + $181.95 = $383.90
Step 2: Find the cost of the tires: $4 \times $9.99 = $39.96
Step 3: Find the difference: $383.90 − $39.96 = $343.94

The three steps above can be written in one equation:

$$(\$201.95 + \$181.95) - (4 \times \$9.99) = \$343.94$$

Bike Bonanza!   Lowest Prices Ever!

Ten speed bike	$181.95	Headlight	$ 8.95	Tires	
Mountain bike	201.95	Taillight	7.35	All-terrain	$9.99
Reflectors		Light package	15.25	Ten-speed	6.38
Red	0.59	Speedometer	3.98	Bell	1.75
White	0.68	Odometer/		Basket	3.89
Yellow	0.49	speedometer	8.00	Seat	7.29
Horn	2.99	Odometer	4.25	Spoke	0.35

Class Work

Write an equation for each word problem. Solve and label.

1. Mr. Connor bought each of his 2 sons a mountain bike for Christmas. He bought an odometer for one bike and a speedometer for the other bike. He also bought 2 all-terrain tires as spares. How much did Mr. Connor spend?

2. Gerald bought a ten-speed bicycle, a basket, and a bell for his mother. He had $325.75 to spend. How much money did he have left?

3. Mrs. Passarelli accidentally bought 4 all-terrain instead of 4 ten-speed tires. If she exchanges the tires, how much money will she get back?

4. Linda bought a mountain bike, 2 all-terrain tires, and a speedometer. She sent in a $50.00 rebate coupon that was included with the bike. How much did she spend after receiving the rebate?

Chapter Review

Write the letter of the property for each equation.

1. $5{,}231 \times 0 = 0$

2. $25 \times 42 = (20 \times 42) + (5 \times 42)$

3. $(20 \times 15) \times 3 = (20 \times 3) \times 15$

4. $24 \times 56 = 56 \times 24$

5. $1 \times 302 = 302$

a. Commutative
b. Identity
c. Zero
d. Distributive
e. Associative

List the factors of each number.

6. 12

7. 36

8. 28

Write *prime* or *composite* for each number.

9. 11

10. 17

11. 21

12. 29

13. 34

14. 43

15. 55

16. 63

List the first 6 multiples of each number.

17. 3

18. 7

19. 9

Mental Math: Write only the answer for each equation.

20. $4 \times 3{,}000 =$

21. $30 \times 700 =$

22. $70 \times 10 =$

23. $400 \times 80 =$

24. $20 \times 500 =$

25. $700 \times 500 =$

Use rounding to estimate. Solve.

26. $\begin{array}{r} 53 \\ \times\ 7 \\ \hline \end{array}$

27. $\begin{array}{r} 64 \\ \times\ 5 \\ \hline \end{array}$

28. $\begin{array}{r} 482 \\ \times\ \ 3 \\ \hline \end{array}$

29. $\begin{array}{r} 9{,}276 \\ \times\ \ \ \ \ 6 \\ \hline \end{array}$

30. $\begin{array}{r} 328 \\ \times\ 57 \\ \hline \end{array}$

31. $\begin{array}{r} \$4.52 \\ \times\ \ 31 \\ \hline \end{array}$

32. $\begin{array}{r} 671 \\ \times\ 76 \\ \hline \end{array}$

33. $\begin{array}{r} 58 \\ \times 92 \\ \hline \end{array}$

34.
$$
\begin{array}{r}
352 \\
\times 489 \\
\hline
\end{array}
$$

35.
$$
\begin{array}{r}
2{,}674 \\
\times\ \ 908 \\
\hline
\end{array}
$$

36.
$$
\begin{array}{r}
\$64.09 \\
\times\ \ 258 \\
\hline
\end{array}
$$

37.
$$
\begin{array}{r}
\$8.76 \\
\times 720 \\
\hline
\end{array}
$$

Write an equation for each word problem. Solve and label.

38. Mr. Newton has made 423 flights. If he flew an average of 387 miles on each flight, about how many miles did he fly in all?

39. The air show ran for 5 days. There was an average of 8,305 tickets sold each day. How many tickets were sold in all?

40. Dot gave Don $0.85 to buy her a candy bar. The candy bar cost $0.50. How much change did he give her?

41. Mrs. Sharp has a budget of $450.00 per month to buy groceries and household supplies. The first three weeks of September she spent $79.00, $117.89, and $93.75. How much does she have left to spend during the rest of the month?

42. Captain Michaels flew to a city that was 2,567 miles away. If he made 3 round-trip visits to this city, how many miles did he fly?

43. Mrs. Cates travels by airplane to many states to sell books. On her last 3 trips, she traveled 789 miles, 1,347 miles, and 901 miles. What is the total number of miles traveled on the 3 trips?

44. Mrs. Cates needs to fly 7,000 miles to earn a free airplane ticket. How many more miles must she fly to earn the ticket?

45. A used car costs $2,975.00. At the beginning of the summer, Veronica had $2,187.45 in the bank. During the summer she earned $687.50. Did she have enough money to buy the car then?

Egyptian Multiplication

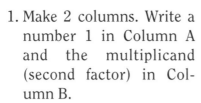

This is the Dornier Do-X, built in 1929. It had 12 engines, paired back to back.
Each of the 12 engines created 600 horsepower.

$$12 \times 600 =$$

1. Make 2 columns. Write a number 1 in Column A and the multiplicand (second factor) in Column B.

A	B
1	600

2. Double the numbers in each column. The last number in Column A should be less than the multiplier (first factor).

A	B
1	600
2	1,200
4	2,400
8	4,800

3. Find numbers in Column A that total the multiplier. Then add the corresponding numbers in Column B.

```
   4    2,400
  +8   +4,800
  12    7,200
```

$12 \times 600 = 7,200$
The Do-X had 7,200 horsepower.

This method works because of the Distributive Property:

$$12 \times 600 =$$
$$(4 \times 600) + (8 \times 600) =$$
$$2,400 + 4,800 = 7,200$$

Solve the following problems using the Egyptian method of multiplication.

1. 13×58

2. 18×63

3. 24×345

Cumulative Review

Write the letter of the correct answer.

1. What is 800,020,019 in expanded form?

   a. 800,000 + 200,000 + 10 + 9
   b. 800,000,000 + 20,000 + 10 + 9
   c. 800,000,000 + 200,000 + 9
   d. not given

2. What is three billion, twenty-three million, two in standard form?

   a. 3,023,000,002
   b. 3,230,000,002
   c. 3,232,000,202
   d. not given

3. What place is the 4 in 82,478,923,076?

   a. thousands
   b. hundred thousands
   c. hundred millions
   d. hundred billions

4. Solve for n.
   $$n - 602 = 331$$

   a. $n = 271$ c. $n = 933$
   b. $n = 371$ d. not given

5. Solve.

   100,000
   − 68,342

   a. 31,658
   b. 31,667
   c. 42,768
   d. not given

6. Choose the correct type of subtraction.

   Last month a photo studio sold 198 photographs with a holiday or plain background. Fifty-seven had a holiday background. How many photographs had a plain background?

   a. take away   c. missing addend
   b. comparing   d. unknown part

7. Which property is represented by $5 \times 7 = 5 \times (3 + 4)$?

   a. Zero   c. Commutative
   b. Identity   d. Distributive

8. Which number is prime?

   a. 6   c. 81
   b. 54   d. not given

9. Solve.

   $7.89
   × 602

   a. $4,248.78
   b. $4,738.78
   c. $4,749.78
   d. not given

10. Use front-end estimation with adjustment to estimate.

    252,578
    +621,042

    a. 870,000
    b. 900,000
    c. 973,620
    d. not given

The Small Plane and Its Parts

Have you ever wondered what all the parts of a small plane are called? You're familiar with the wings and the tail, but could you find the fuselage and the ailerons? Each part of a plane plays an important role in flight.

The fuselage is the body of the plane. Inside the fuselage are the cockpit and all the controls. The cargo, passengers, and pilot ride in this section. Attached to the front of the fuselage is the propeller. The propeller can act as either a driving or braking mechanism, depending on the angle and direction of its large, rotating blades. The wings are attached to the fuselage at the sides, and the tail extends from the rear.

The wings have hinged sections at their edges called ailerons and flaps. The ailerons bank the plane, causing it to turn. The flaps are longer than ailerons, and the pilot uses them to increase lift when taking off or to slow the plane down when landing.

The tail of the plane has several parts that help control the plane in flight. The vertical stabilizer ("fin") keeps the airplane's fuselage aligned with the direction of flight like feathers on an arrow so that it will not veer off course. The rudder is hinged on the back of the vertical stabilizer and helps to keep the plane aligned during turns. The horizontal stabilizer (often called just "the stabilizer") is the crosspiece on the tail and helps keep the plane flying level. It has its own hinged flaps called elevators that adjust the angle of the plane's nose and tail during flight.

CHAPTER
4

Geometry:
Lines and Angles

The propeller acts like a rotating wing: as it spins through the air, it produces lift, or thrust, pulling the airplane forward.

Flaps, used primarily for takeoff and landing, slow an airplane down by increasing drag and enable it to remain flying at lower speeds by increasing lift.

Points, Lines, and Planes

Point
an exact location represented
by a dot

$Q.$ point Q

Line
a straight path of points that
goes on endlessly in both
directions

  $\overleftrightarrow{AB}$

Line segment
a part of a line having
two endpoints

C ———— D $\overline{CD}$

Ray
a part of a line that goes on
endlessly in one direction
from an endpoint

  $\overrightarrow{EF}$

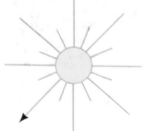

Plane
a set of points that goes on
endlessly in all directions,
forming a flat surface

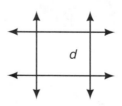 plane d

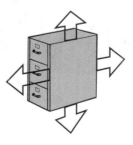

Identify and name each figure.

Example: $\overset{U \quad V}{\longleftrightarrow}$ line, $\overleftrightarrow{UV}$

1. $\overset{M \qquad\qquad O}{\bullet\underline{\hspace{2cm}}\bullet}$

2. $\overset{P \qquad T}{\bullet\underline{\hspace{1.5cm}}}\rightarrow$

3. b

4. $\overset{E}{\bullet}$

Name the geometric figure suggested by the object.

5. edge of a ruler 6. head of a pin 7. cover of a book 8. light from a flashlight

Draw the following figures.

9. line segment *AB* 10. ray *XY* 11. line *QV* 12. point *T*

Use the figure to name each.

13. plane

14. line segment

15. line

16. ray

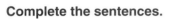

Complete the sentences.

17. A line segment has two _____.

18. A plane goes on endlessly in _____ directions.

19. A line goes on _____ in both directions.

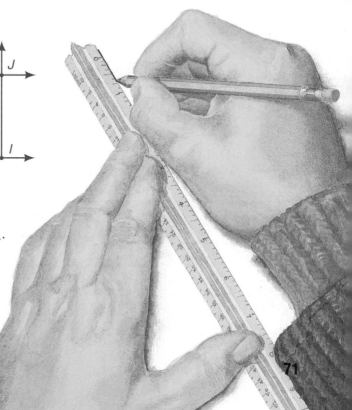

Lines and Angles

Lines

Parallel lines are lines in the same plane that never intersect.

$\overleftrightarrow{AB}$ and $\overleftrightarrow{EF}$ are parallel lines.

Lines in different planes could be nonparallel and still not intersect.

Intersecting lines are lines that have a common point. They form angles.

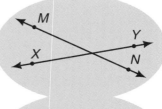

$\overleftrightarrow{MN}$ and $\overleftrightarrow{XY}$ are intersecting lines.

You might see two lines that do not intersect on the page but *will* intersect when they are extended. Such lines are intersecting lines.

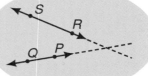

$\overleftrightarrow{SR}$ and $\overleftrightarrow{QP}$ are intersecting lines.

Perpendicular lines are intersecting lines that form right angles.

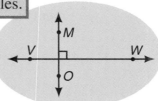

$\overleftrightarrow{MO}$ and $\overleftrightarrow{VW}$ are perpendicular lines.

Angles

The figure formed by two rays with a common endpoint is an angle. The endpoint is the vertex of the angle. (The plural of vertex is vertices.)

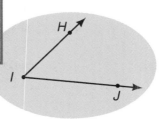

An angle is named by its vertex or by the vertex and 1 point on each ray (the vertex name in the middle). This angle could be named $\angle HIJ$, $\angle JIH$, or $\angle I$.

Identify and name each pair of lines: *parallel, intersecting, perpendicular.*

Example: intersecting, $\overleftrightarrow{AB}$ $\overleftrightarrow{CD}$

1.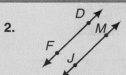

2.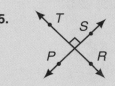

3.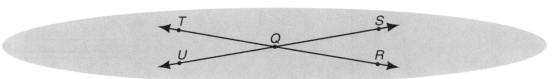

4.

5.

6.

Use the figure to complete the sentences.

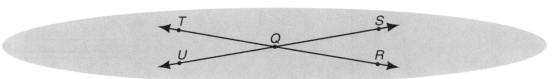

7. The rays that form the sides of ∠*TQS* are _____ and _____.

8. The vertex of ∠*UQR* is _____.

9. The four angles shown here are _____, _____, _____, and _____.

10. The point common to all angles is _____.

Name the angles.

11.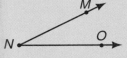

12.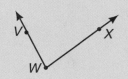

13.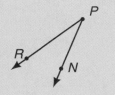

Measuring Angles

This angle measures 90°. It forms a square corner and is called a **right angle.**

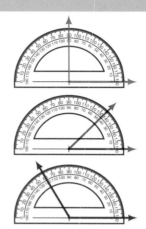

This angle measures 45°. Because it is less than 90°, it is an **acute angle.**

This angle measures 120°. Because it is greater than 90°, and less than 180°, it is an **obtuse angle.**

Angles are measured with a unit called a *degree.* The symbol for degree is °. The protractor has degree markings on it.

Steps for Measuring Angles

1. Place the guide mark on the vertex of the angle.

2. Line up one ray with the zero marking.

3. Move your finger from the zero to the mark where the other ray is.

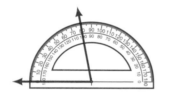

This angle measures 80°.

This angle measures 80°.

Note: You may use either the top or bottom scale on the protractor to measure or construct angles.

Steps for Constructing Angles

1. Draw a ray. Place the guide mark on the endpoint of the ray. Line up the ray with the 0 marking.

2. Draw a point next to the degree mark you are using.

3. Connect the point with the endpoint.

Practice

Identify the type of angle: *right, acute, obtuse.* Use a protractor to measure the angle.

1.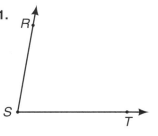

2.

3.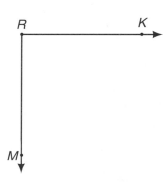

4.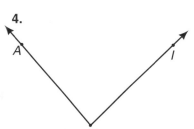

5.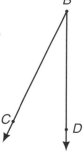

6.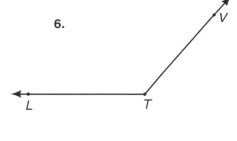

Identify the type of angle for each measurement: *right, acute, obtuse.*

7. $90°$ **8.** $16°$ **9.** $145°$ **10.** $2°$

Use a protractor to construct an angle of each measurement.

11. $90°$ **12.** $56°$ **13.** $35°$ **14.** $95°$

 Chapter 2 Review

Write an equation to demonstrate the Commutative Property for each equation. Solve.

15. $4 + 8 =$ **16.** $7 + 9 =$ **17.** $3 + 7 =$ **18.** $6 + 8 =$

Triangles

Triangles can be classified by their angles.

This triangle has three acute angles. It is an **acute triangle.**

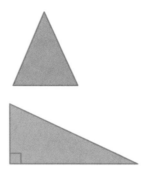

This triangle has two acute angles and one right angle. It is a **right triangle.**

This triangle has two acute angles and one obtuse angle. It is an **obtuse triangle.**

The sum of the measure of the three angles of a triangle is 180°.

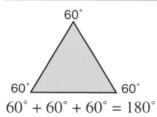

$60° + 60° + 60° = 180°$

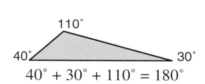

$40° + 30° + 110° = 180°$

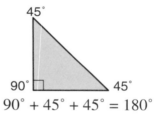

$90° + 45° + 45° = 180°$

If you know the measure of two of the angles of a triangle, you can find the measure of the third angle.

1. Find the sum of the two known angle measurements.

$60° + 90° = 150°$

2. Subtract the sum from 180°.

$180° - 150° = 30°$

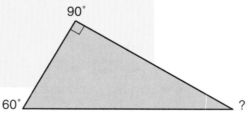

The measure of the third angle is 30°.

Practice

Complete the sentences.

1. Perpendicular lines form _____ angles.
2. Acute angles are _____ than 90°.
3. Obtuse angles are _____ than 90°.

Identify the colored angle in each triangle: *right, acute, obtuse.* Use a protractor to measure the colored angle in each triangle.

4.

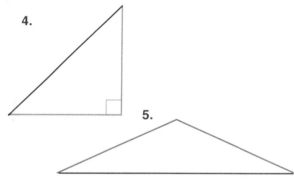

5.

6.

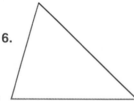

7.

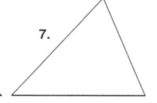

Identify the type of triangle: *right, acute, obtuse.*

8.

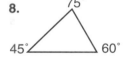

9.

10.

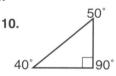

11.

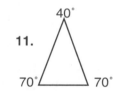

Find the measure of the third angle.

12. Two angles of a triangle measure 50° each. What is the measure of the third angle?

13. A triangle has angles that measure 25° and 55°. What is the measure of the third angle?

14. Bob made a right triangle. If both of the acute angles have the same measurement, what is their measurement?

Circles

A circle is named by its center point. This is circle O.

A **radius** is a line segment whose endpoints are the center point and any point on the circle.

When a radius is named, the center point is the first letter. $\overline{OR}$, $\overline{OS}$, and $\overline{OT}$ are radii of circle O.

A **diameter** is a line segment that connects two points on a circle and passes through the center point. $\overline{TS}$ is a diameter.

A **chord** is a line segment that connects any two points on a circle. $\overline{SU}$, $\overline{VU}$, and $\overline{TS}$ are chords.

A diameter is a chord because both endpoints are on the circle. A radius is not a chord because only one of the endpoints is on the circle.

Steps for Measuring the Central Angles of a Circle

1. Place the protractor along the diameter of the circle, with the guide mark over the center point.

2. Both angles can be measured at the same time.

3. Place the protractor along the diameter of the circle so that the other 2 angles can be measured.

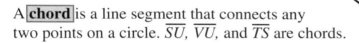
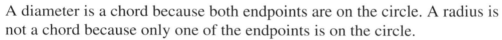
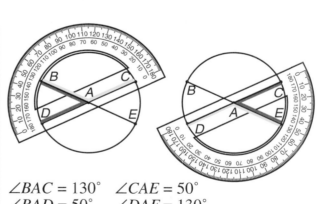

$\angle BAC = 130°$ $\angle CAE = 50°$
$\angle BAD = 50°$ $\angle DAE = 130°$

$$(130 + 50) + (50 + 130) = n$$
$$180 \quad + \quad 180 \quad = 360°$$
$$n = 360°$$

The sum of the measure of the central angles of a circle is 360°.

Practice

Identify each line segment on the circle: *diameter, radius, chord.*

1. $\overline{AF}$
2. $\overline{EC}$
3. $\overline{AG}$
4. $\overline{FD}$
5. $\overline{HB}$
6. Name the circle.

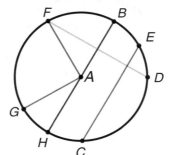

Trace circle *O* from page 78 on your paper. Draw the following line segments on the circle.

7. radius $\overline{QN}$

8. diameter $\overline{XY}$

9. chord $\overline{XV}$

Use a protractor to measure each of the central angles. Write an equation to find the sum of the measurements of the angles for each circle. Solve and label.

10.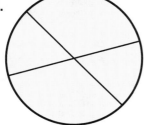

11.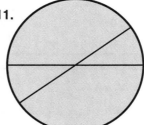

Meet the Challenge!

Use the answers from 10 and 11 to answer the following questions.

12. What do you notice about the measurement of each pair of angles?

13. What do you notice about the measurement of the two acute angles?

14. What do you notice about the measurement of the two obtuse angles?

Circumference of a Circle

> **Circumference** is the distance around a circle.
> If you know the diameter of a circle, you can
> find the circumference of that circle. Multiply
> the diameter by 3.14.

Mary has a round pillow. She wants to put some piping around it. If the diameter of the pillow is 12 inches, how much piping will she need?

diameter = 12 inches   circumference = 37.68 inches
circumference = 3.14 × 12   Mary needs 37.68 inches of piping

---

Jeffrey has a basketball with a circumference of 30 inches. Jeffrey's brother has a basketball hoop with a diameter of 9 inches. Will the basketball fit through the hoop?

3.14 × 9 = 28.26 inches
No, the hoop is too small.

The Fullers bought an above-ground pool. The diameter of the pool is 8 feet. The pool cover their neighbors gave them has a circumference of 26 feet. Is the pool cover large enough to cover the Fullers' new pool?

3.14 × 8 = 25.12 feet
Yes, the cover is large enough.

Did you know . . .

π (pi) is a letter in the Greek alphabet. It is the first letter of the Greek word *peron* ("circumference"). Because of the relationship between the diameter and circumference of a circle, that relationship has been given the name pi.

The exact value of pi has never been found. Computers have taken their calculations to over a million decimal places, but the answer is still not exact. The value of pi is often rounded to 3.1416. If you use 3.14, you will be accurate enough to solve your problems.

circumference = π (3.14) × diameter

Practice

Use a centimeter ruler to find the diameter of these circles. Write an equation to find the circumference of each circle. Use a calculator to solve the problems. Label the answers.

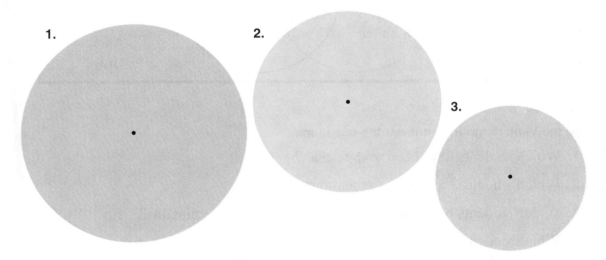

1.

2.

3.

Application

Solve. Your teacher may allow you to use a calculator.

4. The Smiths have a circular flower bed that has a diameter of 18 feet. What is the circumference of the flower bed?

5. The diameter of a bicycle wheel is 26 inches. About how far will it travel when it makes one complete turn? in inches? in feet?

6. Melissa has a round doily that has a diameter of 10 inches. Is a yard of lace enough to go all the way around the edge of the doily?

7. The rope that reaches across the center of a circular swimming pool is 15 meters long. What is the circumference of the swimming pool?

Use a compass to draw a circle for each radius.

8. 25 mm   9. 5 cm   10. 40 mm   11. 2 cm

Venn Diagram

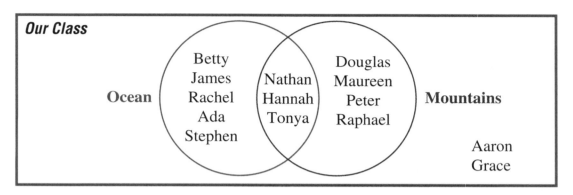

Our Class

Ocean | Betty James Rachel Ada Stephen | Nathan Hannah Tonya | Douglas Maureen Peter Raphael | Mountains

Aaron Grace

Practice

Use the Venn diagram to answer the questions.

1. Which students have been to the ocean?

2. Which students have been to the mountains?

3. Which students have visited both the ocean and the mountains?

4. Which students have been to neither the ocean nor the mountains?

Use the table to make a Venn diagram.

Mrs. Williams's Class		
Name	Hair	Eyes
Sally	red	blue
Morris	brown	brown
Mark	brown	blue
Stephanie	blond	green
Li-Chiu	black	brown
Marcie	red	green
Marius	blond	brown
Leilani	black	brown
Timothy	blond	blue
Jacqui	brown	brown
Noah	brown	green
Valerie	blond	blue
Tracy	brown	brown

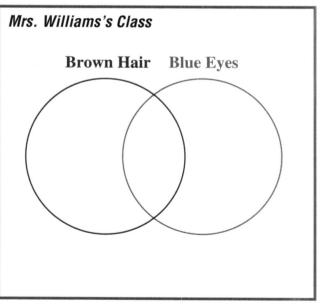

Mrs. Williams's Class

Brown Hair   Blue Eyes

Latitude and Longitude

The horizontal lines are called **latitude lines.** They measure the distance north and south of the equator in degrees.

The vertical lines are called **longitude lines.** They measure the distance east and west of the prime meridian in degrees.

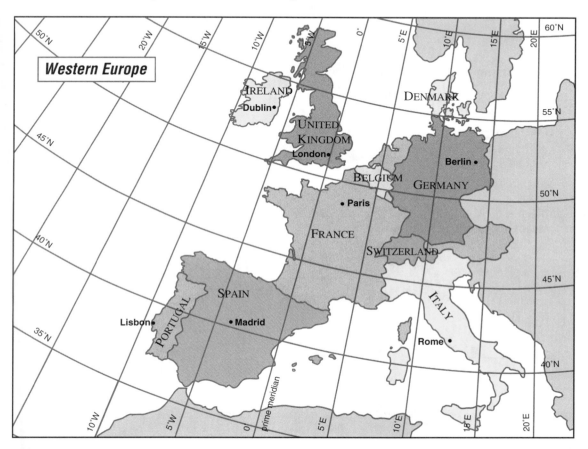

Practice

What country would you be in if you traveled to the following locations?

1. 40° N, 5° W   **2.** 45° N, 10° E   **3.** 50° N, 10° E   **4.** 45° N, 0°

What city would you be in if you traveled to the following locations?

5. 53° N, 7° W   **6.** 51° N, 0°   **7.** 48° N, 2° E   **8.** 52° N, 13° E

Chapter Review

Identify and name each figure: *point, ray, line segment, line, plane.*

Example: M ●——N——▸ *ray,* $\overrightarrow{MN}$

1.

2.

3.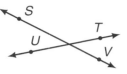

4.

Identify and name each pair of lines: *parallel, intersecting, perpendicular.*

5.

6.

7.

Identify the type of angle: *right, acute, obtuse.* Name each angle. Use a protractor to measure each angle.

Example:  acute, ∠LKJ, 20°

8.

9.

10.

Identify the type of triangle: *right, acute, obtuse.* Find the measure of the unmarked angle.

11. 90° 30°

12. 60° 60°

13. 20° 20°

Use the figure to complete the sentences.

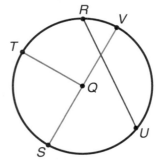

14. $\overline{RU}$ is a _____ of the circle.

15. The diameter shown is _____ .

16. $\overline{QT}$ is a _____ .

17. A circle is named by its _____ .

18. This is circle _____ .

Use a protractor to construct an angle of each measurement.

19. 90°   20. 25°   21. 110°   22. 50°

Write the letter of the correct term.

23. a line segment that has two endpoints on the circle and that passes through the center of the circle

24. a line segment that has two endpoints on the circle

25. a line segment with one endpoint on the circle and with the other endpoint on the center point of the circle

26. an angle with a measurement between 90° and 180°

27. two lines that intersect to form right angles

28. lines in the same plane that never meet

29. a triangle with two acute angles and one right angle

30. a triangle with three acute angles

a. acute triangle
b. parallel lines
c. perpendicular lines
d. diameter
e. right triangle
f. chord
g. obtuse angle
h. radius

Airports

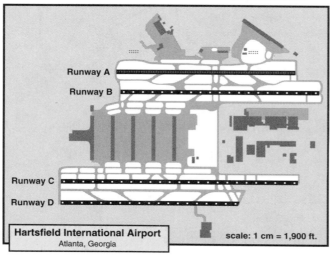

Runway A

Runway B

Runway C

Runway D

Hartsfield International Airport
Atlanta, Georgia

scale: 1 cm = 1,900 ft.

Runway E

Runway F

Runway G

scale: 1 cm = 1,900 ft.

Charlotte/Douglas International Airport
Charlotte, North Carolina

Use the scale to find the approximate length of each runway. Write the equation you used. Your teacher may allow you to use a calculator.

1. A

2. B

3. C

4. D

5. E

6. F

7. G

Use the answers to problems 1 through 7 and the table to answer questions 8 through 13.

8. Which of the runways can the Boeing 747-400 use to take off?

9. Which of the airplanes can land on Runway D? Can the MD-11 land on Runway F?

10. Which of the runways can the MD-80 use to take off?

11. Which of the runways can the MD-11 use to take off?

12. Which of the airplanes will not be able to take off from Runway E?

Airplane	Runway length required for takeoff	Runway length required for landing
Boeing 747-400	11,450 ft.	7,000 ft.
DC-10	10,380 ft.	5,350 ft.
Citationjet	2,960 ft.	2,800 ft.
MD-11	9,600 ft.	6,820 ft.
MD-80	8,075 ft.	5,050 ft.

Cumulative Review

Write the letter of the correct answer.

1. Which sign will make the sentence true?

   $42{,}673{,}892 \bigcirc 42{,}973{,}290$

   a. >
   b. <
   c. =
   d. not given

2. Round 391,762,856 to the nearest one million.

   a. 390,000,000
   b. 391,000,000
   c. 392,000,000
   d. not given

3. Which form represents 62,040,002?

   a. $60{,}000{,}000 + 2{,}000{,}000 + 40{,}000 + 2$
   b. $(6 \times 10{,}000) + (2 \times 1{,}000) + (4 \times 10)$
   c. sixty-two thousand, four hundred
   d. all of the above

4. Use rounding to estimate the answer.

   $48{,}921$
   $-24{,}320$

   a. 23,601
   b. 30,000
   c. 73,241
   d. 20,000

5. Use front-end estimation with adjustment to estimate the answer.

   $591{,}722$
   $+332{,}681$

   a. 820,000
   b. 900,000
   c. 920,000
   d. not given

6. Choose the correct type of subtraction. The church ordered 430 tracts last year. The people used 329 tracts. How many tracts are left?

   a. take away
   b. comparing
   c. missing addend
   d. unknown part

7. What is true about the following set of numbers: 1, 2, 13, 26?

   a. They are factors of 26.
   b. Only 13 is a prime number.
   c. Number 2 is composite.
   d. all of the above

8. Solve.

   $4{,}687$
   $\times \quad 5$

   a. 23,405
   b. 23,435
   c. 24,530
   d. not given

9. What is true about the lines below?

   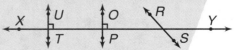

   a. $\overleftrightarrow{UT}$ and $\overleftrightarrow{OP}$ are parallel.
   b. $\overleftrightarrow{XY}$ and $\overleftrightarrow{UT}$ are perpendicular.
   c. $\overleftrightarrow{XY}$ and $\overleftrightarrow{RS}$ are intersecting.
   d. all of the above

10. What is the type of angle?

    a. acute
    b. obtuse
    c. right
    d. not given

George Cayley

George Cayley was the first man to design and build an aircraft that actually left the ground. In 1796 he began his research on flight, carefully studying the flight of birds and trying to apply the same principles to human aviation. By 1799 he had discovered the most important principle of flight: the force called lift. He learned that lift is created anytime air flows over the curved surface of a fixed wing. His studies also showed that an aircraft would need some sort of tail to give it balance.

Cayley got to work applying this principle in his design. After building a successful model glider, he experimented with full-sized gliders, even making one with an engine powered by gunpowder. Cayley never recorded in his journals whether any of these gliders proved able to fly. They all had two things in common: a fixed wing and a moveable tailplane. Both of these inventions are part of aircraft today.

In 1849 Cayley built a triplane glider, a glider with three wings. With a ten-year-old boy aboard, the glider lifted off the ground and flew for a short distance. Four years later, the eighty-year-old Cayley sent his coachman on a flight around his estate in his monoplane glider. Although neither plane had an adequate engine, they did fly successfully for short periods of time.

CHAPTER
5

Decimal Fractions: Addition and Subtraction

Many early aircraft had the stabilizer out in front. Today, forward-mounted stabilizers, or "canards," appear in more designs because they often increase stability and maneuverability, as well as efficiency and safety.

Etched on this silver disk is one of George Cayley's glider designs.

Decimal Fractions: Tenths

The Ones place is the center of the place value system. The decimal point marks the Ones place. The tenths place is to the right of the Ones place.

Decimal fractions can be shown on a number line,

in pictures,

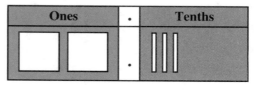

as a common fraction,

$$2\frac{3}{10}$$

or in words.

two and three-tenths

Steps for Comparing Decimal Fractions: Tenths

1. Compare the whole numbers. If the whole numbers are different, the number with the greater whole number is greater. If the whole numbers are the same, go to step 2. $3.7 < 4.1$

2. Compare the tenths. $3.7 > 3.3$

   Annex a zero to help compare if necessary. $3.1 > 3.0$

Steps for Rounding Decimal Fractions to the Nearest Whole Number

1. Find the rounding place (ones).

2. Look at the digit to the right of the rounding place (tenths). If the digit to the right of the rounding place is 5 or more, increase the rounding place by 1. If the digit is less than 5, the rounding place stays the same.

    Remember to drop the digits to the right of the rounding place.

1.2	4.6
1.2	4.6
1	5

Practice

Write a decimal for each picture.

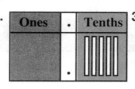
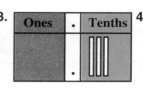
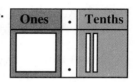

Write a decimal for each common fraction.

5. $\frac{1}{10}$ 6. $\frac{5}{10}$ 7. $\frac{8}{10}$ 8. $\frac{6}{10}$ 9. $2\frac{3}{10}$ 10. $5\frac{1}{10}$ 11. $4\frac{9}{10}$ 12. $6\frac{4}{10}$

Copy and complete each number sentence using a >, <, or =.

13. $1.5 \,\square\, 1.7$ 14. $3.2 \,\square\, 2.3$ 15. $0.8 \,\square\, 0.4$

16. $5.9 \,\square\, 6.1$ 17. $2.0 \,\square\, 2$ 18. $4 \,\square\, 4.7$

Round each decimal to the nearest whole number.

19. 1.9 20. 5.4 21. 3.3 22. 20.5

23. 4.6 24. 12.8 25. 6.2 26. 8.7

Identify the decimals on the number line.

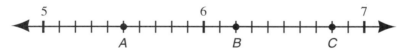

27. What decimal is represented by point *A*?

28. What decimal is represented by point *B*?

29. What decimal is represented by point *C*?

Did you know . . .

Although decimal fractions have been used in China and Arab countries for many centuries, the system we use today was not devised until 1619 by John Napier from Scotland.

Decimal Fractions: Hundredths

The Hundredths place is to the right of the Tenths place.

This frame shows the number one and thirty-seven hundredths.

One and thirty-seven hundredths can be shown on a number line,

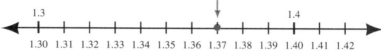

in a picture,

Ones	.	Tenths	Hundredths
	.	‖‖	▫▫▫▫▫▫▫

or as a common fraction. $1\frac{37}{100}$

Steps for Comparing Decimal Fractions: Hundredths

1. Compare the whole numbers. If the whole numbers are the same, go to step 2.

   $4.63 < 5.17$

2. Compare the tenths. If the tenths are the same, go to step 3.

   $4.63 > 4.39$

3. Compare the hundredths.

   $4.63 > 4.61$

   Annex a zero to help compare if necessary.

   $4.63 > 4.60$

Steps for Rounding Decimal Fractions to the Nearest Tenth

| 4.73 |
| 4.73 |
| 4.7 |

1. Find the rounding place (tenths).
2. Look at the digit to the right of the rounding place (hundredths). If the digit to the right of the rounding place is 5 or more, increase the rounding place by 1. If the digit is less than 5, the rounding place stays the same.

| 4.75 |
| 4.75 |
| 4.8 |

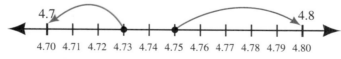

Remember to drop the digits to the right of the rounding place.

Practice

Write the digit for each place in the number. $\boxed{416.29}$

1. hundredths   **2.** tenths   **3.** ones   **4.** hundreds

Write a decimal for each picture.

5. 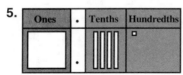   **6.** 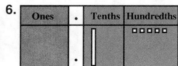   **7.**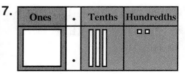

8. 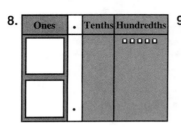   **9.** 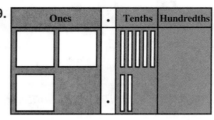   **10.**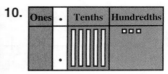

Copy and complete the number sentences using a <, >, or =.

11. 4.78 ☐ 4.79   **12.** 8.75 ☐ 8.90   **13.** 3.85 ☐ 3.09

14. 3.3 ☐ 3.15   **15.** 2.2 ☐ 2.20   **16.** 7.8 ☐ 7.09

Round each decimal to the nearest whole number.

17. 3.1   **18.** 2.5   **19.** 8.7   **20.** 4.4

Round each decimal to the nearest tenth.

21. 3.17   **22.** 7.25   **23.** 4.42   **24.** 12.33

Identify the decimals on the number line.

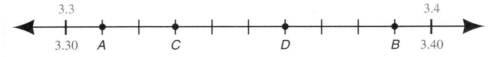

25. What decimal is represented by point *A*?

26. What decimal is represented by point *B*?

27. What decimal is represented by point *C*?

28. What decimal is represented by point *D*?

Decimal Fractions: One Thousandths

The One Thousandths place is to the right of the Hundredths place.

This frame, picture, and number line show the number two and four hundred twenty-six thousandths.

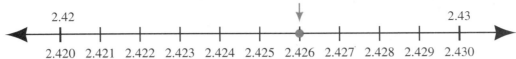

Ones	.	Tenths	Hundredths	One Thousandths

2.42   2.43

2.420 2.421 2.422 2.423 2.424 2.425 2.426 2.427 2.428 2.429 2.430

Steps for Comparing Decimal Fractions: One Thousandths

1. Compare the whole numbers. If the whole numbers are the same, go to step 2. $3.213 < 5.680$

2. Compare the tenths. If the tenths are the same, go to step 3. $3.213 > 3.199$

3. Compare the hundredths. If the hundredths are the same, go to step 4. $3.213 < 3.240$

4. Compare the thousandths. $3.213 < 3.216$

Annex a zero to help compare if necessary.

Steps for Rounding Decimal Fractions to the Nearest Hundredth

1. Find the rounding place (hundredths).

2. Look at the digit to the right of the rounding place (thousandths).

   If the digit to the right of the rounding place is 5 or more, increase the rounding place by 1.

   If the digit is less than 5, the rounding place stays the same.

 Remember to drop the digits to the right of the rounding place.

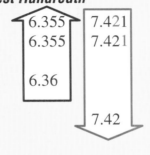

6.355	7.421
6.355	7.421
6.36	
	7.42

Practice

Write a decimal for each picture.

1.

Ones	.	Tenths	Hundredths	One Thousandths
		▌▌		׀׀׀׀

2.

Ones	.	Tenths	Hundredths	One Thousandths
		▌▌▌▌▌	□□□	׀׀׀׀

Write the digit for each place in the number. 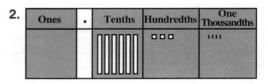 6,751.423

3. tens

4. one thousands

5. one thousandths

6. hundredths

7. tenths

8. hundreds

Identify the decimal on the number line.

3.67   3.68

3.670   A   C   B   3.680

9. What decimal fraction is represented by point *A*?

10. What decimal fraction is represented by point *B*?

11. What decimal fraction is represented by point *C*?

Copy and complete each number sentence using a <, >, or =.

12. 5.178 ☐ 5.2

13. 4.040 ☐ 4.04

14. 3.08 ☐ 3.081

15. 7.15 ☐ 7.2

16. 16.72 ☐ 15.98

17. 9.083 ☐ 9.081

Round the decimal to the nearest—   4.367

18. hundredth.

19. tenth.

20. whole number.

 Chapter 1 Review

Round the number to the nearest—   741,869

21. ten.

22. hundred.

23. one thousand.

24. hundred thousand.

Adding Tenths and Hundredths

Decimal fractions are added in the same way that whole numbers are added. Remember to line up the decimal places before adding and put the decimal point in the answer.

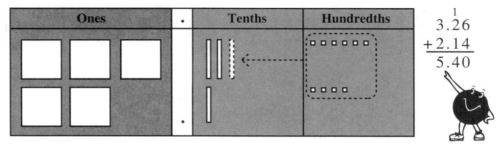

$$\overset{1}{3}.26$$
$$+2.14$$
$$\overline{5.40}$$

To estimate before adding, round each addend to the nearest whole number.

Marla and her mother bought fish at the market. They purchased 5 pounds of salmon and 2.73 pounds of swordfish. How much fish did they purchase in all?

Estimate

$$5$$
$$+3$$
$$\overline{8}$$

Solve

$$5$$
$$+2.73$$
$$\overline{7.73}$$

The answer is reasonable.

5 + 2.73 = 7.73 pounds

Class Work

Use rounding to estimate the sums. Solve.

1. $3.07
   +4.79

2. 6.61
   +2.83

3. 2.89
   +1.43

4. $10.31
   + 2.96

*The fruit of the righteous is a tree of life;
and he that winneth souls is wise.*
                    Proverbs 11:30

Practice

Use rounding to estimate the sums. Solve.

Example: (4)   2.67
                    + 1.23
                    3.90

1. 7.8
   + 8.1

2. 6
   + 2.94

3. $7.95
   + 2.19

4. 4.1
   + 2.78

5. 3.01
   + 5.92

Solve.

6. 15.2
   + 18.7

7. 32
   + 7.07

8. 22.76
   + 13.14

9. $16.49
   + 12.13

10. 41
   + 3.79

Application

Write an equation for each word problem. Solve and label.

11. Mrs. Sears purchased a roast and some vegetables for the church fellowship dinner. The roast cost $9.82 and vegetables cost $3.29. How much did Mrs. Sears spend?

12. Pastor Sears keeps a record of how much gas he purchases for the church van. The first week he bought 8.45 gallons of gas. The second week he bought 10.78 gallons. How many gallons of gas did he purchase in the two weeks?

13. On Saturday, the church bus was driven 21.3 miles for visitation. On Sunday, the bus was driven 33.4 miles to pick up people for church. How many miles was the bus driven on the two days combined?

Lesson 40

Adding One Thousandths

Rename decimal fractions in the same way you have renamed whole numbers. Remember to line up the decimal places before adding and put the decimal point in the answer.

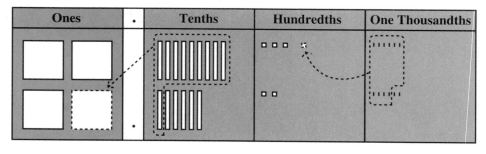

Ones	.	Tenths	Hundredths	One Thousandths

$$2.936$$
$$+1.626$$

Estimate the answer by rounding before adding.

Estimate

$$\begin{array}{r} 3 \\ +2 \\ \hline 5 \end{array}$$

Solve

$$\begin{array}{r} {}^{1}{}^{1} \\ 2.936 \\ +1.626 \\ \hline 4.562 \end{array}$$

Class Work

Write an equation for the word problem. Solve and label.

1. Mandy and Dad cleaned out the garage. They worked for 2.5 hours on Friday afternoon and 3.25 hours on Saturday morning. How many hours did they work in the two days combined?

2. Dad bought two new wrenches. The larger wrench cost $12.79, and the smaller one cost $8.45. How much did Dad spend on new wrenches?

Practice

Use rounding to estimate the sums. Solve.

1. 4.067
    + 3.184

2. 7.079
    + 0.863

3. 1.921
    + 0.252

4. 8.472
    + 5.391

5. 3.62
    + 4.703

6. 0.2
    + 4.579

7. 3.116
    + 2.987

8. 4
    + 3.64

Solve.

9. 58.23
    + 19.897

10. 26.553
    + 12.9

11. 12
     + 27.802

12. 42.039
     + 1.972

Application

Write an equation for each word problem. Solve and label.

13. Mrs. Griggs took David to the doctor. She paid the doctor $49.89 for the exam and $14.21 for medicine. How much did Mrs. Griggs spend?

14. Mr. Yost is a pharmacist. He has a large bottle filled with pills. The full bottle weighs 23.42 pounds. If he adds 3.45 pounds of new pills, what will the bottle weigh?

Write a word problem for the equation. Solve and label.

15. 4.23 + 5.27 =
    Ideas: a relay race, money, metric measures

Chapter 1 Review

16. Write 307,016,580,674 in expanded form.

17. Write 417,092,003,211 in expanded form with multiplication.

Subtracting Tenths and Hundredths

Subtract decimal fractions the same way you subtract whole numbers. Remember to line up the decimal places before subtracting and put the decimal point in the answer.

Joe ran the race in 9.53 seconds. Bob ran the race in 7.64 seconds. How much faster was Bob than Joe?

9.53 − 7.64 =

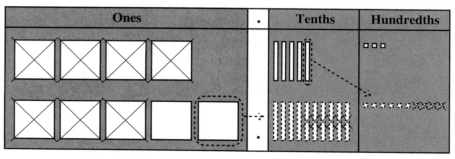

$$\begin{array}{r} \overset{14}{8\ \ \overset{13}{\cancel{4}}\ \cancel{}} \\ \cancel{9}.\cancel{5}\cancel{3} \\ -7.64 \\ \hline 1.89 \end{array}$$

Estimate by rounding to the nearest whole number before subtracting.

Madelynn saved $9.29. She put $2.60 in the special missionary offering. How much does she have left?

Estimate

$$\begin{array}{r} \$9 \\ -3 \\ \hline \$6 \end{array}$$

Solve

$$\begin{array}{r} \overset{8}{\ }\ \overset{12}{\ } \\ \$\cancel{9}.\cancel{2}9 \\ -2.60 \\ \hline \$6.69 \end{array}$$

$9.29 − 2.60 = $6.69

The answer is reasonable.

Annex a zero if needed.

$$\begin{array}{r} 3.9 \\ -2.84 \end{array} \quad \longrightarrow \quad \begin{array}{r} \overset{8\ 10}{\ } \\ 3.\cancel{9}\cancel{0} \\ -2.84 \\ \hline 1.06 \end{array}$$

Class Work

Solve.

1. $58.00
   − 17.32

2. 3.4
   − 1.86

3. 15
   − 9.86

4. $13.43
   − 8.17

Practice

Use rounding to estimate the difference. Solve.

1. $\begin{array}{r} 4.22 \\ -1.99 \\ \hline \end{array}$ 　　2. $\begin{array}{r} 7.81 \\ -6.93 \\ \hline \end{array}$ 　　3. $\begin{array}{r} 7.8 \\ -3.99 \\ \hline \end{array}$ 　　4. $\begin{array}{r} 5.32 \\ -4.2 \\ \hline \end{array}$

5. $\begin{array}{r} 3.06 \\ -1.7 \\ \hline \end{array}$ 　　6. $\begin{array}{r} 8 \\ -2.47 \\ \hline \end{array}$ 　　7. $\begin{array}{r} 9.94 \\ -8.07 \\ \hline \end{array}$ 　　8. $\begin{array}{r} \$14.00 \\ -6.94 \\ \hline \end{array}$

Solve.

9. $\begin{array}{r} 12.29 \\ -1.42 \\ \hline \end{array}$ 　　10. $\begin{array}{r} 28.5 \\ -16.75 \\ \hline \end{array}$

11. $\begin{array}{r} \$30.00 \\ -12.25 \\ \hline \end{array}$ 　　12. $\begin{array}{r} 31.96 \\ -19.2 \\ \hline \end{array}$

13. $\begin{array}{r} 7 \\ -2.58 \\ \hline \end{array}$ 　　14. $\begin{array}{r} 46.29 \\ -18.5 \\ \hline \end{array}$

Application

Write an equation for each word problem. Solve and label.

15. The book Maria wants to buy costs $16.15. She has saved $4.96. How much more does she need to save?

16. Michael ran the race in 10.25 seconds. Stephen ran it in 11.15 seconds. Which boy won the race? How much faster was he?

17. Mr. Rhinehart bought 13.25 acres of land in May. In June he bought 20.4 acres. How many acres did he buy during the two months?

Language Link

18. Explain why four-tenths is equal to forty-hundredths.

Subtracting One Thousandths

Rename decimal fractions in the same way you have renamed whole numbers. Remember to line up the decimal places before subtracting and put the decimal point in the answer.

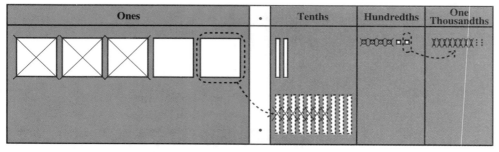

$$\begin{array}{r} 5.260 \\ -3.748 \end{array}$$

Estimate the difference by rounding to the nearest whole number before subtracting.

Estimate

$$\begin{array}{r} 5 \\ -4 \\ \hline 1 \end{array}$$

Solve

$$\begin{array}{r} {\scriptstyle 4\ 12\ 5\ 10} \\ \cancel{5.260} \\ -3.748 \\ \hline 1.512 \end{array}$$

The answer is reasonable.

Remember to line up the decimal places!

Put a decimal point in the answer!

Annex a zero if needed!

Class Work

Solve.

1. $\begin{array}{r} 53.008 \\ -29.872 \end{array}$

2. $\begin{array}{r} 16.97 \\ -\ 3.649 \end{array}$

3. $\begin{array}{r} 108.569 \\ -\ 28.075 \end{array}$

4. $\begin{array}{r} 17 \\ -\ 9.532 \end{array}$

Practice

Use rounding to estimate the difference. Solve.

1. 6.344
    − 2.658

2. 7.253
    − 1.72

3. 8.003
    − 4.75

4. 5
    − 3.68

5. 7.08
    − 4.1

6. 3.621
    − 1.273

7. 9.1
    − 3.264

8. 2.044
    − 1.2

Solve.

9. 37.81
    − 12.259

10. 15.305
    − 11.736

11. 62.007
    − 51.982

12. 19.3
    − 5.972

Application

Write an equation for each word problem. Solve and label.

13. In 1947, Jacqueline Cochran flew a P-51 airplane 469.549 miles per hour. In 1950, R. M. Sharpe flew a Spitfire airplane 322.78 miles per hour. How much faster did Cochran fly than Sharpe?

14. Mr. Newton took his family to an air show. He paid $37.50 for admission to the show and $42.78 for lunch and souvenirs. How much did Mr. Newton spend altogether?

Write a word problem for each equation. Solve and label.

15. 5.35 + 8.61 =   Ideas: running, climbing, skiing

16. 9.421 − 4.352 =   Ideas: bicycle racing, flying model rockets

Chapter 1 Review

Copy and complete each number sentence using a <, >, or =.

17. 47,603,987 ☐ 4,897,603

18. 16,504,033 ☐ 10,000,000 + 6,000,000 + 500,000 + 4,000 + 30 + 3

19. 800,479,328 ☐ eight hundred billion, two hundred eighty thousand, three hundred twenty-eight

Group Problem Solving: Menu Planning

Problem

Your class wants to have a turkey dinner the day before Thanksgiving. The high-school home economics class will prepare the dinner. Your group needs to purchase the main ingredients for the dinner at the lowest price.

Information

Menu

turkey	green beans	iced tea
dressing	cauliflower	cranberry sauce
mashed potatoes	rolls	pumpkin pie

Notes

- Plan on 1 pound of turkey per person.
- Each person will eat 1 serving.
- The home economics class will provide ingredients such as spices, salt, milk, and butter.
- Cups cost $0.89 for a package of 15.
- Plates cost $1.29 for a package of 50.
- A package containing 16 spoons, 16 forks, and 16 knives costs $0.96.
- A package of 100 napkins costs $1.07.

Ingredients	Servings	Cost
Turkey	1 lb. per person	$0.75 per lb.
Dressing	6 per box	$1.29
Mashed potatoes instant boiled potatoes	22 per box $\frac{1}{2}$ lb. per person	2 boxes for $3.00 10 lb. for $1.89
Green beans small can large can	4 per can 26 per can	3 cans for $1.00 $1.90
Cauliflower frozen, box frozen, bag fresh	3 per box 5 per bag 8 per head	2 boxes for $1.19 $2.19 $2.29 per head
Cranberry sauce small can large can	4 per can 8 per can	$0.46 $0.79
Rolls fresh frozen	18 12	$2.25 $1.89

Pumpkin pie
frozen
homemade
  prepared crust
  canned pumpkin
  evaporated milk
  1 egg
	8 per pie
	8 per pie
		$3.34
		
		2 for $0.89
		$0.89
		$0.57
		$0.87 per dozen

Iced tea box of 24 tea bags instant iced tea mix	80 60	$1.69 $3.29

Decide how many people will attend the dinner. Use the chart to answer the questions.

1. How much will it cost to buy the food items for the turkey dinner? Explain your answer.

2. How much will it cost to buy the plates, napkins, cups, spoons, forks, and knives? Explain your answer.

3. What is the total cost of the dinner? Explain your answer.

4. How much money will each student need to pay? Explain your answer.

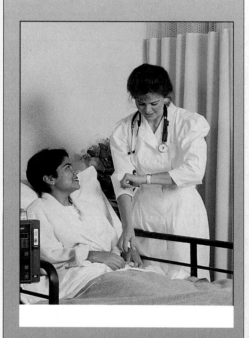

Nurse

Dear Fifth Grade:

I'm glad you asked me how I use math in my job. Many people think nurses merely hand instruments to the doctor and take patients' temperatures. But we do much more than that. Since doctors are usually busy people, they are not always free to check to see that patients are following their orders. We nurses oversee the patients' medical treatments after the doctors have prescribed them.

I often need to use math when I administer medication to a patient. Yesterday Dr. Bowers ordered that one of my patients be given 0.2 grams of a certain medication each day until his condition improves. I found that medicine in our supply room and read the label on the bottle. The medicine only came in tablets of 0.05 grams each. I did some quick division in my head to figure out that I should give my patient 4 of those tablets for his dosage that day.

Sometimes I need to convert units of measurement, a process which is a little trickier. We have charts that help us do the conversions quickly and easily, but it is still important that we be accurate. Doctors' orders are never to be taken lightly. If administered properly, the right medication can bring about a much quicker recovery or even save a life!

Very truly yours,

Karla Schneider
Karla Schneider

Gulf Breeze
Medical
621 Baroco Road
Gulf Breeze, FL 32566

Moore Christian School
334 Tara Lane
Mariposa, CA 95338

Write the digit in each place in the number. (276.832)

1. tenths   **2.** hundredths   **3.** one thousandths   **4.** tens

Write a decimal for each picture.

5. 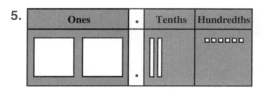 **6.**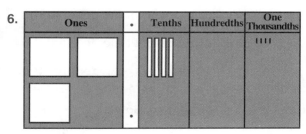

7. 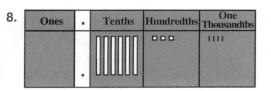 **8.**

Copy and complete each number sentence using a <, >, or =.

9. 26.06 ☐ 26.060   **10.** 8.49 ☐ 8.5   **11.** 17.8 ☐ 17.79

12. 3.697 ☐ 3.698   **13.** 14.307 ☐ 14.4   **14.** 70.899 ☐ 71.2

Round the number 527.649 to the nearest—

15. hundredth.   **16.** tenth.   **17.** ten.   **18.** hundred.

Identify the decimals on the number line.

19. What decimal is represented by point *A?*

20. What decimal is represented by point *B?*

Identify the decimals on the number line.

4.64   4.65
◄——┼——┼——●——┼——●——┼——┼——●——┼——●——┼——►
   4.640   B   A   C   D 4.650

21. What point represents the decimal 4.647?

22. What point represents the decimal 4.642?

23. What point represents the decimal 4.649?

Use rounding to estimate. Solve.

24. 4.65	**25.** $6.24	**26.** 4	**27.** 8.079
−1.389	+3.45	+3.499	−5.867

Solve.

28. $12.79	**29.** 14.79	**30.** 72.349	**31.** 86.328
− 1.68	− 0.306	+ 7.905	+29.31

Write an equation for each word problem. Solve and label.

32. Susan ran the 50-meter dash in 8.73 seconds and the 100-meter dash in 19.43 seconds. What was her combined time for the two races?

33. Max bought a baseball cap for $7.39. If he paid with a ten-dollar bill, how much change did he receive?

34. Major W. R. Payne flew from New York to Paris in 1961, with a speed of 1,089.36 miles per hour. In 1958 Major Burl Davenport flew from London to New York with a speed of 587.457 miles per hour. How much faster did Major Payne fly?

35. Each of the 14 ladies in the women's missionary society collected her goal of $255.00 for the missionary Christmas gift. How much was collected in all?

36. In January $1,256.75 was given to the church building fund. In February $989.35 was given. How much was given in all?

Cumulative Review

Write the letter of the correct answer.

1. What is the value of the 8 in 6,108,679,403?

   a. 800,000
   b. 8,000,000
   c. 80,000,000
   d. not given

2. Round 25,678,932,008 to the nearest ten million.

   a. 25,670,000,000
   b. 25,680,000,000
   c. 25,700,000,000
   d. not given

3. Use rounding to estimate the answer.

   1,730
   +5,801

   a. 7,500
   b. 6,531
   c. 8,000
   d. not given

4. Use rounding to estimate the answer.

   35,676
   −18,413

   a. 20,000
   b. 17,000
   c. 17,362
   d. not given

5. Which property is represented by $43 \times 1 = 43$?

   a. Zero
   b. Identity
   c. Commutative
   d. Distributive

6. Solve.

   7.82
   × 34

   a. 256.96
   b. 265.88
   c. 266.98
   d. not given

7. Which number is composite?

   a. 35
   b. 64
   c. 72
   d. all of the above

8. What is the type of triangle?

   a. acute
   b. obtuse
   c. right
   d. not given

9. Which are chords?

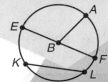

   a. $\overline{AB}$ and $\overline{EF}$
   b. $\overline{AB}$ and $\overline{KL}$
   c. $\overline{EF}$ and $\overline{KL}$
   d. all of the above

10. What term is used for lines that never intersect?

   a. parallel
   b. intersecting
   c. perpendicular
   d. not given

11. Solve.

   $73.32
   − 7.68

   a. $60.64
   b. $64.96
   c. $65.64
   d. not given

12. What digit is in the One Thousandths place in 872.316?

   a. 8
   b. 2
   c. 3
   d. 6

The Wright Brothers

Wilbur and Orville Wright were interested in mechanical things as children. They built their own toys and fixed their friends' bicycles as they were growing up. They loved to experiment with new inventions. Wilbur thought up the ideas, and Orville figured out how to design and make them.

Both boys were extremely interested in the idea of flight. They studied the subject in great detail, reading the writings of George Cayley and Samuel Langley to keep up with current research. In 1899 they began designing their own model gliders, and by 1903 they had come up with a design they believed would actually be able to fly.

The Wrights' airplane, named the *Flyer,* had two 40-foot wings and was powered by a 12-horsepower engine. It had two propellers driven by bicycle chains and a rudder to control the direction of its flight. The two brothers tossed a coin to decide who was going to pilot the aircraft. Wilbur won. Wilbur climbed aboard the plane, and it shot off down its little wooden rail track. When it reached the end of the track, it lifted into the air. But then it angled back so steeply that it could no longer keep flying, and it crashed into the ground.

The Wrights did not give up, however. Three days later, on December 17, 1903, they had the plane repaired and Orville attempted to fly it. This time he controlled the rudder so the plane stayed level, and it flew a distance of 120 feet in 12 seconds. The development of the modern airplane had taken a giant step forward.

CHAPTER

6

Division:
One-Digit Divisors

▲ The first controlled flight of the Wright brothers' airplane, piloted by Orville Wright.

◄ An early flight of the Wright brothers' glider at Kitty Hawk.

Division

Division is used to find the number of equal-sized sets or the number in each set.

$$18 \div 9 = 2$$
dividend divisor quotient

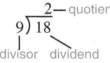
2 — quotient
$9\overline{)18}$
divisor dividend

dividend
$\dfrac{18}{9} = 2$ — quotient
divisor

There can be 2 sets of 9 or 9 sets of 2 in 18.

Division can be used to solve a multiplication equation with a missing factor.

$5 \times n = 30$	$n \times 7 = 56$
$n = 30 \div 5$	$n = 56 \div 7$
$n = 6$	$n = 8$

$4\overline{)33}$ 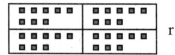   r ▪

Divide the ones.	Multiply.	Subtract.	Write the remainder.	Check by multiplying. Add any remainder.
$\dfrac{8}{4\overline{)33}}$	$\begin{array}{r} 8 \\ 4\overline{)33} \\ 32 \end{array}$	$\begin{array}{r} 8 \\ 4\overline{)33} \\ -32 \\ \hline 1 \end{array}$	$\begin{array}{r} 8\,\text{r1} \\ 4\overline{)33} \\ -32 \\ \hline 1 \end{array}$	$\begin{array}{r} 8 \\ \times\ 4 \\ \hline 32 \\ +\ 1 \\ \hline 33 \end{array}$

Remainders in Problem Solving

Sometimes remainders are dropped.

You have 29 candies to divide equally among 3 friends. How many candies will each person get?

$\begin{array}{r} 9\,\text{r2} \\ 3\overline{)29} \\ -27 \\ \hline 2 \end{array}$

$29 \div 3 = 9\ \text{r2}$ 9 candies

Sometimes the answer will increase by 1.

Lakeisha's mother is organizing a parent fellowship. She expects 76 people to attend. How many tables will she need if 9 people can sit at a table?

$\begin{array}{r} 8\,\text{r4} \\ 9\overline{)76} \\ -72 \\ \hline 4 \end{array}$

If 8 tables are used, 4 people will be without a place to sit.

$76 \div 9 = 8\ \text{r4}$ 9 tables

Practice

Solve. Use multiplication to check your answers.

1. $2\overline{)17}$ **2.** $\frac{12}{4}$ **3.** $27 \div 3$ **4.** $9\overline{)37}$

5. $8\overline{)72}$ **6.** $8\overline{)70}$ **7.** $\frac{25}{5}$ **8.** $8\overline{)48}$

9. $6\overline{)38}$ **10.** $5\overline{)46}$ **11.** $4\overline{)39}$ **12.** $7\overline{)58}$

Write a division equation to find the missing factor. Solve for *n*.

Example: $3 \times n = 27$ $n = 27 \div 3$
$n = 9$

13. $9 \times n = 36$ **14.** $n \times 7 = 14$ **15.** $7 \times n = 21$

16. $n \times 9 = 54$ **17.** $n \times 6 = 48$ **18.** $5 \times n = 20$

Application

Write an equation for each word problem. Solve and label.

19. Mrs. Taylor had 18 apples. She made 3 pies. If she used the same number of apples for each pie, how many apples were used in each pie?

20. Mrs. Burt had 15 sticks of gum. She gave the same number of sticks of gum to each of her 4 children. How many sticks of gum did each child receive?

21. There are 20 students in Mr. Ossen's fifth grade class. If 6 students can ride in each car, how many cars are needed for the field trip?

Did you know . . .

Samuel Pierpont Langley was a pioneer aviator who wanted to be the first man to fly a gas-powered, heavier-than-air machine. In December of 1903, reporters gathered to watch his airplane take off. Unfortunately, his trial flight failed. He was jeered for thinking man could fly. Six days later the Wright brothers flew at Kitty Hawk.

One- and Two-Digit Quotients

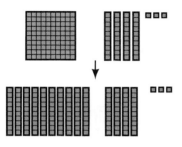

$2\overline{)143}$

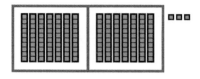

Rename 1 hundred as 10 tens.

$2\overline{)143}$

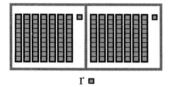

Divide the tens.
Multiply and subtract.

$$\begin{array}{r} 7 \\ 2\overline{)143} \\ -140 \\ \hline 3 \end{array}$$

r ▫

Divide the ones.
Multiply and subtract.
Write the remainder.

$$\begin{array}{r} 71\ r1 \\ 2\overline{)143} \\ -140 \\ \hline 3 \\ -2 \\ \hline 1 \end{array}$$

Check by multiplying.
Add any remainder.

$$\begin{array}{r} 71\ r1 \\ 2\overline{)143} \end{array}$$

$$\begin{array}{r} 71 \\ \times\ 2 \\ \hline 142 \\ +\ \ 1 \\ \hline 143 \end{array}$$

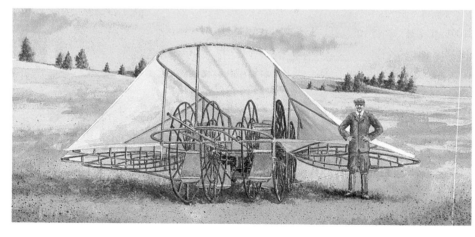

Their appearance and their work was as it were a wheel in the middle of a wheel.
Ezekiel 1:16

The Ezekiel Airship

Practice

Solve. Use multiplication to check your answers.

1. $5\overline{)73}$ 2. $7\overline{)182}$ 3. $6\overline{)59}$ 4. $2\overline{)34}$

5. $4\overline{)364}$ 6. $3\overline{)55}$ 7. $8\overline{)419}$ 8. $8\overline{)610}$

9. $2\overline{)74}$ 10. $5\overline{)61}$ 11. $6\overline{)343}$ 12. $3\overline{)101}$

Write a division equation to find the missing factor. Solve for *n*.

Example: $\quad 5 \times n = 70 \qquad n = 70 \div 5$
$$n = 14$$

$$
\begin{array}{r}
14 \\
5\overline{)70} \\
-50 \\
\hline
20 \\
20 \\
\hline
0
\end{array}
$$

13. $n \times 3 = 18$ 14. $4 \times n = 64$ 15. $n \times 2 = 92$ 16. $5 \times n = 175$

Application

Write an equation for each word problem. Solve and label.

17. A Christian school had purchased 112 dictionaries to distribute evenly among 4 classes. How many dictionaries will each class get?

18. Lai-Ching needs to sell 127 candy bars to earn her way to summer camp. If she sells 9 candy bars per day, how many days will it take her to sell the candy?

19. The youth group at Fellowship Church is preparing 9 care packages for college students. There are 117 candy bars. How many candy bars will be in each care package?

Chapter 3 Review

Solve.

20. $3 \times 5 \times 4 =$ 21. $6 \times 2 \times 2 =$ 22. $4 \times 3 \times 2 =$

One, Two, or Three Digits?

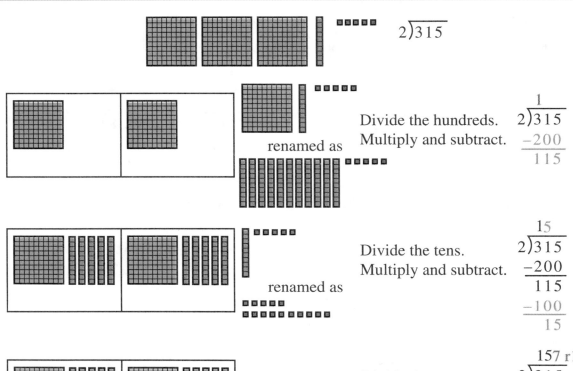

$$2\overline{)315}$$

Divide the hundreds.
Multiply and subtract.

$$\begin{array}{r} 1 \\ 2\overline{)315} \\ -200 \\ \hline 115 \end{array}$$

renamed as

Divide the tens.
Multiply and subtract.

$$\begin{array}{r} 15 \\ 2\overline{)315} \\ -200 \\ \hline 115 \\ -100 \\ \hline 15 \end{array}$$

renamed as

Divide the ones.
Multiply and subtract.
Write the remainder.

$$\begin{array}{r} 157 \text{ r}1 \\ 2\overline{)315} \\ -200 \\ \hline 115 \\ -100 \\ \hline 15 \\ -14 \\ \hline 1 \end{array}$$

r ■

Averages

For the first Sunday in May, the primary Sunday school classes reported attendance of 13, 25, 10, 18, 14, and 22. What was the average class attendance for that Sunday school?

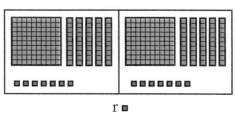

Steps for Finding an Average
1. Add all the numbers.
2. Divide the sum by the number of addends.

$13 + 25 + 10 + 18 + 14 + 22 = 102$

$102 \div 6 = 17$ students

Practice

Solve. Use multiplication to check your answers.

1. $6\overline{)88}$ 2. $2\overline{)194}$ 3. $3\overline{)29}$ 4. $5\overline{)655}$

5. $4\overline{)21}$ 6. $7\overline{)778}$ 7. $3\overline{)117}$ 8. $4\overline{)912}$

9. $6\overline{)35}$ 10. $2\overline{)136}$ 11. $5\overline{)687}$ 12. $8\overline{)476}$

Application

Write an equation for each word problem. Solve and label.

13. A Boeing 747 has 402 seats. A DC-10 has 288 seats. How many more seats does the 747 have than the DC-10?

14. How many seats are in 5 Boeing 747's combined?

15. There are 162 chairs that need to be set up for a fifth grade assembly. If 9 rows of chairs are set up with the same number in each row, how many chairs are in each row?

Find the average length of coastline for each group of states. Your teacher may allow you to use a calculator to check your answers.

16. California, Delaware, Oregon

17. Georgia, Hawaii, Maryland, New York

Length of Coastlines in Miles	
State	Coastline (mi.)
California	840
Delaware	28
Georgia	100
Hawaii	750
Maryland	31
New York	127
Oregon	296

Zero in the Quotient

> ## Zero in the Quotient
> When there are not enough tens or ones to divide, write a zero in that place.
> (A zero is not needed if it is the first digit.)

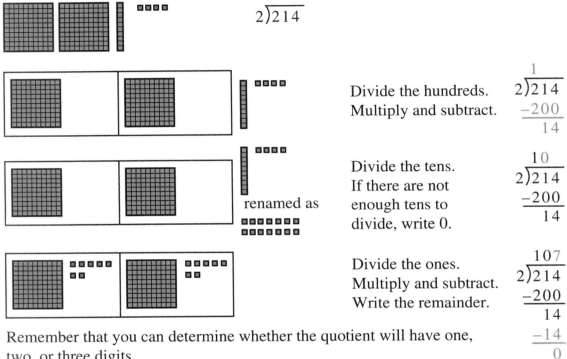

$$2\overline{)214}$$

Divide the hundreds.
Multiply and subtract.

$$\begin{array}{r} 1 \\ 2\overline{)214} \\ -200 \\ \hline 14 \end{array}$$

Divide the tens.
If there are not
enough tens to
divide, write 0.

$$\begin{array}{r} 10 \\ 2\overline{)214} \\ -200 \\ \hline 14 \end{array}$$

Divide the ones.
Multiply and subtract.
Write the remainder.

$$\begin{array}{r} 107 \\ 2\overline{)214} \\ -200 \\ \hline 14 \\ -14 \\ \hline 0 \end{array}$$

renamed as

Remember that you can determine whether the quotient will have one, two, or three digits.

$$\overset{X\,X\,X}{2\overline{)315}}$$ There are enough hundreds to divide.

$$\overset{X\,X}{3\overline{)265}}$$ There are enough tens to divide.

$$\overset{X}{5\overline{)37}}$$ There are not enough tens to divide.

*Teaching and admonishing one another
in psalms and hymns and spiritual songs,
singing with grace in your hearts to the Lord.*
Colossians 3:16

Practice

Mark the places where the digits of each quotient will be. Do not solve.

1. $3\overline{)719}$　　　2. $8\overline{)83}$　　　3. $6\overline{)207}$　　　4. $8\overline{)56}$

Solve. Use multiplication to check your answers.

5. $2\overline{)816}$　　　6. $3\overline{)905}$　　　7. $6\overline{)60}$　　　8. $2\overline{)41}$

9. $3\overline{)73}$　　　10. $4\overline{)921}$　　　11. $5\overline{)900}$　　　12. $7\overline{)763}$

Write a division equation to find the missing factor. Solve for *n*.

$$\text{Example:}\quad 5 \times n = 75 \qquad n = 75 \div 5$$
$$n = 15$$

$$\begin{array}{r} 15 \\ 5\overline{)75} \\ -50 \\ \hline 25 \\ -25 \\ \hline 0 \end{array}$$

13. $2 \times n = 600$　　14. $n \times 4 = 804$　　15. $3 \times n = 120$　　16. $n \times 8 = 864$

Application

Write equations for the word problems. Solve and label.

17. Mr. McKinley stacked the new hymnbooks on the table. If there are 60 hymnbooks stacked in 5 equal piles, how many hymnbooks are in each pile?

18. If each package of pencils costs $1.59, how much do 12 packages cost?

19. Althea saved $59.62 from babysitting. Her brother Marcus saved $38.24 from his paper route. How much more money did Althea save?

20. Attendance at choir practice was 45 the first week, 39 the second week, 46 the third week, and 38 the fourth week. What was the average attendance at choir practice?

Compatible Numbers

Compatible numbers are numbers that are easy to use together. To estimate a division problem with a four-digit dividend, think of compatible numbers.

$$3\overline{)8,426}$$

I can think of the basic fact.
$6 \div 3 = 2$; so
$6,000 \div 3 = 2,000$

Divide the thousands. Multiply and subtract.	Divide the hundreds. Multiply and subtract.	Divide the tens. Multiply and subtract.	Divide the ones. Multiply and subtract. Write the remainder.
$\begin{array}{r} 2, \\ 3\overline{)8,751} \\ -6,000 \\ \hline 2,751 \end{array}$	$\begin{array}{r} 2,9 \\ 3\overline{)8,751} \\ -6,000 \\ \hline 2,751 \\ -2,700 \\ \hline 51 \end{array}$	$\begin{array}{r} 2,91 \\ 3\overline{)8,751} \\ -6,000 \\ \hline 2,751 \\ -2,700 \\ \hline 51 \\ -30 \\ \hline 21 \end{array}$	$\begin{array}{r} 2,917 \\ 3\overline{)8,751} \\ -6,000 \\ \hline 2,751 \\ -2,700 \\ \hline 51 \\ -30 \\ \hline 21 \\ -21 \\ \hline 0 \end{array}$

Think

$2\overline{)1,870} \longrightarrow \overset{900}{2\overline{)1,800}}$

$$\begin{array}{r} 935 \\ 2\overline{)1,870} \\ -1,800 \\ \hline 70 \\ -60 \\ \hline 10 \\ -10 \\ \hline 0 \end{array}$$

Think

$5\overline{)2,630} \longrightarrow \overset{500}{5\overline{)2,500}}$

$$\begin{array}{r} 526 \\ 5\overline{)2,630} \\ -2,500 \\ \hline 130 \\ -100 \\ \hline 30 \\ -30 \\ \hline 0 \end{array}$$

Practice

Estimate using compatible numbers. Solve.   *Example:* $6\overline{)576}$ (100)

$$\begin{array}{r} 96 \\ 6\overline{)576} \\ -540 \\ \hline 36 \\ -36 \\ \hline 0 \end{array}$$

1. $7\overline{)2,947}$ 2. $4\overline{)2,364}$ 3. $8\overline{)6,584}$ 4. $6\overline{)614}$

5. $2\overline{)638}$ 6. $9\overline{)3,780}$ 7. $5\overline{)1,540}$ 8. $3\overline{)931}$

Application

Find the average for the word problem. Label the answer.

9. A school had 48 students enrolled in kindergarten, 42 enrolled in first grade, 29 enrolled in second grade, and 33 enrolled in third grade. What is the average enrollment in these grades?

Write an equation for each word problem. Solve and label.

10. If 9 students read an average of 650 pages each in one semester, what is the total number of pages read?

11. Nine students in Mrs. Shumate's class read a total of 3,402 pages in one semester. If each student read the same number of pages, how many pages did each student read?

12. Mrs. Dickson's class collected 8,205 pennies for the missionary gift. Mrs. Vaughn's class collected 9,352. How many more pennies did they collect than their combined goal of 15,000 pennies?

Chapter 3 Review

Use the Distributive Property to write a new equation. Solve.

Example: $5 \times 73 = (5 \times 70) + (5 \times 3) =$
$350 \quad + \quad 15 \quad = 365$

13. $4 \times 39 =$ 14. $7 \times 92 =$ 15. $8 \times 21 =$

Dividing Money

Divide money the same way you divide whole numbers. Remember to write the dollar sign and decimal point in the quotient.

$$\$3.72 \div 3 = \$1.24$$

Divide the one-dollar bills.	Divide the dimes.	Divide the pennies.

Rename 1 dime as 10 pennies.

Remember to use a zero as a place holder if there are not enough one-dollar bills to divide.

```
        $0.82
    8)$6.56
     -640
       16
      -16
        0
```

Averages

Each week in May the Dodson family spent the following amounts for groceries: week 1, $58.62; week 2, $65.13; week 3, $56.49; and week 4, $68.52. What was the average cost of a week's groceries?

Steps for finding an average:
1. Add all the numbers.
   $58.62 + $65.13 + $56.49 + $68.52 = $248.76
2. Divide the sum by the number of addends.
   $248.76 ÷ 4 = $62.19

Practice

Solve.

1. $5\overline{)\$2.15}$ 2. $6\overline{)\$17.04}$ 3. $4\overline{)\$6.08}$ 4. $2\overline{)\$0.08}$

5. $8\overline{)\$0.96}$ 6. $9\overline{)\$98.55}$ 7. $6\overline{)\$298.98}$ 8. $5\overline{)\$60.00}$

Application

Write equations for the word problems. Solve and label.

9. Mrs. Brown has $28.50 to buy each of her 3 children a gift. She wants to spend the same amount on each child. How much can she spend on each gift?

10. A bag of potato chips costs $0.99 on sale. If you save $0.09 by buying it on sale, what is the regular price of the chips?

11. Doris spent $45.16 on Christmas presents. Jerry spent $52.91. How much more did Jerry spend than Doris?

12. Three of Anthony's friends helped him put rubber bands around the newspapers he delivers. If each of the 4 boys prepared 48 newspapers, how many newspapers were prepared altogether?

13. Four girls went shopping. Lisa spent $18.04, Meredith spent $7.95, Miriam spent $20.55, and Leticia spent $14.34. What was the average spent by each girl?

Write a word problem for the equation. Solve and label.

14. $16.50 ÷ 3 =

 Ideas: clothes, food, gifts

Division: Alternative Forms

Division problems can be solved without zeros.

Modified Traditional Form (with zeros)

$$
\begin{array}{r}
149\ \text{r}1 \\
4\overline{)597} \\
-400 \\
\hline
197 \\
-160 \\
\hline
37 \\
-36 \\
\hline
1
\end{array}
$$

Traditional Form (without zeros)

$$
\begin{array}{r}
149\ \text{r}1 \\
4\overline{)597} \\
-4 \\
\hline
19 \\
-16 \\
\hline
37 \\
-36 \\
\hline
1
\end{array}
$$

1. Divide the hundreds.
2. Multiply $4 \times 1 = 4$ hundreds.
3. Subtract.
4. Combine the tens (use an arrow).
5. Divide the tens.
   Multiply and subtract.
6. Combine the ones (use an arrow).
7. Divide the ones.
   Multiply, subtract, and write the remainder.

Short Form

Division problems can be solved using a short form. When using the short form of division, there are neither zeros nor arrows.

1. Divide the hundreds.
   Multiply and subtract mentally.
2. Add the remaining hundreds to the tens.
3. Divide the tens.
   Multiply and subtract mentally.
4. Add the remaining tens to the ones.
5. Divide the ones.
   Multiply and subtract mentally.
   Write the remainder.

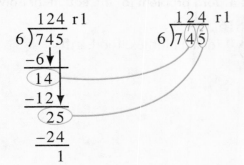

Traditional (without zeros)

$$
\begin{array}{r}
124\ \text{r}1 \\
6\overline{)745} \\
-6 \\
\hline
14 \\
-12 \\
\hline
25 \\
-24 \\
\hline
1
\end{array}
$$

Short

$$
\begin{array}{r}
124\ \text{r}1 \\
6\overline{)745}
\end{array}
$$

Practice

Use the traditional form (without zeros) to solve the problems.

1. $2\overline{)12,589}$ **2.** $4\overline{)7,988}$ **3.** $5\overline{)20,618}$ **4.** $6\overline{)1,726}$

5. $3\overline{)879}$ **6.** $8\overline{)3,173}$ **7.** $7\overline{)2,429}$ **8.** $9\overline{)6,147}$

Use the short form of division to solve the problems.

9. $4\overline{)394}$ **10.** $8\overline{)1,426}$ **11.** $5\overline{)1,594}$ **12.** $8\overline{)95}$

13. $3\overline{)6,021}$ **14.** $6\overline{)834}$ **15.** $2\overline{)\$9.58}$ **16.** $8\overline{)\$7.12}$

Write a word problem about the picture.
Solve and label.

17.

Meet the Challenge!

Fill in the missing numbers.

18.

$$
\begin{array}{r}
\square\square\ r\ \square \\
3\overline{)2\square\square} \\
-\underline{\square4\square} \\
17 \\
-\underline{\square\square} \\
\square
\end{array}
$$

If/Then

IF my people, which are called by my name, shall humble themselves, and pray, and seek my face, and turn from their wicked ways;

THEN will I hear from heaven, and will forgive their sin, and will heal their land.

II Chronicles 7:14

Class Work

RUN the following program. Enter information from the word problem below to calculate Jane's average and to answer the questions. (Your teacher may allow you to use a calculator.)

```
5 S=0
10 INPUT "HOW MANY ADDENDS";A
20 FOR I=1 TO A
30 INPUT "ENTER ADDEND: ",B
40 S=S+B
50 NEXT I
60 AV=S/A
70 PRINT "THE AVERAGE IS";AV
80 INPUT "DO YOU WANT TO DO ANOTHER? Y OR N";C$
90 IF C$="Y" THEN GOTO 5
100 END
```

Grading Scale	
A	94-100
B	86-93
C	78-85
D	70-77

Jane's math scores for the semester are 72, 76, 81, 92, and 94. The teacher uses the following grading scale.

1. What is Jane's average?

2. Will she pass math?

3. Will Jane's letter grade change if she scores 89 on her next test?

Multistep Word Problems

Application

Write an equation for each word problem.

1. Jerusha spent $19.75 on a sweater and $15.95 on a matching skirt. Mary found the same outfit on sale for $30.00. How much more did Jerusha pay?

2. Miss Cameron and Mrs. Harris baked cookies for vacation Bible school. They put 3 cookies in each sandwich bag. If Miss Cameron baked 72 cookies and Mrs. Harris baked 57 cookies, how many bags were there in all?

3. Uncle Bob picked 18 pumpkins. Jesse picked 7 pumpkins. If each pumpkin weighs about 14 pounds, about how many pounds of pumpkins did Uncle Bob and Jesse pick?

4. Alex picked 7 dozen apples. His mother uses 8 apples to make an apple pie. How many apples will be left if she makes 3 apple pies?

5. Roger's Auto Repair charges $18.50 to change the oil and oil filter in a car. How much will Mr. Hambrick save by buying an oil filter for $3.50, oil for $8.00, and doing the work himself?

6. Amanda picked 12 pounds of apples. Her brother John picked 17 pounds. If both of them pick the same amount of apples each day for 5 days, how many pounds of apples will be picked in all?

7. Mother uses 24 apples to make a jar of applesauce. If there are 3 apples per pound, how many jars of applesauce can mother make using the apples John and Amanda picked?

Composer

Dear Fifth Grade:

Thanks for taking an interest in how a songwriter uses math. I use math much more than you might think! Every song I write must have a time signature. That's a means of telling the person playing or singing the song how fast it should go. As I hear a melody in my head, I usually sit at the piano with my pencil and put all the notes on paper first, without worrying about the time signature. Then I go back and divide each line into measures and determine at what rate the song should be played.

Yesterday I was working on a song called "Thy Lovingkindness." It had a 6/8 time signature. That means there are six beats to every measure, and an eighth note gets 1 beat. Normally, an eighth note gets only half a beat in 4/4 or 3/4 time. Therefore, all my note values were doubled. Some notes are worth one beat, some two, and some only a half or fourth of a beat. I had to make sure every measure had six beats. Getting it all to work out can be tricky sometimes! But it's worth it when you have a beautiful song to show for all your effort.

Sincerely yours,

Brian Richards

Brian Richards

Richards Music Service
1600 Happy Hollow Rd. / Carrollton, GA 30116

Moore Christian School
334 Tara Lane
Mariposa, CA 95338

Chapter Review

Use compatible numbers to estimate. Write the letter of the best estimate.

1. $4\overline{)327}$ a. 80
              b. 90
              c. 800

2. $8\overline{)3,578}$ a. 40
               b. 400
               c. 4,000

3. $9\overline{)62,528}$ a. 540
                 b. 2,000
                 c. 7,000

Solve.

4. $\dfrac{63}{9}$

5. $\dfrac{24}{8}$

6. $32 \div 4$

Solve. Use multiplication to check your answers.

7. $9\overline{)252}$

8. $8\overline{)1,909}$

9. $3\overline{)86}$

10. $5\overline{)\$0.75}$

11. $5\overline{)\$67.85}$

12. $8\overline{)\$729.04}$

13. $5\overline{)6,025}$

14. $3\overline{)986}$

Write a division equation to find the missing factor. Solve for *n*.

15. $7 \times n = 42$

16. $n \times 4 = 648$

17. $6 \times n = 114$

Use short division to solve the problems.

18. $5\overline{)1,344}$

19. $7\overline{)25,201}$

20. $8\overline{)749}$

21. $3\overline{)573}$

Write equations for the word problems. Solve and label.

22. In their first 4 basketball games, the Warriors scored 85 points, 73 points, 66 points, and 72 points. What was the Warriors' average number of points per game?

23. The Jones family traveled 567 miles in 9 hours. What was their average speed in miles per hour?

24. Every week night, Dad jogs around the block 5 times. The distance around the block is 473 meters. How many meters does Dad jog each night?

25. The school program ran for 3 nights. The attendance was 197 on Tuesday, 132 on Thursday, and 342 on Friday. How many more people attended on Friday than on Tuesday and Thursday combined?

Use the table to answer the questions. Write the equations you use.

26. What was the average number of visitors each night in 1935?

27. What was the average number of visitors each night in 1945?

28. How many more people came to the fair in 1950 than in 1945?

29. What was the combined number of visitors for 1935 and 1940?

30. What was the average number of visitors each night for all the years combined?

Visitors to the County Fair

Year	Number of nights	Number of visitors
1935	7	945
1940	5	2,398
1945	8	7,935
1950	9	11,342

Write the letter of the correct answer.

1. The numbers in the box are ordered from least to greatest. Which number is missing?

   a. 28,614,039
   b. 28,624,930
   c. 29,614,978
   d. not given

28,642,301
29,624,892
29,732,890

2. Which of the forms below represents 400,000,003?

   a. 400,000,000 + 3
   b. $(4 \times 100,000,000) + (3 \times 1)$
   c. four hundred million, three
   d. all of the above

3. Solve.
   $$\begin{array}{r} 88,908 \\ -\,43,862 \\ \hline \end{array}$$

   a. 44,450
   b. 45,046
   c. 45,766
   d. not given

4. Solve for *n*.

   $280 - n = 62$

   a. $n = 218$
   b. $n = 222$
   c. $n = 228$
   d. not given

5. Which property represents $6 \times 8 = 8 \times 6$?

   a. Zero
   b. Identity
   c. Commutative
   d. Distributive

6. Solve.
   $$\begin{array}{r} 4,892 \\ \times\quad 43 \\ \hline \end{array}$$

   a. 162,356
   b. 210,356
   c. 220,530
   d. not given

7. Mrs. Kay has a circular rug with a diameter of 8 feet. What is the rug's circumference?

   a. 25.12 feet
   b. 26.13 feet
   c. 27.14 feet
   d. not given

8. What is the measure of the third angle?

   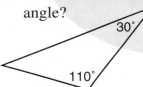

   a. 30°
   b. 40°
   c. 50°
   d. 60°

9. Solve.
   $$\begin{array}{r} 32.6 \\ +\,483.02 \\ \hline \end{array}$$

   a. 515.62
   b. 5156.2
   c. 616.02
   d. not given

10. Use short division.

    $8\overline{)3954}$

    a. 472 r1
    b. 483
    c. 494 r2
    d. not given

Preflight Inspection

The first concern of every pilot is safety. Once a pilot is in flight, it may be too late to notice a problem. Safety in the air requires careful observation on the ground. Before a flight, the pilot should walk around his plane and check it thoroughly to make sure all of its parts are in proper condition to fly. A pilot should always use a check list to be sure he doesn't leave out an important step.

Pilots usually start by opening the door of the cockpit and checking to make sure all the control switches are off. They turn on a master switch that allows them to read the fuel gauges for the two wing tanks. They carefully inspect the wings, pulling down the ailerons to check them for freedom of movement. They walk down the side of the plane and around the tail, then back up the other side, checking the surface of the plane for dents or cracks. They check the fuel and the oil to see that they are free from water or sediment. They finish by walking around the nose of the plane and checking the propeller for nicks or dents. After he has started the engine, the pilot must check oil pressure and other indicators to be sure the engine is running properly. He also checks to make sure the controls move freely. Just before he moves on the runway, the pilot performs an engine run-up, to be sure the engine functions properly at higher speeds.

If a pilot discovers a problem during the inspection, he should take care of it while still on the ground. A careful preflight check will go a long way toward ensuring safety in the air.

CHAPTER

7

Common Fractions

Aircraft that are used for commercial purposes must have a detailed inspection every 100 hours of engine time, in addition to the annual inspections required for all aircraft.

Checking the oil during the pre-flight inspection prevents the engine from seizing up.

133

Common Fractions

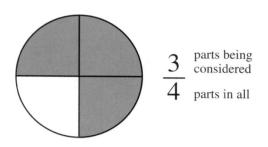

$$\frac{3}{4}$$ parts being considered

parts in all

> The **numerator** is the digit(s) above the fraction bar that tells the number of parts being considered.

> The **denominator** is the digit(s) below the fraction bar that tells the number of equal parts in all and names the parts.

This circle has been divided into four equal parts. Each part is one-fourth. The three red parts are being considered.

> The digits 3 and 4 are the *terms* of the fraction $\frac{3}{4}$.

A fraction can name part of a whole   *or*   part of a set.

$\frac{1}{2}$ part eaten
parts in all

One-half of the pie has been eaten.

$\frac{2}{5}$ red apples
apples in all

Two-fifths of the apples are red.

A fraction can be shown on a number line.

When comparing fractions that have denominators that are the same, the fraction with the greater numerator has the greater value.

   >

$$\frac{4}{6} \qquad > \qquad \frac{2}{6}$$

When comparing fractions that have numerators that are the same, the fraction with the lesser denominator has the greater value.

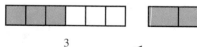 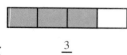

$$\frac{3}{6} \qquad < \qquad \frac{3}{4}$$

Practice

Write the word that will complete each sentence.

1. The _____ tells the number of equal parts in all and names the parts.

2. The _____ tells how many parts are being considered.

3. If two fractions have the same denominator, the fraction with the greater _____ is the greater fraction.

4. The numerator and the denominator are the _____ of a fraction.

Write the fraction that tells what part is colored.

5.   6.   7.   8.

Copy and complete each number line by filling in the missing fractions.

9.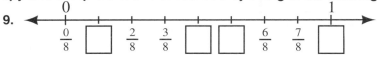

10.

Complete each number sentence using a < or >.

11. $\frac{17}{25}$ ☐ $\frac{14}{25}$ 12. $\frac{6}{8}$ ☐ $\frac{6}{12}$ 13. $\frac{1}{5}$ ☐ $\frac{3}{5}$

14. $\frac{7}{9}$ ☐ $\frac{7}{10}$ 15. $\frac{8}{9}$ ☐ $\frac{5}{9}$ 16. $\frac{1}{4}$ ☐ $\frac{3}{4}$

Application

Write a fraction to answer the question.

17. Mrs. Bernard had a dozen eggs. She used 5 of them in a cake. What part of the eggs is left?

Equivalent Fractions

Equivalent fractions name the same part of a whole or set. *Equivalent* means "equal value."

$$\frac{1}{2} = \frac{5}{10}$$

You can use the Identity Property of Multiplication to find equivalent fractions in higher terms.

When 1 is a factor in a multiplication equation, the product is the other factor.

To find an equivalent fraction for $\frac{1}{4}$, multiply $\frac{1}{4}$ by a fractional name for 1. (The numerator and denominator are the same, but not 0 or 1.)

$$\frac{1}{4} = \frac{1 \times 2}{4 \times 2} = \frac{2}{8}$$

$$\frac{1}{4} = \frac{2}{8}$$

Notice that the *terms* are higher in the second fraction.

Class Work

Multiply to find two equivalent fractions in higher terms.

1. $\frac{2}{3} = \frac{2 \times 2}{3 \times 2} =$

$\frac{2}{3} = \frac{2 \times 4}{3 \times 4} =$

2. $\frac{3}{5} =$

$\frac{3}{5} =$

3. $\frac{4}{7} =$

$\frac{4}{7} =$

Practice

Write the equivalent fraction in higher terms.

1.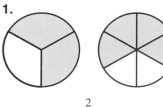

$$\frac{2}{3}$$

2.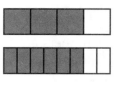

$$\frac{3}{4}$$

3.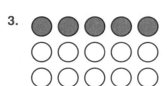

$$\frac{1}{3}$$

Write an equation to rename each fraction in higher terms.

Example: $\frac{3}{7} = \frac{3 \times 2}{7 \times 2} = \frac{6}{14}$

4. $\frac{1}{5}$

5. $\frac{3}{4}$

6. $\frac{1}{6}$

7. $\frac{4}{5}$

8. $\frac{3}{8}$

9. $\frac{1}{2}$

10. $\frac{2}{5}$

11. $\frac{4}{9}$

Write *true* or *false* for each number sentence.

12. $\frac{2}{5} = \frac{4}{10}$

13. $\frac{3}{8} = \frac{1}{12}$

14. $\frac{7}{9} = \frac{21}{28}$

15. $\frac{3}{4} = \frac{12}{16}$

Prime and Composite Numbers

> A **prime number** is a number with exactly 2 factors.
> These factors are the number itself and 1.

2 is a prime number. It has exactly 2 factors: 1 and 2.

$$\boxed{1} \times \boxed{2} = 2$$

The first 5 prime numbers are 2, 3, 5, 7, and 11.
Can you tell why 6 is *not* prime?

> A **composite number** is a number
> that has more than 2 factors.

6 is a composite number. It has 4 factors: 1, 2, 3, and 6.

$$\boxed{1} \times \boxed{6} = 6 \qquad\qquad \boxed{2} \times \boxed{3} = 6$$

Eratosthenes of Cyrene lived about 200 years before the birth of Christ. He was the head librarian at Alexandria, and was well known as a mathematician, astronomer, and geographer. He is remembered for calculating the circumference of the earth and for devising a system called the "Sieve of Eratosthenes" for finding prime numbers.

Use the "Sieve of Eratosthenes" to find the prime numbers to 100.

1. List the numbers 1 through 100.
2. Shade the 1; it is neither prime nor composite.
3. Circle the 2; it is prime.
   Cross out all the multiples of 2.
4. Circle the 3; it is prime.
   Cross out all the multiples of 3.
5. Circle the 5; it is prime.
   Cross out all the multiples of 5.
6. Circle the 7; it is prime.
   Cross out all the multiples of 7.
7. Circle all the numbers that are not crossed out.
   The circled numbers are prime.

Practice

Use a hundred grid and Eratosthenes' "sieve" to answer the problems.

1. List the prime numbers to 100.

2. Explain why 2 is the only even prime number.

Write *prime* or *composite* for each number.

3. 14   4. 23   5. 76   6. 43   7. 47

List the factors for each number and write *prime* or *composite*.

8. 5   9. 12   10. 9   11. 17

Language Link

12. Your friend needs to find all the prime numbers less than 100, but he has never heard of the Sieve of Eratosthenes. Write a letter to your friend explaining how to find prime numbers using this method.

Chapter 4 Review

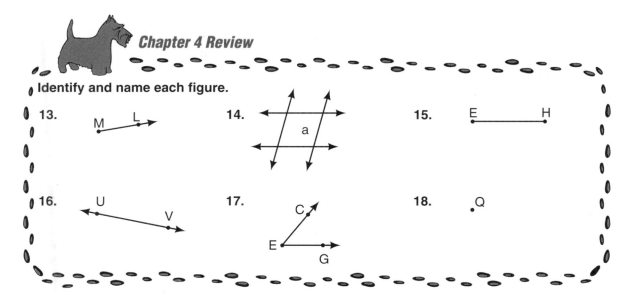

Identify and name each figure.

13. M L

14. a

15. E H

16. U V

17. C E G

18. Q

Common Factors

> **Factors** are the numbers multiplied together to find a product.
> **Common factors** are factors that are the same for each number.

Factors can be listed in pairs   or   from least to greatest.

The factors of 54	The factors of 72
1, 54	1, 72
2, 27	2, 36
3, 18	3, 24
6, 9	4, 18
	6, 12
	8, 9

54: 1, 2, 3, 6, 9, 18, 27, 54
72: 1, 2, 3, 4, 6, 8, 9, 12, 18, 24, 36, 72

The common factors for 54 and 72 are 1, 2, 3, 6, 9, and 18.

> The **greatest common factor** is the greatest
> factor that is the same for each number.

The greatest common factor of 54 and 72 is 18.

Divisibility Rules for 2, 3, 5, and 10

- Even numbers are divisible by 2 (2 is a factor).
- If the sum of the digits is divisible by 3, the number is divisible by 3 (3 is a factor).
- Numbers with a 5 or a 0 in the Ones place are divisible by 5 (5 is a factor).
- Numbers with a 0 in the Ones place are divisible by 10 (10 is a factor).

Steps for Renaming Common Fractions in Lower Terms

1. List the factors of each number from least to greatest.

   28: 1, 2, 4, 7, 14, 28
   42: 1, 2, 3, 6, 7, 14, 21, 42

   $$\frac{28}{42} = \frac{?}{?}$$

2. Find the common factors.

   $$\left.\begin{matrix} 28 \\ 42 \end{matrix}\right\} \; 1, 2, 7, 14$$

3. Divide the numerator and the denominator by a common factor (a fractional name for 1).

   $$\frac{28 \div 2}{42 \div 2} = \frac{14}{21} \quad \text{or} \quad \frac{28 \div 7}{42 \div 7} = \frac{4}{6} \quad \text{or} \quad \frac{28 \div 14}{42 \div 14} = \frac{2}{3}$$

Practice

Write *prime* or *composite* for each number.

1. 7   **2.** 11   **3.** 9   **4.** 8   **5.** 12

Follow the directions to find the greatest common factor.

6. List the prime numbers less than 10.

7. List the factors of 26 from least to greatest.

8. List the factors of 39 from least to greatest.

9. List the common factors of 26 and 39 from least to greatest.

10. What is the greatest common factor (GCF) of 26 and 39?

List the factors of each number. Underline the common factors. Circle the greatest common factor (GCF).

Example: 4 and 12

4: 1, 2, ④
12: 1, 2, 3, ④, 6, 12

11. 9 and 81

12. 21 and 63

13. 10 and 45

Write an equation to rename the fractions in lower terms.

Example: $\dfrac{15}{30}$ $\dfrac{15 \div 5}{30 \div 5} = \dfrac{3}{6}$

14. $\dfrac{12}{27}$ **15.** $\dfrac{16}{24}$ **16.** $\dfrac{18}{30}$

17. $\dfrac{15}{40}$ **18.** $\dfrac{14}{28}$ **19.** $\dfrac{8}{10}$

20. $\dfrac{24}{30}$ **21.** $\dfrac{12}{22}$ **22.** $\dfrac{36}{54}$

Factor Trees

> **Factors** are the numbers that are multiplied together to find a product.

The factors of 6 are 2, 3, and 6.

$\boxed{1} \times \boxed{6} = 6 \qquad \boxed{2} \times \boxed{3} = 6$

The factors of 12 are 2, 3, 4, 6, and 12.

Remember! Because 1 is a factor of every number, it is not necessary to name it in a list of factors.

$\boxed{1} \times \boxed{12} = 12 \qquad \boxed{2} \times \boxed{6} = 12 \qquad \boxed{3} \times \boxed{4} = 12$

Factor trees are used to find the prime factors of a number.

Notice that the prime factors do not change when the number is factored a different way.

You can find the greatest common factor (GCF) of two numbers using factor trees.

1. Use factor trees to find the prime factors of both numbers.

2. List the prime factors of each number from least to greatest.

   24: 2, 2, 2, 3
   36: ②②③ 3

3. Circle the prime factors in the second list that are common to both numbers.

4. Multiply the common (circled) factors.

   $2 \times 2 \times 3 = 12$
   The GCF of 24 and 36 is 12.

Practice

List the factors of each number from least to greatest.

1. 15

2. 18

3. 21

Write *prime* or *composite* for each number.

4. 7

5. 9

6. 3

7. 10

Copy and complete the factor trees.

8.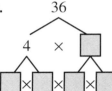

9.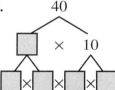

10.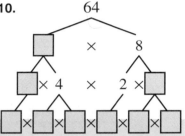

Use the factor trees to find the answers.

11. List the prime factors of 36 and 40 from least to greatest.

12. List the common prime factors of 36 and 40 from least to greatest.

13. What is the GCF of 36 and 40?

14. List the prime factors of 40 and 64 from least to greatest.

15. List the common prime factors of 40 and 64 from least to greatest.

16. What is the GCF of 40 and 64?

17. List the prime factors of 36 and 64 from least to greatest.

18. List the common prime factors of 36 and 64 from least to greatest.

19. What is the GCF of 36 and 64?

Make a factor tree for each number.

20. 20

21. 32

Use the factor trees to find the answers.

22. List the common prime factors of 20 and 32 from least to greatest.

23. What is the GCF of 20 and 32?

Lowest Terms

Steps for Renaming a Fraction in Lower Terms

1. Choose a common factor for the terms of the fraction.
2. Divide by a fractional name for 1 using a common factor.

$$\frac{24 \div 2}{32 \div 2} = \frac{12}{16}$$

Think: 12 and 16 can be divided by 2.

$$\frac{12 \div 2}{16 \div 2} = \frac{6}{8}$$

Think: 6 and 8 can be divided by 2.

$$\frac{6 \div 2}{8 \div 2} = \frac{3}{4}$$

$\frac{3}{4}$ is $\frac{24}{32}$ renamed in lowest terms.

To rename a fraction in *lowest* terms, divide the terms of the fraction by their greatest common factor.

1. Find the greatest common factor (GCF).

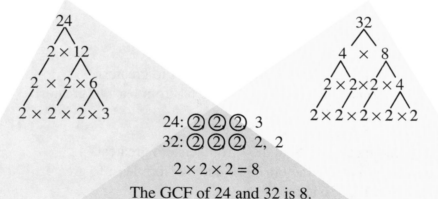

$$\begin{array}{c} 24 \\ 2 \times 12 \\ 2 \times 2 \times 6 \\ 2 \times 2 \times 2 \times 3 \end{array}$$

$$\begin{array}{c} 32 \\ 4 \times 8 \\ 2 \times 2 \times 2 \times 4 \\ 2 \times 2 \times 2 \times 2 \times 2 \end{array}$$

24: ②②② 3
32: ②②② 2, 2

$2 \times 2 \times 2 = 8$

The GCF of 24 and 32 is 8.

2. Divide both the numerator and the denominator by the greatest common factor.

$$\frac{24 \div 8}{32 \div 8} = \frac{3}{4}$$

Finding the greatest common factor before dividing is especially helpful when working with fractions that are in higher terms, such as $\frac{84}{120}$.

Practice

Make a factor tree for each number.

1. 28

2. 50

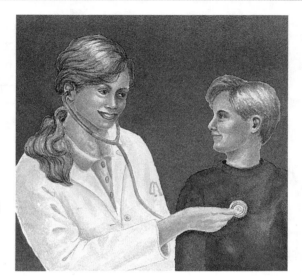

Use the factor trees to find the answers.

3. List the prime factors of 28 and 50 from least to greatest.

4. List the common prime factors of 28 and 50 from least to greatest.

5. What is the GCF of 28 and 50?

Rename in lowest terms.

6. $\frac{30}{54}$

7. $\frac{6}{15}$

8. $\frac{18}{28}$

9. $\frac{22}{50}$

10. $\frac{24}{40}$

11. $\frac{10}{12}$

12. $\frac{24}{60}$

13. $\frac{28}{50}$

Application

Answer each question. Rename the answer in lowest terms.

14. Mrs. Fox bought one dozen eggs. Nine of the eggs broke when they fell off the car seat on the way home. What fraction of the eggs broke?

15. Mrs. Rose baked two dozen cookies. Her family ate 16 of the cookies at lunch. What fraction of the cookies did they eat?

 Chapter 4 Review

Find the measurement of the unmarked angle in each triangle. Your teacher may allow you to use a calculator to check your answers.

16.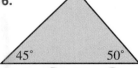
45° 50°

17.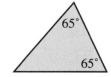
65°
65°

18.
50° 90°

When comparing unlike fractions, the fractions need to be renamed so they have common denominators. To find the common denominator, find the least common multiple (LCM). The LCM will become the common denominator.

$$\frac{4}{15} \ \square \ \frac{7}{20}$$

1. Find the prime factors of the denominators using factor trees.

2. List the prime factors of each denominator from least to greatest.

$$15: \ 3, \ 5$$
$$20: \ 2, \ 2, \ 5$$

3. Circle each factor in the list in which it appears most.

There are more 3s in the first list.

There are more 2s in the second list.

The 5 may be circled in either list, but not both.

4. Multiply the circled factors. The product is the LCM.

$$3 \times 2 \ \times \ 2 \times 5 \ =$$
$$(3 \times 2) \times (2 \times 5) \ =$$
$$6 \ \times \ 10 \ = \ 60$$

5. Rename the fractions using the LCM as the lowest common denominator.

$$\frac{4 \ \times \ n}{15 \ \times \ n} = \frac{?}{60} \qquad \begin{array}{c} n = 60 \div 15 \\ n = 4 \end{array} \qquad \frac{4 \ \times \ 4}{15 \ \times \ 4} = \frac{16}{60}$$

$$\frac{7 \ \times \ n}{20 \ \times \ n} = \frac{?}{60} \qquad \begin{array}{c} n = 60 \div 20 \\ n = 3 \end{array} \qquad \frac{7 \ \times \ 3}{20 \ \times \ 3} = \frac{21}{60}$$

6. Compare the fractions.

$$\frac{16}{60} < \frac{21}{60} \quad \text{so} \quad \frac{4}{15} < \frac{7}{20}$$

Practice

Make a factor tree for each number.

1. 9   **2.** 14   **3.** 12   **4.** 10   **5.** 8

Use the factor trees to find the answers.

6. List the prime factors of 9 and 12 from least to greatest.

7. What is the LCM of 9 and 12?

8. List the prime factors of 8 and 14 from least to greatest.

9. What is the LCM of 8 and 14?

10. List the prime factors of 8 and 10 from least to greatest.

11. What is the LCM of 8 and 10?

Complete each number sentence using a < or >.

12. $\frac{3}{4}$ ◯ $\frac{3}{8}$ **13.** $\frac{1}{2}$ ◯ $\frac{6}{8}$ **14.** $\frac{5}{7}$ ◯ $\frac{2}{14}$

15. $\frac{5}{8}$ ◯ $\frac{1}{2}$ **16.** $\frac{9}{10}$ ◯ $\frac{9}{12}$ **17.** $\frac{7}{10}$ ◯ $\frac{4}{5}$

Rename as fractions with common denominators using the LCM. Write another number sentence and complete each number sentence using a > or <.

18. $\frac{5}{12}$ ◯ $\frac{3}{7}$

19. $\frac{2}{3}$ ◯ $\frac{9}{16}$

20. $\frac{4}{14}$ ◯ $\frac{7}{20}$

Improper Fractions and Mixed Numbers

An **improper fraction** is equal to or greater than 1.
(The numerator is greater than or equal to the denominator.) $\dfrac{9}{9}$ $\dfrac{12}{7}$

A **mixed number** is the sum of a whole number and a fraction.
(It has a whole number part and a fraction part.) $4\dfrac{5}{8}$

A **proper fraction** has a value less than 1.
(The numerator is less than the denominator.) $\dfrac{3}{5}$

Renaming an Improper Fraction As a Mixed Number

$$\frac{8}{3} = ?$$

Find out the number of wholes using repeated subtraction

$$\frac{8}{3} - \frac{3}{3} - \frac{3}{3} = \frac{2}{3}$$

or divide. $\frac{8}{3}$ means $8 \div 3 = 2\frac{2}{3}$

Renaming a Mixed Number As an Improper Fraction

$$3\frac{1}{4} = ?$$

Find out the number of fraction pieces in the wholes using repeated addition

$$\frac{4}{4} + \frac{4}{4} + \frac{4}{4} + \frac{1}{4} = \frac{13}{4}$$

or multiplication. $\left(3 \times \frac{4}{4}\right) + \frac{1}{4} = \frac{13}{4}$

Steps for Comparing Mixed Numbers

Compare whole numbers.

$$6\frac{2}{3} > 3\frac{9}{10}$$

If whole numbers are the same, compare the fractions.

If there are like denominators, compare the numerators.

$$4\frac{1}{3} < 4\frac{2}{3}$$

If there are like numerators, compare the denominators.

$$3\frac{2}{4} > 3\frac{2}{5}$$

If the numerators are unlike and the denominators are unlike, rename so that the fractions have a common denominator.

$$2\frac{3}{7} \;\square\; 2\frac{8}{35}$$

$$2\frac{15}{35} > 2\frac{8}{35}$$

Practice

Write a mixed number and an improper fraction for each picture.

1.

2.

3.

Rename each improper fraction as a mixed number.

4. $\frac{5}{3}$ 5. $\frac{17}{8}$ 6. $\frac{11}{2}$ 7. $\frac{14}{5}$

8. $\frac{26}{5}$ 9. $\frac{18}{7}$ 10. $\frac{81}{10}$ 11. $\frac{25}{3}$

Rename each mixed number as an improper fraction.

12. $5\frac{1}{2}$ 13. $2\frac{5}{6}$ 14. $6\frac{1}{5}$ 15. $7\frac{3}{5}$

Complete each number sentence using a >, <, or =.

16. $\frac{4}{9} \bigcirc \frac{6}{20}$ 17. $2\frac{3}{5} \bigcirc 2\frac{2}{7}$ 18. $7\frac{7}{9} \bigcirc 8\frac{4}{5}$

19. $1\frac{12}{15} \bigcirc 1\frac{4}{5}$ 20. $\frac{10}{13} \bigcirc \frac{23}{24}$ 21. $3\frac{1}{6} \bigcirc 3\frac{2}{8}$

Application

Solve and label.

22. Sally picked 5 half-bushels of apples. How many bushels does she have?

23. Mrs. Jones bought 10 bags of coffee. Each bag held one-half pound. How many pounds of coffee did she buy?

Coordinate Graph

> **Ordered pairs** are two numbers that locate a point on a graph. The first number indicates the point's horizontal location, and the second number indicates the point's vertical location on a graph.

Class Work

Use the coordinate graph to complete the table.

1.

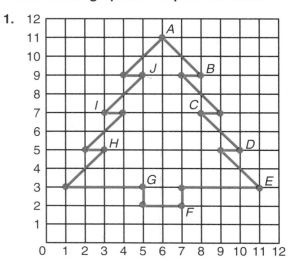

Point	Ordered Pair
A	(6, 11)
B	
C	
D	
E	
F	
G	
H	
I	
J	

Graph each point on graph paper. Connect the dots in order to form a graph.

2. $(2, 2) \rightarrow (5, 2) \rightarrow (5, 1) \rightarrow (7, 1) \rightarrow (7, 2) \rightarrow (10, 2) \rightarrow (10, 3) \rightarrow (7, 4) \rightarrow$
   $(7, 6) \rightarrow (12, 6) \rightarrow (12, 7) \rightarrow (7, 9) \rightarrow (7, 11) \rightarrow (6, 12) \rightarrow (5, 11) \rightarrow$
   $(5, 9) \rightarrow (0, 7) \rightarrow (0, 6) \rightarrow (5, 6) \rightarrow (5, 4) \rightarrow (2, 3) \rightarrow (2, 2)$

Meet the Challenge!

Graph and connect the points. Do not connect the last point of a section with the first point of the next section.

3. Part 1 $(1, 4) \rightarrow (6, 4) \rightarrow (7, 5) \rightarrow (8, 6) \rightarrow (12, 6) \rightarrow (13, 5) \rightarrow (13, 3)$
         $(12, 2) \rightarrow (8, 2) \rightarrow (7, 3) \rightarrow (6, 4)$
   Part 2 $(10, 6) \rightarrow (10, 7) \rightarrow (6, 8) \rightarrow (5, 7) \rightarrow (14, 7) \rightarrow (14, 6) \rightarrow (10, 7)$
   Part 3 $(6, 1) \rightarrow (12, 1) \rightarrow (13, 2)$
   Part 4 $(8, 2) \rightarrow (8, 1)$
   Part 5 $(11, 2) \rightarrow (11, 1)$
   Part 6 $(1, 5) \rightarrow (1, 3)$

Too Little or Too Much?

Class Work

> Write an equation for each word problem. Solve and label. (If there is too little information, decide what is needed and supply the information before solving the problem.)

1. A quart of milk costs $0.69, a half gallon costs $1.27, and a gallon costs $2.19. How much more do 2 half gallons of milk cost than 1 whole gallon of milk?

2. Becky bought three kinds of cereal. Each box of cereal had a mass of 567 grams. The first box cost $3.59, the second box cost $3.65, and the third box cost $3.74. What was the combined mass of the three boxes of cereal?

3. Miss McCord's class had a special work period to finish the science projects. Kathy finished her project 10 minutes before the end of the period. How long did Kathy work on her project that day?

4. A package of 8 ice-cream sandwiches costs $1.68. Mrs. Coburn bought 2 packages. What is the cost of each ice-cream sandwich in the package?

5. Each of the students in the fifth grade brought $0.50 to buy Mr. Luther a birthday present. How much money did the students collect to spend on the present?

6. Mr. Matthews used 115 gallons of gas to drive from Greenville, South Carolina, to Barstow, California. He traveled 2,564 miles in 5 days. How many miles will he travel in all if he returns to Greenville by the same route?

7. The Davenports' car needs 4 new tires. In one store they are $45.00 each, and in another store there is a special sale of 2 tires for $75.00. If the tires are of the same quality, which is the better buy? How much will the tires cost?

8. Miss Stallings jogs 3 miles and does 20 sit-ups each day. How many miles does she jog in 14 days?

9. After the game the team went to a fast-food restaurant to eat dinner. If each team member spent $3.87 for his meal, how much money did the team spend in all?

Aircraft Technician

Dear Fifth Grade:

A small airplane is a little like a seesaw—it has to be balanced. The point at which the plane balances is referred to as the center of gravity, which is like the center point on a seesaw. If the center of gravity, or C.G., is too far forward, the plane will tend to fly with its nose up, making it impossible for the pilot to control. Or if the C.G. is too far back, the nose will be tilting down toward the ground. Every time a new piece of equipment is added, the plane's weight will change, making the center of gravity different. Most of my opportunities to use math come when I'm figuring out weight and balance. For the plane to be balanced, the C.G. needs to be figured using a mathematical formula.

Every so often we need to replace the "O" rings in a plane's engines. When deciding how many "O" rings to order for a plane, I multiply. On a plane with a six-cylinder engine, each cylinder has one nozzle, and there are two "O" rings on each nozzle. Instead of walking up to the plane and counting how many replacements we need, I know that six times two equals twelve "O" rings. I then multiply the number of engines on the plane by the product. For a twin-engine plane, I would multiply two times twelve. I need 24 "O" rings. Years ago I learned the multiplication facts, and I still use them.

Respectfully yours,

Wayne Rapp

Wayne Rapp

AEROENGINEERING
907 Mehus Street
Minneapolis, MN 55409

Moore Christian School
334 Tara Lane
Mariposa, CA 95338

Chapter Review

Copy and complete the number line by filling in the missing fractions.

1.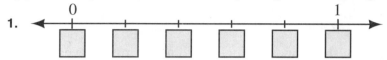

Write *prime* or *composite* for each number.

2. 63

3. 31

4. 5

5. 25

Make a factor tree for each number.

6. 28

7. 32

8. 27

9. 45

10. List the prime factors of 28 and 32 from least to greatest.

11. What is the greatest common factor of 28 and 32?

12. List the prime factors of 27 and 45 from least to greatest.

13. What is the greatest common factor of 27 and 45?

14. List the prime factors of 28 and 32 from least to greatest.

15. What is the least common multiple of 28 and 32?

16. List the prime factors of 27 and 45 from least to greatest.

17. What is the least common multiple of 27 and 45?

Rename each fraction in lowest terms.

18. $\frac{3}{9}$

19. $\frac{25}{50}$

20. $\frac{24}{60}$

21. $\frac{10}{80}$

22. $\frac{8}{12}$

23. $\frac{28}{40}$

24. $\frac{27}{45}$

25. $\frac{18}{30}$

Complete each number sentence using a < or >.

26. $\frac{2}{3} \bigcirc \frac{4}{5}$

27. $\frac{3}{8} \bigcirc \frac{7}{8}$

28. $3\frac{5}{6} \bigcirc 3\frac{5}{9}$

29. $4\frac{3}{10} \bigcirc 2\frac{3}{4}$

30. $5\frac{1}{9} \bigcirc 5\frac{6}{18}$

31. $\frac{3}{4} \bigcirc \frac{14}{20}$

32. $\frac{5}{8} \bigcirc \frac{5}{12}$

33. $\frac{2}{3} \bigcirc \frac{3}{4}$

34. $\frac{7}{10} \bigcirc \frac{9}{10}$

Rename the fractions with a common denominator to answer each question.

35. Bob ate $\frac{3}{8}$ of an apple pie. John ate $\frac{5}{12}$ of a strawberry pie. Who ate more pie?

36. Last year Martine saved $\frac{2}{5}$ of the money needed to go to camp. This year she saved $\frac{3}{7}$ of the money for camp. Which year did she save a greater part of her camp enrollment money?

37. Mrs. Collins bought 4 packages of sandwich meat. Each package held one-half pound of meat. How many pounds of sandwich meat did she buy?

Use the table to answer the questions.

Distance Run

	Monday	Tuesday	Wednesday	Thursday	Friday
Jill	$\frac{4}{10}$ mi.	$\frac{3}{5}$ mi.	$\frac{5}{10}$ mi.	$\frac{3}{12}$ mi.	$\frac{4}{6}$ mi.
Lauren	$\frac{5}{12}$ mi.	$\frac{3}{6}$ mi.	$\frac{2}{3}$ mi.	$\frac{2}{4}$ mi.	$\frac{8}{10}$ mi.

38. Who ran farther on Monday?

39. Who ran farther on Tuesday?

40. Who ran farther on Wednesday?

41. Who ran farther on Thursday?

42. Who ran farther on Friday?

Cumulative Review

Write the letter of the correct answer.

1. Round 609,489,743,820 to the nearest ten billion.
   a. 6,900,000,000
   b. 600,000,000,000
   c. 610,000,000,000
   d. not given

2. Choose the correct equation.
   Matt made some cookies. Eight were eaten and 5 are left. How many cookies did he make in all?
   a. $n = 8 - 5$ c. $n = 13 - 8$
   b. $n - 8 = 5$ d. not given

3. $6,000 \times 40 =$
   a. 240,000
   b. 2,400,000
   c. 24,000,000
   d. not given

4. What is a set of points that go on endlessly in *all* directions to form a flat surface?
   a. point   c. ray
   b. line segment   d. plane

5. What is the name of the figure?

   a. $\overline{AB}$ c. $\overrightarrow{AB}$
   b. $\overline{BA}$ d. both *a* and *b*

6. Which sign will make the sentence true?

   4.06 ◯ 4.60

   a. >   c. =
   b. <   d. not given

7. What decimal fraction is represented by point *A*?

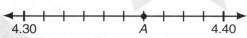

   a. 4.35   c. 4.36
   b. 4.37   d. not given

8. Which equation would you use to check the division problem?

   $$4\overline{)39}\quad 9\text{ r}3$$

   a. $(4 \times 3) + 9$
   b. $(4 + 9) \times 3$
   c. $(4 \times 9) + 3$
   d. not given

9. Solve for *n*.

   $2 \times n = 800$

   a. $n = 400$
   b. $n = 600$
   c. $n = 1,000$
   d. not given

10. What is $\frac{2}{5}$ renamed in higher terms?
    a. $\frac{4}{10}$ c. $\frac{6}{15}$
    b. $\frac{8}{20}$ d. all of the above

Cockpit Instruments

If you have ever been inside a small plane, you have noticed the rows of round clock faces on the instrument panel in front of you. But, as you probably guessed, these are not all clocks. Each one gives the pilot a different piece of information about his plane. Using all of these instruments together, a pilot can make sure his plane is working properly. He can also use his instruments to determine his position in the air, even when he cannot see outside.

One of the most important instruments, the airspeed indicator, measures the velocity of air as it rushes past the plane. The vertical speed indicator measures the plane's rate of climb. The altimeter is an instrument that measures how high the plane is flying in thousands and hundreds of feet. The turn-and-bank indicator helps the pilot straighten out the plane after a turn. The artificial horizon shows the pilot a tiny picture of where the plane is in relation to the horizon so he can keep it flying level. The tachometer shows the speed of the engine. Every plane has gauges to measure the amount, pressure, and temperature of its fuel and oil. Planes also have a means of navigating by radio signals from the ground when visibility is limited. Pilots call this VOR navigation.

Before a pilot has his instrument rating, he is not allowed to fly in extremely low visibility conditions. But after he has learned how to guide the plane by its instruments, he is capable of flying even in inclement weather if necessary.

Measurement: Metric

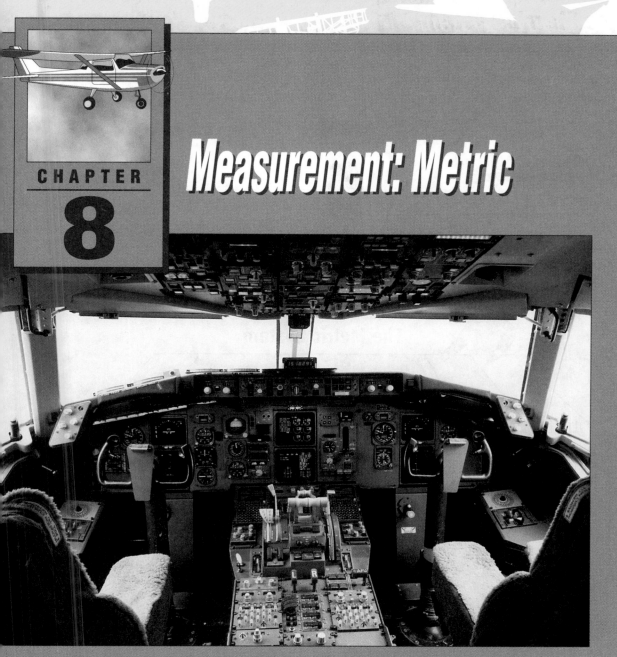

Although this commercial airliner cockpit is much more complex than that of a small plane, the basic instruments found in the smaller cockpit are all here too.

The Metric System

The metric system of measurement, based on the number 10, is used throughout the world. It is divided into linear, capacity, and mass units.

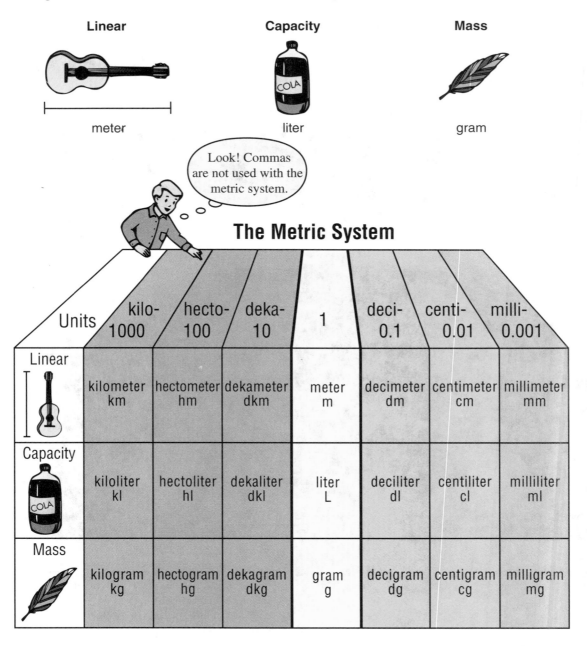

Linear	Capacity	Mass
meter	liter	gram

Look! Commas are not used with the metric system.

The Metric System

Units	kilo- 1000	hecto- 100	deka- 10	1	deci- 0.1	centi- 0.01	milli- 0.001
Linear	kilometer km	hectometer hm	dekameter dkm	meter m	decimeter dm	centimeter cm	millimeter mm
Capacity	kiloliter kl	hectoliter hl	dekaliter dkl	liter L	deciliter dl	centiliter cl	milliliter ml
Mass	kilogram kg	hectogram hg	dekagram dkg	gram g	decigram dg	centigram cg	milligram mg

Practice

Use the chart on page 158 to answer the questions.

1. What is the basic unit of capacity?

2. What is the basic unit of length?

3. What is the basic unit of mass?

Write the prefix of each word. Write the number it represents.

Example: hectometer *hecto-; 100*

4. decimeter   5. hectoliter   6. milligram   7. dekaliter   8. centimeter

Write the unit represented by each symbol.

9. mg   10. cg   11. dkl   12. hl   13. dg   14. kg

15. hm   16. hg   17. ml   18. km   19. dkg   20. cm

Write the prefix for each number.

21. 0.001   22. 10   23. 1000   24. 0.01

Write the symbol of the unit you would use to measure.

25. the distance to the moon   26. amount of water in a bathtub

27. mass of an airplane   28. height of a building

29. length of an ant   30. medicine in an eyedropper

Chapter 6 Review

Write a division equation to find the missing factor. Solve for *n*.

31. $4 \times n = 20$ 32. $n \times 5 = 100$ 33. $n \times 6 = 78$ 34. $9 \times n = 153$

Units of Length

This chart shows metric units of length.

kilometer (1000 meters) km	hectometer (100 meters) hm	dekameter (10 meters) dkm	meter (1 meter) m	decimeter (0.1 meters) dm	centimeter (0.01 meters) cm	millimeter (0.001 meters) mm

1 m

The distance from a man's left shoulder to the end of his right hand is about 1 meter.

1 cm

The width of a fingernail is about 1 centimeter.

The width of one wire of a paper clip is about 1 millimeter.

1 mm

The length of 10 soccer fields is 1 kilometer.

100 m

To rename larger units as smaller units, multiply.

Timothy ran 5 kilometers. How many meters did he run?

$$5 \text{ km} = \underline{\hspace{1cm}} \text{ m}$$
$$5 \times 1000 = 5000$$
$$5 \text{ km} = \underline{5000} \text{ m}$$

Think: 1 km = 1000 m

To rename smaller units as larger units, divide.

Tracy pulled weeds from a row of plants 7000 millimeters long. How many meters long is the row?

$$7000 \text{ mm} = \underline{\hspace{1cm}} \text{ m}$$
$$7000 \div 1000 = 7$$
$$7000 \text{ mm} = \underline{7} \text{ m}$$

Think: 1000 mm = 1 m

Practice

Use a centimeter ruler. Measure to the nearest centimeter.

1.

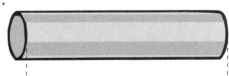

2.

Use a centimeter ruler. Measure to the nearest millimeter.

3.

4.

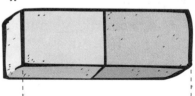

Rename the metric units of length. Your teacher may allow you to use a calculator.

5. 2 km = _____ m

6. 3.746 m = _____ mm

7. 47.36 m = _____ cm

8. 2225 m = _____ km

9. 45 cm = _____ m

10. 2.376 km = _____ m

11. 320 mm = _____ m

12. 3829 mm = _____ m

13. 86 m = _____ cm

Write the unit that would be used to measure each object (*millimeter, centimeter, meter, kilometer*).

14. the length of a book

15. the length of a house

16. the width of a nickel

Centimeters and Millimeters

Centimeters and millimeters are metric units used to measure small lengths.

1 centimeter (cm) = 10 millimeters (mm)

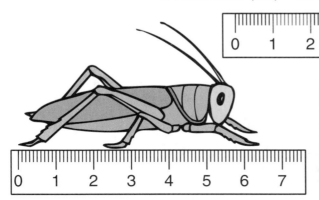

This grasshopper measures 6 centimeters and 4 millimeters.
This can be written:
- as centimeters and millimeters (6 cm 4 mm)
- as millimeters (64 mm)
- as a decimal (6.4 cm)

Multiply to rename centimeters as millimeters.

Debbie's caterpillar measures 5 cm. How many millimeters long is it?

$$5 \text{ cm} = \underline{} \text{ mm}$$
$$5 \times 10 = 50$$
$$5 \text{ cm} = \underline{50} \text{ mm}$$

John's caterpillar measures 5.9 cm. How many millimeters long is it?

$$5.9 \text{ cm} = \underline{} \text{mm}$$
$$5.9 \times 10 = 59$$
$$5.9 \text{ cm} = \underline{59} \text{ mm}$$

Divide to rename millimeters as centimeters.

Carrie's lizard measures 160 mm. How many centimeters long is it?

$$160 \text{ mm} = \underline{} \text{ cm}$$
$$160 \div 10 = 16$$
$$160 \text{ mm} = \underline{16} \text{ cm}$$

Matthew's lizard measures 96 mm. How many centimeters long is it?

$$96 \text{ mm} = \underline{} \text{ cm}$$
$$96 \div 10 = 9.6$$
$$96 \text{ mm} = \underline{9.6} \text{ cm}$$

Practice

Estimate each length to the nearest centimeter. Measure to the nearest centimeter and millimeter.

Example: ├─────────────────┤

(4 cm)   3 cm 9 mm

1.

2.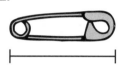

3.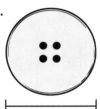

Rename the millimeters as centimeters and millimeters. Then rename as centimeters. Your teacher may allow you to use a calculator.

Example: 48 mm = _4_ cm _8_ mm = _4.8_ cm

4. 37 mm = _____ cm _____ mm = _____ cm

5. 152 mm = _____ cm _____ mm = _____ cm

6. 95 mm = _____ cm _____ mm = _____ cm

7. 397 mm = _____ cm _____ mm = _____ cm

Rename the units of length.

8. 2 cm = _____ mm

9. 7 mm = _____ cm

10. 16 cm = _____ mm

11. 39 cm = _____ mm

12. 60 mm = _____ cm

13. 150 mm = _____ cm

Write the unit that would be used to measure each distance (*meter, centimeter, millimeter*).

14. the distance from the ceiling to the floor

15. the length of a tennis court

16. the width of a ring

17. the length of a worm

Metric Units of Capacity

Capacity is the amount a container will hold. The *liter* (L) is the basic metric unit of capacity. The *milliliter* (ml) is a metric unit of capacity used to measure small amounts.

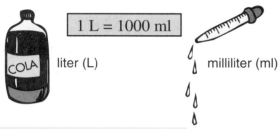

1 L = 1000 ml

liter (L)   milliliter (ml)

Multiply to rename liters as milliliters.

Josiah has 2 liters of soft drink. How many milliliters of soft drink does Josiah have?

$$2 \text{ L} = \underline{} \text{ ml}$$
$$2 \times 1000 = 2000$$
$$2 \text{ L} = \underline{\text{ 2000 }} \text{ ml}$$

Divide to rename milliliters as liters.

Mrs. Henry poured 7218 milliliters of punch into the punch bowl. How many liters of punch are in the bowl?

$$7218 \text{ ml} = \underline{} \text{ L}$$
$$7218 \div 1000 = 7.218$$
$$7218 \text{ ml} = \underline{\text{ 7.218 }} \text{ L}$$

Temperature is measured in degrees Celsius (°C) in the metric system.

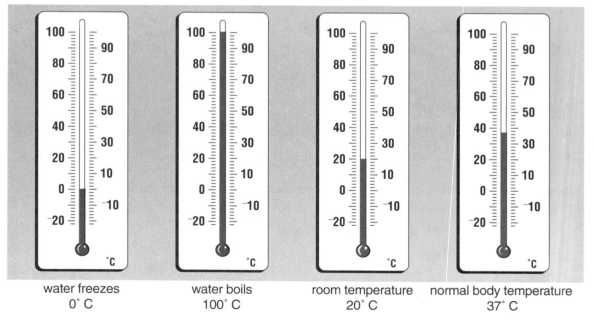

| water freezes 0° C | water boils 100° C | room temperature 20° C | normal body temperature 37° C |

Practice

Write the unit that would be used to measure each capacity (*milliliter, liter*).

1. paint for a house
2. lemonade for a party
3. 5 drops of food coloring
4. water to fill an aquarium
5. juice to fill a baby's bottle
6. cup of hot chocolate

Rename the units of capacity. Your teacher may allow you to use a calculator.

7. 8 L = _____ ml
8. 600 ml = _____ L
9. 7722 ml = _____ L
10. 7000 ml = _____ L
11. 17.493 L = _____ ml
12. 215 ml = _____ L
13. 18013 ml = _____ L
14. 9 L = _____ ml
15. 4.823 L = _____ ml

Write the temperature.

16.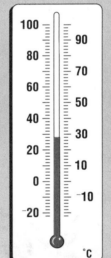
17.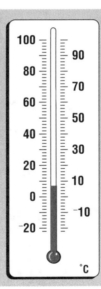
18.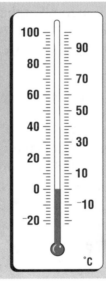
19.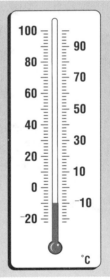

Write the letter of the more sensible temperature for each activity.

20. playing football   a. ⁻10° C   b. 18° C
21. swimming in the ocean   a. 30° C   b. 0° C
22. cross-country skiing   a. ⁻8° C   b. 25° C
23. shoveling snow   a. ⁻2° C   b. 30° C

Metric units of mass include milligram, gram, and kilogram.

| 1 crystal of salt | a dollar bill | a bunch of bananas |
| 1 mg | 1 g | 1 kg |

$$1000 \text{ mg} = 1 \text{ g} \qquad 1000 \text{ g} = 1 \text{ kg}$$

Multiply to rename larger units as smaller units.

Gloria bought a potted plant that has a mass of 3 kilograms. What is the mass of the plant in grams?

$3 \text{ kg} = \underline{\hspace{1cm}} \text{ g}$
$3 \times 1000 = 3000$
$3 \text{ kg} = \underline{3000} \text{ g}$

Divide to rename smaller units as larger units.

Russ used equipment that has a mass of 93278 grams. What is the mass of the equipment in kilograms?

$93278 \text{ g} = \underline{\hspace{1cm}} \text{ kg}$
$93278 \div 1000 = 93.278$
$93278 \text{ g} = \underline{93.278} \text{ kg}$

Practice

Write the unit that would be used to measure each object (*milligram, gram, kilogram*).

1. a nickel   **2.** a bag of cement   **3.** a snowflake   **4.** a horse

5. a grain of sand   **6.** a clothes iron   **7.** a paper clip   **8.** a calculator

Rename the units of mass. Your teacher may allow you to use a calculator.

9. 1085 mg = _____ g   **10.** 0.113 g = _____ mg   **11.** 6899 mg = _____ g

12. 7900 g = _____ kg   **13.** 3 kg = _____ g   **14.** 12 kg = _____ g

15. 0.045 kg = _____ g   **16.** 7.897 g = _____ mg   **17.** 6392 g = _____ kg

---

Catch of the Day - Fishing trip results!

Fisherman	Fish	Mass
Andrea	trout	1.5 kg
Eileen	salmon	1.6 kg
Howard	bass	1900 g
Jon	perch	2400 g

Use the chart to answer the questions. Your teacher may allow you to use a calculator.

18. What was the mass of Howard's fish in kilograms?

19. What was the mass of Eileen's fish in grams?

20. What was the mass of Jon's fish in kilograms?

21. What was the mass of Andrea's fish in grams?

Meet the Challenge!

22. Jenny found a rock with a mass of 4 kilograms. What is the mass of the rock in milligrams?

Adding and Subtracting Metric Units

Metric units can be added or subtracted as individual units or as decimals.

Addition

The Statue of Liberty is 46 m 5 cm tall from her feet to the top of the torch. The pedestal is 46 m 94 cm high. What is the overall height including the pedestal?

$$
\begin{array}{r}
46 \text{ m } 5 \text{ cm} \\
+46 \text{ m } 94 \text{ cm} \\
\hline
92 \text{ m } 99 \text{ cm}
\end{array}
\qquad \text{or} \qquad
\begin{array}{r}
46.05 \text{ m} \\
+46.94 \text{ m} \\
\hline
92.99 \text{ m}
\end{array}
$$

Subtraction

The Statue of Liberty is 33 m 45 cm tall from her feet to the top of her head. The entire statue is 46 m 5 cm tall. How much height is added by the upraised arm and torch?

Remember
1 m = 100 cm

$$
\begin{array}{r}
\overset{5}{} \quad \overset{105}{} \\
46 \text{ m } 5 \text{ cm} \\
-33 \text{ m } 45 \text{ cm} \\
\hline
12 \text{ m } 60 \text{ cm}
\end{array}
\qquad \text{or} \qquad
\begin{array}{r}
\overset{5}{} \overset{10}{} \\
46.05 \text{ m} \\
-33.45 \text{ m} \\
\hline
12.60 \text{ m}
\end{array}
\quad \text{or } 12.6 \text{ m}
$$

Class Work

Write an equation for the word problem. Solve and label.

1. The overall mass of the statue is 204000 kilograms. The copper skin is 91000 kilograms of the mass. What is the mass of the rest of the statue?

Did you know . . .

A metric ton is equivalent to 1000 kg. The copper skin of the Statue of Liberty has a mass of 91 metric tons. The framework of the statue has a mass of 113 metric tons. What is the overall mass of the statue in metric tons?

Practice

Solve.

1. $\begin{array}{r} 7.05 \text{ m} \\ + 3.49 \text{ m} \\ \hline \end{array}$

2. $\begin{array}{r} 3.518 \text{ L} \\ - 2.154 \text{ L} \\ \hline \end{array}$

3. $\begin{array}{r} 9 \text{ m} \quad 76 \text{ cm} \\ - 8 \text{ m} \quad 23 \text{ cm} \\ \hline \end{array}$

4. $\begin{array}{r} 6 \text{ m} \quad 15 \text{ cm} \\ + 2 \text{ m} \quad 28 \text{ cm} \\ \hline \end{array}$

5. $\begin{array}{r} 8 \text{ L} \quad 163 \text{ ml} \\ + 2 \text{ L} \quad 515 \text{ ml} \\ \hline \end{array}$

6. $\begin{array}{r} 15 \text{ kg} \quad 315 \text{ g} \\ - 5 \text{ kg} \quad 198 \text{ g} \\ \hline \end{array}$

7. $\begin{array}{r} 9 \text{ m} \quad 42 \text{ cm} \\ + 10 \text{ m} \quad 63 \text{ cm} \\ \hline \end{array}$

8. $\begin{array}{r} 12 \text{ L} \quad 213 \text{ ml} \\ - 8 \text{ L} \quad 176 \text{ ml} \\ \hline \end{array}$

Application

Write an equation for each word problem. Solve and label.

9. Liberty's old emergency elevator was 64.5 meters high. A new elevator, installed during the statue's renovation in the 1980s, is 29 meters high. How much shorter is the new elevator?

10. Each eye of the Statue of Liberty is 0.76 meters wide. What is the width of both eyes?

Language Link

11. Explain why 15 m 4 cm is equal to 15.04 m.

Chapter 6 Review

Solve.

12. $3\overline{)4,365}$

13. $7\overline{)5,201}$

14. $9\overline{)8,746}$

15. $5\overline{)9,306}$

Miles to Kilometers

You may have seen signs telling you how many miles you must travel before you reach your destination. Sometimes signs will tell the distance in kilometers. You can use your computer to convert miles to kilometers.

Class Work

Enter the program below into the computer.

```
10 REM    RENAME MILES TO KILOMETERS
20 INPUT "NUMBER OF MILES"; MI
25 PRINT
30 LET KM=MI*1.61
40 PRINT "MILES", "KILOMETERS"
50 PRINT MI, KM
55 PRINT
60 INPUT "DO YOU WANT TO DO ANOTHER? Y OR N"; A$
65 PRINT
70 IF A$="Y" THEN GOTO 20
80 END
```

RUN the program to find the answers to the problems. If a computer is not available, you may use a calculator.

$$kilometers = miles \times 1.61$$

1. Atlanta, Ga., to Chicago, Ill.   674 miles = _____ kilometers

2. Chicago, Ill., to Los Angeles, Calif.   2,054 miles = _____ kilometers

3. Los Angeles, Calif., to Denver, Colo.   1,059 miles = _____ kilometers

4. Denver, Colo., to Washington, D.C.   1,616 miles = _____ kilometers

5. Washington, D.C., to New York, N.Y.   233 miles = _____ kilometers

Meet the Challenge!

6. How many kilometers would you travel if you flew from Los Angeles to London, England (5,439 miles), and then from London to Vienna, Austria (771 miles)?

Map and Scale

Class Work

Use the map, the scale, and your centimeter ruler to solve the problems. Measure to the nearest millimeter, add the measurements, round to the nearest centimeter, and then use the scale.

1. On Monday, the Ortegas traveled from Indianapolis, Indiana, to Nashville, Tennessee. On Tuesday, they traveled to Greenville, Mississippi. How far did the Ortegas travel on Monday and Tuesday?

2. Randall went by train from Richmond, Virginia, to Norfolk, Virginia; and then he went to Dover, Delaware. How far did Randall travel?

3. Mrs. Fox lives in Charleston, West Virginia. Her sister lives in Tampa, Florida. About how many kilometers will she travel per day if she makes the trip in two days and travels the same distance each day?

4. The Butlers traveled from Memphis, Tennessee, to Dover, Delaware, for their vacation. Their neighbors, the Smiths, traveled from Memphis to Charleston, South Carolina. How much farther did the Butlers travel than the Smiths?

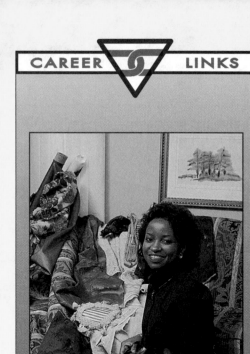

Interior Decorator

Dear Fifth Grade:

When I got your letter asking me how I use math in my job, I had to think about that for a minute. Then I remembered a decorating job I did for a very particular customer. Miss Jackson wanted her home to be decorated in a style she called neo-Victorian. I took lots of measurements throughout her home before I started decorating it. I measured the length and width of the windows so I could choose curtains, measured the rooms that needed to be wallpapered so I would know how much paper to use, and measured spaces on the wall where I felt mirrors or pictures would look nice.

We began with the kitchen. Miss Jackson had already chosen her kitchen wallpaper; it was striped with a floral border at the top. Near the end of the job, she began to get very nervous because she was afraid I was going to run out of paper. I was glad I had taken careful measurements! I finished the last panel, and there were still some scraps of paper left over. She checked my work thoroughly for mistakes. I was very relieved when she told me she was satisfied with the job! From that point on, she never questioned anything else I did. The most important thing about measuring is to be accurate. Measure something three or four times if you're not sure you did it correctly. Being off by two inches can ruin a wallpaper job!

Cordially yours,

Rita Henderson
Rita Henderson

Henderson
Interiors
P.O Box 151 · Cookeville, TN 38501

Moore Christian School
334 Tara Lane
Mariposa, CA 95338

Write the unit that would be used to measure each length (*kilometer, meter, centimeter, millimeter*).

1. thickness of a penny

2. distance from London to Rome

3. length of a car

4. length of your foot

5. height of the Statue of Liberty

6. width of a blade of grass

Write the unit that would be used to measure each capacity (*liter, milliliter*).

7. water in a fishbowl

8. water in a bathtub

9. tea in a cup

Write the unit that would be used to measure each mass (*kilogram, gram, milligram*).

10. a mouse 11. a grain of rice 12. a tractor 13. a person 14. a pencil

Rename the metric units.

15. 5 km = _____ m

16. 2000 mm = _____ m

17. 1 m = _____ cm

18. 4000 m = _____ km

19. 5 L = _____ ml

20. 7000 g = _____ kg

21. 8 kg = _____ g

22. 6000 ml = _____ L

23. 3 cm = _____ mm

Write the letter of the correct answer.

24. 831 cm = _____ m   a. 8.31   b. 0.0831   c. 800.31

25. 1.796 kg = _____ g   a. 17.96   b. 0.0976   c. 1796

26. 4765 m = _____ km   a. 4765   b. 0.4765   c. 4.765

27. 71 mm = _____ cm   a. 7100   b. 7.1   c. 0.071

Use a centimeter ruler. Measure to the nearest centimeter and millimeter.

28. |—————————————————————|

29. |————————————————|

Write the temperature.

30.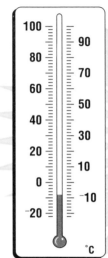

31.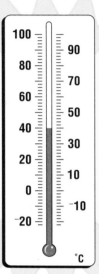

32.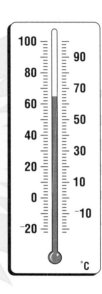

Solve.

33. $\begin{array}{r} 6.21 \text{ m} \\ - 3.54 \text{ m} \\ \hline \end{array}$

34. $\begin{array}{r} 82 \text{ m } 41 \text{ cm} \\ + 40 \text{ m } 78 \text{ cm} \\ \hline \end{array}$

35. $\begin{array}{r} 24.353 \text{ L} \\ + 11.212 \text{ L} \\ \hline \end{array}$

36. $\begin{array}{r} 6 \text{ m } 57 \text{ cm} \\ - 2 \text{ m } 22 \text{ cm} \\ \hline \end{array}$

Write an equation for each word problem. Solve and label.

37. Dr. Harris told Mr. Markham to cut fat from his diet. Mr. Markham had a mass of 101.35 kg. After 8 weeks he had a mass of 97.854 kg. How much did Mr. Markham's mass decrease?

38. To get to Grandma's house, the Markhams drove 145.253 km before lunch and 85.088 km after lunch. How far did they drive in all?

39. How much farther did the Markhams drive in the morning than in the afternoon?

40. Gail needs 12 L of punch for a party. She has 7 L 500 ml. How much more punch does she need?

Cumulative Review

Write the letter of the correct answer.

1. Round 93,462,980 to the nearest thousand.
   a. 93,000,000
   b. 93,500,000
   c. 93,463,000
   d. not given

2. Choose the correct type of subtraction.

   Ken has 8 screws. He needs 17 screws. How many more screws does he need?

   a. take away
   b. missing addend
   c. comparing
   d. unknown part

3. The numbers 1, 2, 3, 6, 9, and 18 are factors of what number?
   a. 6
   b. 9
   c. 12
   d. 18

4. What is a line segment whose end points are the center of a circle and any point on the circle?
   a. radius
   b. diameter
   c. chord
   d. angle

5. Solve.

   $$18 - 6.382$$

   a. 11.382
   b. 11.618
   c. 12.728
   d. not given

6. Solve.

   $$6 \overline{)1,800}$$

   a. 300
   b. 500
   c. 400
   d. 600

7. Solve.

   $$4 \overline{)328}$$

   a. 62
   b. 82
   c. 64
   d. 84

8. The Beck family traveled 1,540 miles on vacation. If they traveled for 5 days, what is the average number of miles they traveled each day?
   a. 308 miles
   b. 408 miles
   c. 508 miles
   d. not given

9. What is $\frac{15}{35}$ renamed in lower terms?
   a. $\frac{1}{5}$
   b. $\frac{2}{8}$
   c. $\frac{3}{7}$
   d. not given

10. Which is not a unit of mass?
    a. milligram
    b. hectogram
    c. kilogram
    d. dekameter

Pilot Talk

If you were to listen to the talk on a pilot's radio, you might think you were hearing a foreign language. Pilots often use code words and special expressions to mean certain things. For example, pilots and air traffic controllers all memorize the phonetic alphabet. The phonetic alphabet substitutes words for letters whenever a letter occurs by itself. Letters sound similar when heard over a radio. If words are used instead of letters, sounds can be distinguished more easily. For example, if a pilot had to say "B-15," he would say "Bravo-15." Another term used is "niner" to distinguish the number nine from the number five.

Pilots identify their planes by their registration numbers. They give the type of plane, a set of three or four numbers, and the final letter at the end of the registration number. The number "Skyhawk 976D" would sound like this: "Skyhawk niner seven six Delta."

Before taking off and before landing, the pilot has to radio the control tower for "clearance," or permission. Air traffic controllers at large airports have special radar that allows them to see whether a certain air space is clear for a plane to enter it. Air traffic controllers at small airports usually have to go by sight. They will direct the plane safely to an open runway when it is ready to land. It is vitally important that pilots listen and follow the controller's instructions. It could even be a matter of life or death.

Division: Two-Digit Divisors

The pilots of these two aircraft, flying very close at speeds above 300 mph, must maintain communications with each other and controllers to fly safely.

Controllers in this air force control center use radar and other tools to direct flight operations.

177

Division: Multiples of Ten

If the divisor is a multiple of 10, decide where to start, then think of the basic fact.

Two-digit dividend $20\overline{)80}$

Step 1
Decide where to start.

$$\overset{\textbf{x}}{20\overline{)80}}$$

There are not enough tens to divide into 20 groups. Divide the ones.

Step 2
Think of the basic fact.

$8 \div 2 = 4$

Step 3
Multiply, subtract, and write the remainder.

$$\begin{array}{r} 4 \\ 20\overline{)80} \\ -80 \\ \hline 0 \end{array}$$

Three-digit dividend $80\overline{)734}$

Step 1
Decide where to start.

$$\overset{\textbf{x}}{80\overline{)734}}$$

There are not enough hundreds or tens to divide into 80 groups. Divide the ones.

Step 2
Think of the basic fact.

$72 \div 8 = 9$

Step 3
Multiply, subtract, and write the remainder.

$$\begin{array}{r} 9 \text{ r}14 \\ 80\overline{)734} \\ -720 \\ \hline 14 \end{array}$$

Use multiplication to check your answer.

Multiply the quotient and the divisor. Add any remainder. The answer will be the dividend.

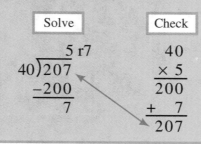

Solve

$$\begin{array}{r} 5 \text{ r}7 \\ 40\overline{)207} \\ -200 \\ \hline 7 \end{array}$$

Check

$$\begin{array}{r} 40 \\ \times\ 5 \\ \hline 200 \\ +\quad 7 \\ \hline 207 \end{array}$$

Practice

Solve. Use multiplication to check your answers.

1. $50\overline{)150}$

2. $40\overline{)82}$

3. $10\overline{)20}$

4. $80\overline{)320}$

5. $30\overline{)60}$

6. $30\overline{)274}$

7. $20\overline{)87}$

8. $70\overline{)424}$

9. $60\overline{)180}$

Application

Write an equation for each word problem. Solve and label.

10. Peggy's older sister has 210 wedding invitations to send. If she addresses 30 invitations each day, how many days will it take to address all the invitations?

11. Mrs. Turner earns $56.00 a day. How much does she earn in 10 days?

12. The air distance between London and Chicago is 3,958 miles. The air distance between London and New York is 3,469 miles. How much farther is it from London to Chicago than from London to New York?

13. Tom's soccer team made a total of 27 goals during the season. What was the average number of goals for each game if the team played 9 games?

14. If you use 20 stamps a month, how many months will 85 stamps last?

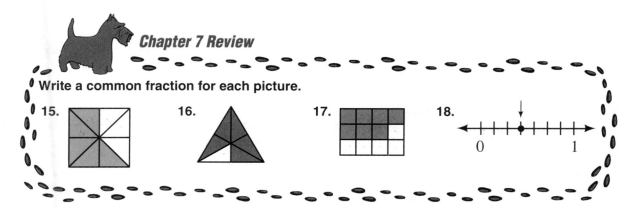

Chapter 7 Review

Write a common fraction for each picture.

15.

16.

17.

18.

0   1

Rounding the Divisor

When the divisor has two digits, decide where to start,
then round the divisor to the nearest 10 and think of the basic fact.

$$36\overline{)212}$$

Decide where to start.	Round the divisor to the nearest 10.	Think of the basic fact.	Multiply, subtract, and write the remainder.

$$\overset{x}{36\overline{)212}}$$

 40

$$36\overline{)212}$$

$20 \div 4 = 5$

$$\begin{array}{r} 5\,r\,32 \\ 36\overline{)212} \\ -180 \\ \hline 32 \end{array}$$

 Remember: Use multiplication to check your answer. Multiply the quotient times the divisor. Add any remainder.

$$\begin{array}{r} 36 \\ \times\ 5 \\ \hline 180 \\ +\ 32 \\ \hline 212 \end{array}$$

Division can be used to find a missing factor.

Gretchen walked the same number of miles each week for 52 weeks.
She walked 416 miles in all. How many miles did she walk each week?

Solve for n.

$$52 \times n = 416$$
$$n = 416 \div 52$$
$$n = 8 \text{ miles}$$

$\longrightarrow$

50

$$\overset{x}{52\overline{)416}}$$

$40 \div 5 = 8$

$$\begin{array}{r} 8 \\ 52\overline{)416} \\ -416 \\ \hline 0 \end{array}$$

Practice

Solve. Use multiplication to check your answers.

1. $19\overline{)53}$

2. $36\overline{)177}$

3. $23\overline{)77}$

4. $72\overline{)576}$

5. $25\overline{)70}$

6. $54\overline{)270}$

7. $49\overline{)306}$

8. $22\overline{)90}$

9. $21\overline{)148}$

Copy each equation. Write a division equation to find the missing factor. Solve for *n*.

Example: $n \times 18 = 144$ $n = 144 \div 18$ $\begin{array}{r} 8 \\ 18\overline{)144} \\ -144 \\ \hline 0 \end{array}$
$n = 8$

10. $53 \times n = 371$

11. $n \times 12 = 48$

12. $33 \times n = 99$

Application

Write an equation for each word problem. Solve and label.

13. A farmer raised an average of 86 bushels of corn on each of his 104 acres. How many bushels of corn did he raise?

14. Mrs. Sharp earned 523 bonus points with the class book club. If she can purchase 1 book for the class library for 35 points, how many books can she purchase?

15. Mr. Murr is making flower beds. He puts 48 plants in each bed. He has 300 plants in all. How many complete flower beds can he make?

16. How long will it take a car traveling an average of 52 miles per hour to travel 468 miles?

17. Calvary Christian School has 672 students. If 45 of the students attend the preschool, how many attend the elementary, junior high, and high school?

Adjusting One-Digit Quotients

Adjust the quotient *up* when the remainder is the same or greater than the divisor.

Remainder Same As Divisor

$$\begin{array}{r} 7 \\ 27\overline{)216} \\ -189 \\ \hline 27 \end{array}$$

adjust to

$$\begin{array}{r} 8 \\ 27\overline{)216} \\ -216 \\ \hline 0 \end{array}$$

$21 \div 3 = 7$

Remainder Greater Than Divisor

$$\begin{array}{r} 6 \\ 19\overline{)136} \\ -114 \\ \hline 22 \end{array}$$

adjust to

$$\begin{array}{r} 7 \text{ r}3 \\ 19\overline{)136} \\ -133 \\ \hline 3 \end{array}$$

$12 \div 2 = 6$

Adjust the quotient *down* when the product is greater than the dividend.

$$\begin{array}{r} 2 \\ 22\overline{)43} \\ -44 \end{array}$$

adjust to

$$\begin{array}{r} 1 \text{ r}21 \\ 22\overline{)43} \\ -22 \\ \hline 21 \end{array}$$

$4 \div 2 = 2$

Use division to find the missing factor.

Mr. Watson kept track of the number of miles he rode on his exercise bike. He rode 465 miles in 93 days. If he rode the same number of miles each day, how far did he ride each day?

$$93 \times n = 465$$
$$n = 465 \div 93$$
$$n = 5 \text{ miles}$$

$$\begin{array}{r} 5 \\ 93\overline{)465} \\ -465 \\ \hline 0 \end{array}$$

Did you know . . .

The British/French supersonic transport (the Concorde) can fly faster than 1,000 miles per hour!

Practice

Solve. Use multiplication to check your answers.

1. $15 \overline{)70}$

2. $14 \overline{)56}$

3. $49 \overline{)344}$

4. $36 \overline{)198}$

5. $17 \overline{)136}$

6. $51 \overline{)99}$

7. $62 \overline{)364}$

8. $83 \overline{)544}$

9. $13 \overline{)40}$

Copy each equation. Write a division equation to find the missing factor. Solve for *n*.

10. $28 \times n = 56$

11. $76 \times n = 684$

12. $n \times 42 = 252$

Application

Use the chart to write an equation for each question. Solve and label. Your teacher may allow you to use a calculator.

13. How many packages of red pencils are for sale in the store?

14. How many erasers are in each package?

15. How many packages of thumbtacks are for sale?

16. How many ballpoint pens are in each package?

Maxwell Office Supply Inventory

Item	Number of packages	Number in each package	Total number of items
erasers	18		72
red pencils		12	168
ballpoint pens	32		192
thumbtacks		25	425

17. What is the total number of items listed on the inventory?

Division: The Traditional Form

Decide where to start.

$$\begin{array}{r} \text{x x} \\ 24\overline{)293} \end{array}$$

Follow the steps to divide.

Modified Traditional Form (with zeros)	Traditional Form (without zeros)
$$\begin{array}{r} 12\ \text{r5} \\ 24\overline{)293} \\ -240 \\ \hline 53 \\ -48 \\ \hline 5 \end{array}$$	1. Divide the tens. 2. Multiply $24 \times 1 = 24$. 3. Subtract. 4. Combine the ones (use an arrow). 5. Divide the ones. Multiply, subtract, and write the remainder. $\qquad \begin{array}{r} 12\ \text{r5} \\ 24\overline{)293} \\ -24\downarrow \\ \hline 53 \\ -48 \\ \hline 5 \end{array}$

$$\begin{array}{r} \text{x} \\ 72\overline{)651} \end{array}$$

If there is a one-digit quotient, the forms will be the same.

$$\begin{array}{r} 9\ \text{r3} \\ 72\overline{)651} \\ -648 \\ \hline 3 \end{array}$$	$$\begin{array}{r} 9\ \text{r3} \\ 72\overline{)651} \\ -648 \\ \hline 3 \end{array}$$

Class Work

Use the traditional form of division to solve these problems.

1. $42\overline{)885}$ 2. $32\overline{)995}$ 3. $56\overline{)472}$ 4. $61\overline{)985}$

Practice

Mark the places where the digits of the quotient will be. Do not solve the problems.

Example: $28\overline{)219}$ with x marked above

1. $36\overline{)517}$
2. $19\overline{)79}$
3. $25\overline{)196}$
4. $23\overline{)843}$

Solve the problems using the traditional form (without zeros). Use multiplication to check your answers.

5. $44\overline{)398}$
6. $35\overline{)511}$
7. $73\overline{)862}$
8. $54\overline{)435}$

9. $42\overline{)957}$
10. $62\overline{)310}$
11. $21\overline{)886}$
12. $11\overline{)674}$

Application

Write an equation for each word problem. Solve and label.

13. A total of 128 students went on the fifth grade field trip. Sixty-nine of the students were girls. How many were boys?

14. Twelve baseball teams played on the summer league. There were 12 boys on each team. How many boys played in the summer league?

15. Winnie has a goal of reading 35 pages each day until she has finished her book. If the book has 231 pages, how many days will Winnie take to finish it?

16. Mr. Hall wants to plant 117 tomato plants in his back field. If he places 22 plants in each row, how many rows will he make?

Use the table to answer the questions. Write the equations you use.

17. What is the average number of visitors to the elementary school for the years listed?

18. What is the average number of visitors to the high school for the years listed?

Visitors to Open House		
Elementary School	Junior High	High School
1996 489	294	371
1997 502	321	363
1998 557	339	403

19. On the average, how many more people visited the elementary school than the high school each year?

20. What is the combined number of visitors for all 3 schools in 1998?

Adjusting Two-Digit Quotients

Adjust the quotient *up* when the remainder is the same as the divisor.

Miss Lumm bought 380 stickers at the beginning of the school year. If she gives the same number of stickers to each of her 19 students, how many will each student receive?

```
 20       1       adjust to       20
      19)380      ─────────→  19)380
          -19                    -38↓
           19                      0
```

Adjust the quotient *up* when the remainder is greater than the divisor.

The 27 students in Miss Ruiz's class ran a total of 877 laps at the jog-a-thon. What was the average number of laps run by each of the students?

```
 30        2      adjust to       32 r13
      27)877      ─────────→  27)877
          -54                    -81↓
           33                      67
                                  -54
                                   13
```

Adjust the quotient *down* when the product is greater than the dividend.

Fourteen of Miss Ruiz's students participated in the reading contest. These students read a total of 437 books. What was the average number of books read by each of the 14 students?

```
 10        4      adjust to       31 r3
      14)437      ─────────→  14)437
          -56                    -42↓
                                   17
                                  -14
                                    3
```

Practice

Solve the problems using the traditional form (without zeros). Your teacher may allow you to use a calculator to check your answers.

1. $34\overline{)125}$

2. $52\overline{)678}$

3. $47\overline{)293}$

4. $34\overline{)620}$

5. $47\overline{)999}$

6. $29\overline{)899}$

7. $88\overline{)690}$

8. $17\overline{)743}$

9. $23\overline{)598}$

10. $17\overline{)136}$

11. $12\overline{)310}$

12. $43\overline{)903}$

Application

Write an equation for each word problem. Solve and label.

13. According to Genesis 6:16, Noah's ark had 3 floors. If the area of each floor was 3,375 ft.^{2}, what would be the combined area of all 3 floors?

14. Three students brought in some packages of cookies that had a total of 252 cookies. If each package had 36 cookies, how many packages did they bring?

15. The auditorium seats 500 people. By 7:15, 387 people had arrived for the program. How many more people could still be seated for the program?

16. How many feet of ribbon does Sue have if she has 168 inches of ribbon?

17. Ten cases of soft drink each held 24 cans. One hundred eight cans were cherry flavor. The rest were strawberry flavor. How many cans of soft drink were strawberry?

Three-Digit Quotients

Steps for Solving a Division Problem with a Four- or Five-Digit Dividend

1. Determine the number of places in the quotient.
2. Round the divisor.
3. Divide.
4. Multiply and subtract.
5. Combine the tens (use an arrow).
6. Divide the tens; multiply and subtract.
7. Combine the ones (use an arrow).
8. Divide the ones; multiply, subtract, and write the remainder.

$$\begin{array}{r} \textbf{x x x} \\ 21\overline{)3{,}297} \end{array}$$

$$\begin{array}{r} (20)\quad 157 \\ 21\overline{)3{,}297} \\ \underline{-21}\downarrow \\ 119 \\ \underline{-105}\downarrow \\ 147 \\ \underline{-147} \\ 0 \end{array}$$

Adjusting the Quotient

Sometimes you will need to adjust the quotient.
- Adjust the quotient *up* when the remainder is the same or greater than the divisor.
- Adjust the quotient *down* when the product is greater than the dividend.

$$\begin{array}{r} \textbf{x x x} \\ 32\overline{)21{,}492} \end{array}$$

$$\begin{array}{r} (30)\quad 7 \\ 32\overline{)21{,}492} \\ -224 \end{array}$$

adjust to →

$$\begin{array}{r} 671 \text{ r}20 \\ 32\overline{)21{,}492} \\ \underline{-192}\downarrow \\ 229 \\ \underline{-224}\downarrow \\ 52 \\ \underline{-32} \\ 20 \end{array}$$

Practice

Solve. Your teacher may allow you to use a calculator to check your answers.

1. $74\overline{)15,836}$
2. $16\overline{)5,200}$
3. $86\overline{)46,064}$

4. $66\overline{)8,986}$
5. $34\overline{)16,264}$
6. $28\overline{)7,748}$

7. $58\overline{)3,625}$
8. $18\overline{)4,763}$
9. $87\overline{)74,582}$

Application

Write an equation for each word problem. Solve and label.

10. Jason bought 4 boards that are 230 cm long and 7 boards that are 345 cm long. How many boards did he buy?

11. Jason needs to cut boards that are 32 cm long. If he cuts these pieces from a board that measured 230 cm, how many 32-cm pieces will he have?

12. What length would a board need to be if Jason cut exactly 11 pieces with nothing left ove? (Remember, each piece is 32 cm long.)

Meet the Challenge!

Solve.

13.

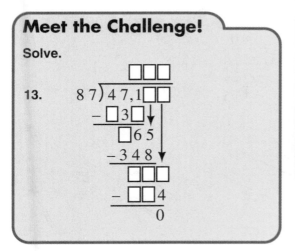

Zero in the Quotient

Zero in the Quotient

When there are not enough tens or ones to divide, write a 0 in that place.

Zero in the Ones Place

Decide where to start.

$$\begin{array}{r} \times\times \\ 12\ \overline{)124} \end{array}$$

Divide the tens.
Multiply and subtract.
Combine the ones.

$$\begin{array}{r} 1 \\ 12\overline{)124} \\ -12\downarrow \\ \hline 4 \end{array}$$

Divide the ones.
If there are not enough
ones to divide, write a 0
in the quotient.
Write the remainder.

$$\begin{array}{r} 10\ \text{r}4 \\ 12\overline{)124} \\ -12\downarrow \\ \hline 4 \end{array}$$

Zero in the Tens Place

Decide where to start.

$$\begin{array}{r} \times\times\times \\ 23\overline{)9,315} \end{array}$$

Divide the hundreds.
Multiply and subtract.
Combine the tens.

$$\begin{array}{r} 4 \\ 23\overline{)9,315} \\ -92\downarrow \\ \hline 11 \end{array}$$

Divide the tens.
If there are not enough
tens to divide, write
a 0 in the quotient.
Combine the ones.

$$\begin{array}{r} 40 \\ 23\overline{)9,315} \\ -92\downarrow\downarrow \\ \hline 115 \end{array}$$

Divide the ones.
Multiply and subtract.
Write the remainder.

$$\begin{array}{r} 405 \\ 23\overline{)9,315} \\ -92\downarrow\downarrow \\ \hline 115 \\ -115 \\ \hline 0 \end{array}$$

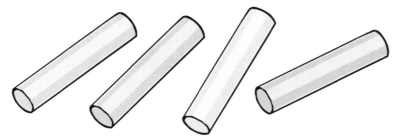

Practice

Solve. Use multiplication to check your answers.

1. $24\overline{)7{,}368}$ 2. $25\overline{)768}$ 3. $53\overline{)8{,}480}$ 4. $14\overline{)562}$

5. $62\overline{)139}$ 6. $55\overline{)22{,}495}$ 7. $29\overline{)2{,}913}$ 8. $28\overline{)2{,}016}$

Copy each equation. Write a division equation to find the missing factor.
Solve for *n*.

9. $n \times 31 = 9{,}455$ 10. $49 \times n = 882$ 11. $n \times 16 = 3{,}248$

Application

Use the chart to write an equation for each question. Solve and label. Your
teacher may allow you to use a calculator.

12. What is the total number of packages of marbles?

13. How many rubber bands are in a package?

14. What is the total number of pieces of chalk?

15. What is the total number of packages of pins?

Item	Number of items	Number of items in each package	Number of packages
marbles	7,400	20	
rubber bands	10,750		43
chalk		500	25
paper clips	4,800		16
pins	18,600	200	

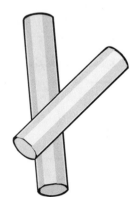

Chapter 7 Review

Rename each fraction in lowest terms.

16. $\frac{5}{15}$ 17. $\frac{24}{36}$ 18. $\frac{30}{45}$ 19. $\frac{20}{80}$

How Many Digits?

Determine how many digits will be in the quotient.

Mr. Arden has 286 stickers to divide equally among 36 students. How many stickers will each student receive?

There are 2 hundreds. There are 28 tens. There are not enough hundreds or tens to divide into 36 groups. There are 286 ones. There are enough ones to divide into 36 groups. The quotient will have one digit.

$$\begin{array}{r} x \\ 36\overline{)286} \end{array} \qquad \begin{array}{r} 7\ \text{r}34 \\ 36\overline{)286} \\ -252 \\ \hline 34 \end{array}$$

$286 \div 36 = 7$ stickers

Sixty-one students participated in the reading contest. They read a total of 5,673 pages. What was the average number of pages read?

There are 5 thousands. There are 56 hundreds. There are not enough thousands or hundreds to divide into 61 groups. There are 567 tens. There are enough tens to divide into 61 groups. The quotient will have two digits.

$$\begin{array}{r} x\ x \\ 61\overline{)5,673} \end{array} \qquad \begin{array}{r} 93 \\ 61\overline{)5,673} \\ -549\downarrow \\ \hline 183 \\ -183 \\ \hline 0 \end{array}$$

$5,673 \div 61 = 93$ pages

A total of 7,614 pennies were brought to chapel for the missionary penny drive. If 54 students brought pennies, what was the average number of pennies each student brought?

$$\begin{array}{r} x\ x\ x \\ 54\overline{)7,614} \end{array} \qquad \begin{array}{r} 141 \\ 54\overline{)7,614} \\ -54\downarrow \\ \hline 221 \\ -216\downarrow \\ \hline 54 \\ -54 \\ \hline 0 \end{array}$$

There are 7 thousands. There are not enough thousands to divide into 54 groups. There are 76 hundreds. There are enough hundreds to divide into 54 groups. The quotient will have three digits.

$7,614 \div 54 = 141$ pennies

Practice

Determine how many digits will be in the quotient. Write the letter of the correct answer.

1. $18 \overline{)4,140}$

   a. one digit
   b. two digits
   c. three digits

2. $22 \overline{)1,606}$

   a. one digit
   b. two digits
   c. three digits

3. $24 \overline{)294}$

   a. one digit
   b. two digits
   c. three digits

4. $29 \overline{)145}$

   a. one digit
   b. two digits
   c. three digits

Solve. Use multiplication to check your answers.

5. $81 \overline{)5,184}$

6. $65 \overline{)45,639}$

7. $43 \overline{)25,800}$

8. $74 \overline{)1,628}$

9. $13 \overline{)111}$

10. $25 \overline{)510}$

11. $93 \overline{)98,462}$

12. $47 \overline{)5,011}$

Application

Write a word problem for the equation. Solve and label.

13. $1,845 \div 23 =$

   Ideas: newspapers, pieces of paper, candies

Chapter 7 Review

Find the LCM of each pair of numbers. (Refer to page 134 for an example.)

14. 6, 14

15. 12, 15

16. 20, 22

Division: Dollars and Cents

> Divide money in the same way you divide whole numbers.
> Place a dollar sign and a decimal point in the quotient.

Cara spent $2.94 on 14 pencils. What was the cost of each pencil?

If there are are not enough one-dollar bills to divide, use a 0 as a place holder.

$$\begin{array}{r} \$0.21 \\ 14\overline{)\$2.94} \\ -28\downarrow \\ \overline{14} \\ -14 \\ \overline{0} \end{array}$$

$2.94 \div 14 = \$0.21$

Remember to place a 0 in the quotient if needed.

There are not enough ten-dollar bills to divide.
Divide the one-dollar bills.
Multiply and subtract.
Combine the dimes.

$$\begin{array}{r} \$2. \\ 27\overline{)\$55.08} \\ -54\downarrow \\ \overline{10} \end{array}$$

There are not enough dimes to divide.
Write a zero in the quotient.
Combine the pennies.

$$\begin{array}{r} \$2.0 \\ 27\overline{)\$55.08} \\ -54\downarrow\downarrow \\ \overline{108} \end{array}$$

$55.08 \div 27 = \$2.04$

Divide the pennies.
Multiply and subtract.

$$\begin{array}{r} \$2.04 \\ 27\overline{)\$55.08} \\ -54\downarrow\downarrow \\ \overline{108} \\ -108 \\ \overline{0} \end{array}$$

Remember to adjust the quotient if needed.

If the remainder is the same as or greater than the divisor, adjust *up*.
If the product is greater than the dividend, adjust *down*.

$$\begin{array}{r} \text{20} \$2.3 \\ 23\overline{)\$52.21} \\ -46\downarrow \\ 62 \\ -69 \end{array}$$

(greater than the dividend)

adjust to →

$$\begin{array}{r} \$2.27 \\ 23\overline{)\$52.21} \\ -46\downarrow \\ 62 \\ -46\downarrow \\ \overline{161} \end{array}$$

Practice

Solve. Your teacher may allow you to use a calculator to check your answers.

1. $21\overline{)\$23.73}$ **2.** $45\overline{)\$8.10}$ **3.** $18\overline{)\$1.44}$ **4.** $13\overline{)\$4.03}$

5. $50\overline{)\$12.00}$ **6.** $32\overline{)\$93.44}$ **7.** $93\overline{)\$1.86}$ **8.** $22\overline{)\$10.56}$

9. $64\overline{)\$42.24}$ **10.** $23\overline{)\$5.29}$ **11.** $24\overline{)\$9.36}$ **12.** $35\overline{)\$83.65}$

Application

Write an equation for each word problem. Solve and label.

13. Kaylee purchased a gift for her mother's birthday for a total of $13.46. How much change did she receive from a twenty-dollar bill?

14. Mandy paid $62.25 to rent a small airplane. She flew the plane for 75 minutes. How much did she pay for each minute?

15. Mr. Newton is installing carpet in Mandy's room. If he paid $13.95 for each square yard of carpet, how much did he pay for 12 square yards?

16. Troop 519 collected $126.50 from 23 scouts to cover the cost of the supper for an overnight camping trip. How much did each boy pay?

Language Link

17. Division can be thought of as repeated subtraction. Explain why this is so. Give an example for your explanation.

Group Problem Solving: Estimating Beans

Problem

Your school is having an estimating contest. In the school office is a gallon jar full of dried pinto beans. The class whose estimate is closest to the number of dried beans in the jar wins an ice cream party. Your group needs to estimate the number of dried beans in the jar.

Information

Use one of the following methods to estimate the number of dried beans in the gallon jar. You will be given a quart jar full of dried pinto beans. You may not count the total number of beans in the quart jar. Your teacher will provide any materials you will need. The procedures for estimating the number of beans are incomplete. Use problem-solving skills to complete the procedure. After estimating the number of beans in your quart jar, estimate the number of beans in a gallon jar.

Method 1

1. Measure out a handful of dried beans.

2. Count the number of dried beans in a handful.

3. Count the number of handfuls in a quart jar.

Method 2

1. Determine the volume of 1 dried bean.

2. Determine the volume of the quart jar.

Method 3

1. Find the mass of the quart jar full of dried beans in grams or kilograms.

2. Find the mass of the empty quart jar in grams or kilograms.

3. Find the mass of 4 beans in grams or kilograms.

Method 4

1. Measure out a cup of dried beans.

2. Count the number of dried beans in a cup.

3. Find the number of cups in the quart jar.

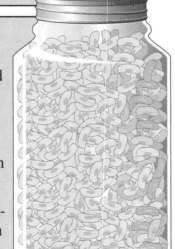

Answer the questions.

1. About how many dried beans are in a quart jar? Explain your answer.

2. How can you estimate the number of dried beans in a gallon jar?

3. About how many beans are in a gallon jar? Explain your answer.

4. How can your class use the groups' estimates to determine a class estimate?

Air Traffic Controller

Dear Fifth Grade:

I was glad to hear from you! I'd be happy to tell you how I use math in my job. I have a computer that does most of my math for me, but there are times when I have to use it a little myself. I have to make sure planes are kept at safe distances from each other so we don't have any collisions in the air. When several planes at a time are getting ready to land, we sometimes need to put them in a holding pattern. This means they fly in separate, oval-shaped lanes in a protected zone several miles from the airport until it is their turn to land. The lanes are stacked on top of one another, about 1,000 feet apart. So I have to be aware of each plane's position in the holding pattern and add by 1,000s to tell each new plane at what altitude to stop its descent to join the pattern.

I also need to know some geometry. When a pilot is making a turn to approach the runway, I need to tell him the proper angle to turn so that he will line up all right. We had an especially busy evening last week, and at one point I was trying to direct three planes into the holding pattern at the proper times and altitudes while I helped another pilot who was disoriented in some fog. My job is one that requires close concentration and is often pretty stressful! It helps to take breaks every few hours, leave the control room, and just relax for a while. That always helps me be ready to come back and concentrate.

Sincerely,

Jim Nelson
Jim Nelson

New Bern
Airport
995 Airport Road
New Bern, NC 28562

USA 32

Moore Christian School
334 Tara Lane
Mariposa, CA 95338

Mark the places where the digits of the quotient will be. Do not solve.

1. $29\overline{)862}$
2. $54\overline{)387}$
3. $17\overline{)138}$
4. $64\overline{)826}$

Copy each equation. Write a division equation to find the missing factor. Solve for n.

5. $21 \times n = 63$
6. $n \times 52 = 5{,}356$
7. $47 \times n = 1{,}786$

Solve. Use multiplication to check your answers.

8. $60\overline{)480}$
9. $30\overline{)186}$
10. $70\overline{)210}$

11. $23\overline{)78}$
12. $35\overline{)492}$
13. $54\overline{)687}$

14. $87\overline{)3{,}516}$
15. $14\overline{)2{,}912}$
16. $23\overline{)1{,}265}$

17. $8\overline{)\$112.72}$
18. $12\overline{)\$70.80}$
19. $24\overline{)\$78.00}$

Write an equation for each word problem. Solve and label.

20. How many more people live in Maui County than in Kauai County?

21. What is the difference in population between the largest county and the smallest county?

22. What is the population of the three smallest counties combined?

1990 Hawaiian Population

Counties	Population
Hawaii	120,317
Honolulu	836,231
Kalawao	130
Kauai	51,177
Maui	100,374

Write an equation for each word problem. Solve and label.

23. The community club bought 352 ounces of hamburger meat for the annual picnic. There are 16 ounces in a pound. How many pounds of meat did the club purchase?

24. Greg's brother is 1.74 meters tall. Greg is 1.22 meters tall. How much taller is Greg's brother than Greg?

25. Grace Christian School has an enrollment of 397 elementary students, 93 junior high students, and 215 high school students. What is the total enrollment of the school?

26. The office sold 175 tickets for each night of the school play. The play ran for 4 nights. How many tickets were sold in all?

Five schools kept track of the books students read during part of a school year. Use the table to answer the questions. Write any equations you use.

School	Weeks	Books
Bethany Christian	29	4,782
Grace Christian	30	896
Judson Academy	25	2,975
Taylor Memorial	18	7,835
Faith Christian	31	1,829

27. What is the average number of books read each week at Judson Academy?

28. There are 96 students at Faith Christian School. If each read the same number of books, about how many books did each student read?

29. What is the combined total of books read for Judson Academy and Taylor Memorial School?

30. How many more books did the students at Taylor Memorial School read than those at Grace Christian School?

Cumulative Review

Write the letter of the correct answer.

1. What is one million, ten thousand, seven hundred forty in standard form?
   a. 1,007,040
   b. 1,010,740
   c. 1,100,704
   d. not given

2. Use front-end estimation with adjustment to estimate the answer.

   $$\begin{array}{r} 78,874 \\ +11,689 \\ \hline \end{array}$$

   a. 69,000
   b. 79,000
   c. 89,000
   d. not given

3. Solve.

   $$\begin{array}{r} 4,687 \\ \times \quad 4 \\ \hline \end{array}$$

   a. 16,648
   b. 17,704
   c. 18,748
   d. not given

4. What angle measures less than 90°?
   a. acute
   b. obtuse
   c. right
   d. not given

5. Solve.

   $$\begin{array}{r} \$14.84 \\ -\ 3.96 \\ \hline \end{array}$$

   a. $10.88
   b. $11.12
   c. $12.08
   d. not given

6. Solve.

   $$3)\overline{\$0.69}$$

   a. $0.12
   b. $0.23
   c. $0.26
   d. not given

7. Which sign will make the sentence true? $\frac{3}{4} \bigcirc \frac{3}{8}$
   a. >
   b. <
   c. =
   d. not given

8. Complete the equation.
   $$5 \text{ km} = \underline{\quad} \text{ m}$$
   a. 50 m
   b. 5000 m
   c. 500 m
   d. not given

9. What unit would you use to measure the wings of a fly?
   a. km
   b. m
   c. cm
   d. mm

10. Solve.

    $$50)\overline{92}$$

    a. 1 r7
    b. 1 r42
    c. 10 r4
    d. not given

11. What is $\frac{25}{50}$ in lowest terms?
    a. $\frac{1}{2}$
    b. $\frac{1}{25}$
    c. $\frac{1}{4}$
    d. not given

12. Solve.

    $$\begin{array}{r} 48 \\ \times 36 \\ \hline \end{array}$$

    a. 1,248
    b. 432
    c. 1,728
    d. not given

Airports

Airports are perhaps the world's busiest places. In large international airports, people are always coming from and going to different countries. Planes are taking off and landing and being repaired. Thousands of people are working to see that all the passengers and their luggage have smooth flights. And in small airports, planes have to be serviced and directed, and pilots have to make all the arrangements for their flights.

A large airport is almost like a little city in itself. It has shops, restaurants, and banks, and many people work there. Agents behind counters send luggage off to be stored in the belly of the plane and tell people where to find the plane for their flight. Security officials use x-ray machines and metal detectors to check passengers and

their bags for weapons. Mechanics work on planes that need repairs, and they inspect each plane before it leaves the ground. Air traffic controllers direct the planes, telling pilots when and where to take off and land. Customs officials check passports and bags of passengers taking international flights. Most large airports need people to work various shifts day and night, because flights arrive and depart at all hours.

Both large and small airports serve important purposes for different types of flights. Whether an airport is equipped with luxuries or with only a few short runways, it is a necessity for the pilots who use it.

CHAPTER
10

Common Fractions: Addition and Subtraction

At today's large airports, passengers can board aircraft, like this Boeing 727, through enclosed gangways, so they never have to go out in the weather.

Many check-in counters are needed to serve thousands of passengers.

Adding Like Fractions

$\dfrac{5}{8}$ The numerator is the number of parts being discussed.
The denominator is the number of parts in all; it names the parts.

To add like fractions, add the numerators.
The denominator does not change.

John ate $\frac{1}{8}$ of a pan of brownies. His sister ate $\frac{1}{8}$ of the brownies, and his dad ate $\frac{2}{8}$ of the brownies. How much of the pan of brownies did they eat in all?

This problem can be shown in five ways:

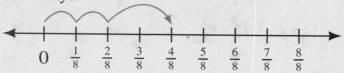

1 eighth	$\frac{1}{8}$
1 eighth	$\frac{1}{8}$
+2 eighths	$+\frac{2}{8}$
4 eighths	$\frac{4}{8}$

Simplify the answer by renaming the fraction in lowest terms.

$$\frac{1}{8} + \frac{1}{8} + \frac{2}{8} = \frac{4}{8}$$

$$\frac{4 \div 4}{8 \div 4} = \frac{1}{2} \text{ of the pan}$$

Anne bought one dozen doughnuts. Five-twelfths of the doughnuts were jelly filled. One-twelfth of the doughnuts was cream filled. The rest of the doughnuts were not filled. What part of the doughnuts were filled?

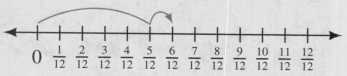

5 twelfths	$\frac{5}{12}$
+1 twelfth	$+\frac{1}{12}$
6 twelfths	$\frac{6}{12}$

Simplify the answer by renaming the fraction in lowest terms.

$$\frac{5}{12} + \frac{1}{12} = \frac{6}{12}$$

$$\frac{6 \div 6}{12 \div 6} = \frac{1}{2} \text{ of the doughnuts}$$

Practice

Solve. Simplify the answer by renaming in lowest terms.

1. $\frac{4}{9} + \frac{1}{9} =$

2. $\frac{1}{6} + \frac{1}{6} =$

3. $\frac{1}{12} + \frac{5}{12} + \frac{1}{12} =$

4. $\frac{2}{8} + \frac{2}{8} =$

5. $\frac{7}{20} + \frac{5}{20} + \frac{3}{20} =$

6. $\frac{3}{11} + \frac{2}{11} + \frac{5}{11} =$

7. $\frac{4}{15} + \frac{2}{15} =$

8. $\frac{3}{7} + \frac{2}{7} =$

9. $\frac{5}{16} + \frac{3}{16} =$

Application

Write an equation to find how far (in miles) Bill ran each day. Simplify the answer.

Day	Before lunch	After lunch	Total
10. Monday	$\frac{3}{10}$ mi.	$\frac{4}{10}$ mi.	mi.
11. Tuesday	$\frac{5}{10}$ mi.	$\frac{4}{10}$ mi.	mi.
12. Wednesday	$\frac{3}{10}$ mi.	$\frac{3}{10}$ mi.	mi.
13. Thursday	$\frac{3}{10}$ mi.	$\frac{5}{10}$ mi.	mi.
14. Friday	$\frac{2}{10}$ mi.	$\frac{2}{10}$ mi.	mi.

Adding Mixed Numbers

Steps for Adding Mixed Numbers

1. Add the fractions.
2. Add the whole numbers.
3. Rename if necessary.

On Monday Joel rode his bike $3\frac{3}{10}$ miles to a park to play ball. On Tuesday Joel rode $2\frac{6}{10}$ miles to a friend's house. How far did he ride both days combined?

Step 1
Add the fractions.

$$3\frac{3}{10}$$
$$+ 2\frac{6}{10}$$
$$\overline{\frac{9}{10}}$$

Step 2
Add the whole numbers.

$$3\frac{3}{10}$$
$$+ 2\frac{6}{10}$$
$$\overline{5\frac{9}{10}}$$

The answer is in lowest terms. Renaming is not necessary.

$$3\frac{3}{10} + 2\frac{6}{10} = 5\frac{9}{10} \text{ miles}$$

If the answer is not in lowest terms, renaming is necessary to simplify it.

Joel rides $2\frac{5}{10}$ miles to fish at the pond, and $1\frac{7}{10}$ miles farther to his grandma's house. How far does he ride in all?

Step 1
Add the fractions.

$$2\frac{5}{10}$$
$$+ 1\frac{7}{10}$$
$$\overline{\frac{12}{10}}$$

Step 2
Add the whole numbers.

$$2\frac{5}{10}$$
$$+ 1\frac{7}{10}$$
$$\overline{3\frac{12}{10}}$$

Step 3
Rename if necessary.

$$3\frac{12}{10} = 3 + \frac{12}{10} =$$
$$3 + (12 \div 10) =$$
$$3 + \quad 1\frac{2}{10} \quad = 4\frac{2}{10} = 4\frac{1}{5}$$

$$10\overline{)12} \quad \begin{array}{r} 1 \\ \hline -10 \\ \hline 2 \end{array}$$

$$2\frac{5}{10} + 1\frac{7}{10} = 4\frac{1}{5} \text{ miles}$$

Practice

Copy and complete each number wheel. Add the center number to each number in the second ring. Write the answers in the third ring. Simplify the answer in the outer ring if necessary. Part of problem number one has been done for you.

1.

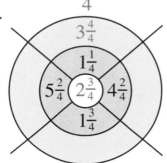

2.

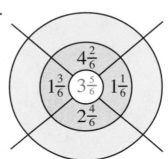

Solve. Simplify the answer by renaming in lowest terms.

3. $3\frac{2}{5} + 4\frac{1}{5} =$

4. $5\frac{7}{12} + 4\frac{8}{12} =$

5. $6\frac{5}{8} + 3\frac{6}{8} =$

6. $2\frac{1}{3} + 4\frac{2}{3} =$

7. $5\frac{2}{9} + 2\frac{7}{9} =$

8. $1\frac{2}{8} + 2\frac{1}{8} =$

Application

Write an equation for each word problem. Solve. Simplify and label the answer.

9. Isabelle made a cake that called for $2\frac{1}{2}$ cups of flour. She's now making cookies that call for $3\frac{1}{2}$ cups of flour. How much flour will she use in all?

10. Isabelle made punch for a party using $1\frac{3}{4}$ quarts of fruit punch and $1\frac{1}{4}$ quarts of lemonade. How much punch was made in all?

Subtracting Like Fractions

> To subtract like fractions, subtract the numerators.
> The denominator does not change.

Camille has 1 yard of fabric to use for a skirt she is making. The directions call for $\frac{3}{4}$ of a yard. How much material will she have left over?
(Hint: 1 yard = $\frac{4}{4}$ yard)

$$\begin{array}{r} 4 \text{ fourths} \\ - \ 3 \text{ fourths} \\ \hline 1 \text{ fourth} \end{array}$$

$$\begin{array}{r} \frac{4}{4} \\ - \ \frac{3}{4} \\ \hline \frac{1}{4} \end{array}$$

$$\frac{4}{4} - \frac{3}{4} = \frac{1}{4} \text{ yard}$$

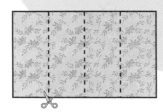

> Camille will have $\frac{1}{4}$ yard left.

Grant needs to have $\frac{9}{12}$ of his support raised by April for a summer mission trip. If he has $\frac{5}{12}$ of the support now, how much more does he need before April?

$$\begin{array}{r} 9 \text{ twelfths} \\ - \ 5 \text{ twelfths} \\ \hline 4 \text{ twelfths} \end{array}$$

$$\begin{array}{r} \frac{9}{12} \\ - \ \frac{5}{12} \\ \hline \frac{4}{12} \end{array}$$

$$\frac{9}{12} - \frac{5}{12} = \frac{4}{12}$$

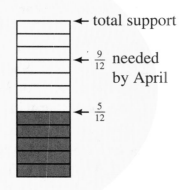

← total support

← $\frac{9}{12}$ needed by April

← $\frac{5}{12}$

Renaming is necessary: $\frac{4 \div 4}{12 \div 4} = \frac{1}{3}$

$$\frac{9}{12} - \frac{5}{12} = \frac{1}{3} \text{ of his support}$$

> Grant needs $\frac{1}{3}$ of his support.

Practice

Solve. Simplify the answer by renaming in lowest terms.

1. $\frac{7}{8} - \frac{3}{8} =$

2. $\frac{5}{6} - \frac{1}{6} =$

3. $\frac{9}{10} - \frac{3}{10} =$

4. $\frac{13}{15} - \frac{4}{15} =$

5. $\frac{8}{9} - \frac{7}{9} =$

6. $\frac{7}{12} - \frac{5}{12} =$

7. $\frac{13}{20} - \frac{7}{20} =$

8. $\frac{8}{11}$
   $-\frac{4}{11}$
   ‾‾‾‾‾

9. $\frac{7}{8}$
   $-\frac{5}{8}$
   ‾‾‾‾‾

10. $\frac{3}{6}$
    $-\frac{2}{6}$
    ‾‾‾‾‾

11. $\frac{9}{10}$
    $-\frac{5}{10}$
    ‾‾‾‾‾

Application

Use the chart to write an equation for each word problem. Solve. Simplify and label the answer.

12. How much more of the class would rather have pepperoni than Italian sausage?

13. How much more of the class would rather have sausage than mushrooms?

14. How much more of the class would rather have green peppers than onions?

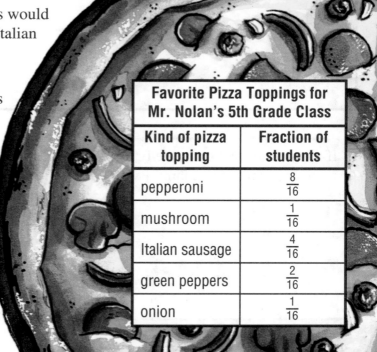

Favorite Pizza Toppings for Mr. Nolan's 5th Grade Class	
Kind of pizza topping	Fraction of students
pepperoni	$\frac{8}{16}$
mushroom	$\frac{1}{16}$
Italian sausage	$\frac{4}{16}$
green peppers	$\frac{2}{16}$
onion	$\frac{1}{16}$

Subtracting Mixed Numbers

Step 1	Step 2	Step 3
Subtract the fractions.	Subtract the whole numbers.	Simplify the answer if necessary.

$$6\frac{9}{10}$$
$$-\,2\frac{3}{10}$$
$$\frac{6}{10}$$

$$6\frac{9}{10}$$
$$-\,2\frac{3}{10}$$
$$4\frac{6}{10}$$

$$4\frac{6}{10} = 4 + \frac{6}{10} =$$
$$4 + \left(\frac{6 \div 2}{10 \div 2}\right) =$$
$$4 + \frac{3}{5} = 4\frac{3}{5}$$

$$6\frac{9}{10} - 2\frac{3}{10} = 4\frac{3}{5}$$

If there is not enough in the first fraction (minuend), renaming is necessary.

Step 1	Step 2	Step 3
Subtract the fractions. Rename 1 whole as a fraction if necessary.	Subtract the whole numbers.	Simplify the answer if necessary.

$$\overset{7\frac{6}{6}}{\cancel{8\frac{1}{6}}} = 7\frac{7}{6}$$
$$-\,4\frac{5}{6} = -\,4\frac{5}{6}$$
$$\frac{2}{6}$$

$$7\frac{7}{6}$$
$$-\,4\frac{5}{6}$$
$$3\frac{2}{6}$$

$$3\frac{2}{6} = 3 + \frac{2}{6} =$$
$$3 + \left(\frac{2 \div 2}{6 \div 2}\right) =$$
$$3 + \frac{1}{3} = 3\frac{1}{3}$$

If there is no fraction in the first number (minuend), rename 1 whole.

$$\overset{5\frac{7}{7}}{\cancel{6}} = 5\frac{7}{7}$$
$$-\,4\frac{3}{7} = -\,4\frac{3}{7}$$
$$1\frac{4}{7}$$

If there is no fraction in the subtrahend (second number), it is not necessary to rename.

$$4\frac{5}{8}$$
$$-\,3$$
$$1\frac{5}{8}$$

Practice

Simplify.

1. $3\frac{4}{10}$

2. $\frac{18}{4}$

3. $9\frac{4}{20}$

4. $\frac{20}{14}$

Solve. Simplify the answer.

5. $8\frac{3}{4}$
$-\ 2\frac{1}{4}$

6. $23\frac{8}{9}$
$-\ 17\frac{2}{9}$

7. $6\frac{1}{3}$
$-\ 4\frac{2}{3}$

8. 5
$-\ 3\frac{2}{7}$

9. 3
$-\ 1\frac{5}{8}$

10. $6\frac{1}{5}$
$-\ 1\frac{3}{5}$

11. 8
$-\ 4\frac{2}{3}$

12. $7\frac{1}{8}$
$-\ 3\frac{3}{8}$

Application

Write an equation for each word problem. Solve. Simplify and label the answer.

13. Janelle had $4\frac{1}{8}$ yards of string. She used $\frac{3}{8}$ of a yard of string to tie a package. How many yards of string are left?

14. Weston ran a race in $9\frac{7}{10}$ seconds. Bethany's time was $10\frac{1}{10}$ seconds. How much faster did Weston run than Bethany?

15. Philip and Noah ran a 200-yard relay race. Their combined time was 23 seconds. Philip's time was $11\frac{6}{10}$ seconds. What was Noah's time?

 Chapter 2 Review

Solve.

16. $29,000$
$-18,643$

17. $70,000$
$-25,879$

18. $10,000$
$-\ 4,631$

19. $300,706$
$-\ 16,398$

Adding Unlike (Related) Fractions

Fractions are related if one of the denominators is a multiple of the other denominator.

$$\frac{1}{2} + \frac{3}{4} =$$

$\frac{1}{2}$ is related to $\frac{3}{4}$ because 4 is a multiple of 2 $(2 \times 2 = 4)$.

Find a common denominator before adding the fractions.

$$\frac{1}{2} = \frac{1 \times 2}{2 \times 2} = \frac{2}{4}$$

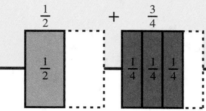

$$+ \frac{3}{4} = \qquad + \frac{3}{4}$$
$$\frac{5}{4} = 1\frac{1}{4}$$

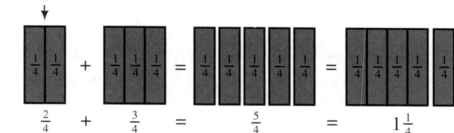

$$\frac{2}{4} \quad + \quad \frac{3}{4} \quad = \quad \frac{5}{4} \quad = \quad 1\frac{1}{4}$$

Class Work

Solve. Simplify the answer.

Example:

$$\frac{2}{3} = \frac{2 \times 2}{3 \times 2} = \frac{4}{6}$$
$$+ \frac{3}{6} \qquad\qquad + \frac{3}{6}$$
$$\frac{7}{6} = 1\frac{1}{6}$$

1. $\frac{4}{10}$
$+ \frac{4}{5}$

2. $\frac{3}{4}$
$+ \frac{5}{8}$

3. $\frac{1}{3}$
$+ \frac{3}{9}$

Practice

Solve. Simplify the answer.

1. $\frac{2}{5} + \frac{3}{10} =$

2. $\frac{5}{6} + \frac{5}{12} =$

3. $\frac{1}{2} + \frac{1}{6} =$

4. $\begin{array}{r} \frac{7}{8} \\ + \frac{3}{4} \\ \hline \end{array}$

5. $\begin{array}{r} \frac{6}{15} \\ + \frac{2}{3} \\ \hline \end{array}$

6. $\begin{array}{r} \frac{9}{14} \\ + \frac{4}{7} \\ \hline \end{array}$

7. $\begin{array}{r} \frac{3}{8} \\ + \frac{1}{2} \\ \hline \end{array}$

8. $\begin{array}{r} \frac{1}{3} \\ + \frac{8}{9} \\ \hline \end{array}$

9. $\begin{array}{r} \frac{8}{10} \\ + \frac{1}{2} \\ \hline \end{array}$

10. $\begin{array}{r} \frac{9}{12} \\ + \frac{3}{4} \\ \hline \end{array}$

11. $\begin{array}{r} \frac{1}{4} \\ + \frac{8}{16} \\ \hline \end{array}$

Application

Write an equation for each word problem. Solve. Simplify and label the answer.

12. Malía used $\frac{3}{4}$ teaspoon of baking powder in making pancakes and $\frac{1}{8}$ teaspoon baking powder when making cookies. How much baking powder did she use in the two recipes?

13. Malía used $\frac{1}{2}$ cup of brown sugar and $\frac{3}{4}$ cup of granulated sugar in making cookies. How many cups of sugar did she use in all?

Did you know . . .

A Boeing 747-400 burns 3,361 gallons of fuel per hour!

Least Common Multiple

> The **least common multiple** is the lowest multiple, other than 0, that is the same for two or more numbers. The least common multiple is referred to as the LCM.

To find the LCM, list multiples of each number. The lowest multiple that is the same is the least common multiple (LCM).

6: 0, 6, 12, ⑱, 24, 30, ㊱, 42, 48, ㊄④   18, 36, and 54 are common multiples

9: 0, 9, ⑱, 27, ㊱, 45, ㊄④   18 is the *least* common multiple (LCM)

You can also use factor trees to find the LCM of two numbers.

1. Find the prime factors of the numbers, using factor trees.

2. List the prime factors of each number from least to greatest.

    30: 2, 3, 5

    36: 2, 2, 3, 3

3. Circle each factor in the list it appears most often.

    30: 2, 3, ⑤

    36: ②, ②, ③, ③

4. Multiply the circled factors. The product is the LCM.

    $5 \times 2 \times 2 \times 3 \times 3 =$

    $(5 \times 2) \times (2 \times 3) \times 3 =$

    $(10 \times 6) \times 3 =$

    $60 \times 3 = 180$

The LCM of 30 and 36 is 180.

Practice

List the multiples for each number to find the least common multiple (LCM).

1. 8, 10   **2.** 4, 9   **3.** 9, 12

Follow the steps for using factor trees on page 214 to find the least common multiple for each pair of numbers.

4. 28, 16   **5.** 45, 30   **6.** 15, 20   **7.** 7, 12

Language Link

8. Find the LCM of 12 and 18 both ways: first list the multiples to find the LCM, then use factor trees to find the LCM. Tell which method you prefer and explain why.

In all thy ways acknowledge him and he shall direct thy paths.
Proverbs 3:6

Meet the Challenge!

9. Bryan, Kristin, Lauren, and Jill take horse riding lessons. Bryan has a lesson every Saturday. Kristin has a lesson every other Saturday. Lauren has a lesson every third Saturday, and Jill has a lesson every fourth Saturday. How many weeks will pass before all four children have a lesson on the same Saturday?

Adding Unlike Fractions

Fractions must have a common denominator before they can be added. There are many ways to find a common denominator.

Method A: Multiply Denominators Together

If both denominators are prime or one denominator is prime and the other denominator is not a multiple of it (unrelated denominators), multiply the denominators together to find the least common denominator.

$$\frac{1}{10} + \frac{2}{3} =$$

1. Multiply. $\qquad\qquad\qquad\qquad 10 \times 3 = 30$

2. Rename both fractions, using the $\qquad \frac{1 \times 3}{10 \times 3} = \frac{3}{30} \qquad \frac{2 \times 10}{3 \times 10} = \frac{20}{30}$
   product as the denominator.

3. Add the fractions; simplify if necessary. $\qquad \frac{3}{30} + \frac{20}{30} = \frac{23}{30}$

Method B: Find the LCM

If neither number is prime, use prime factors to find the least common multiple. The least common multiple will be the least common denominator of the renamed fractions.

$$\frac{3}{10} + \frac{1}{4} =$$

1. Find the prime factors of the denominators, using factor trees.

$$10 \qquad\qquad 4$$

$$2 \times 5 \qquad\quad 2 \times 2$$

2. List the prime factors of each denominator from least to greatest.

$$10\text{: } 2, 5$$
$$4\text{: } 2, 2$$

3. Circle each factor in the list it appears most often.

$$10\text{: } 2, \text{⑤}$$
$$4\text{: } \text{②, ②}$$

4. Multiply the circled factors. The product is the LCM.

$$5 \times 2 \times 2 = 20$$

5. Rename the fractions, using the LCM as the least common denominator.

$$\frac{3 \times 2}{10 \times 2} = \frac{6}{20} \qquad \frac{1 \times 5}{4 \times 5} = \frac{5}{20}$$

6. Add the fractions.

$$\frac{6}{20} + \frac{5}{20} = \frac{11}{20}$$

Practice

Multiply denominators to find a common denominator. Solve. Simplify the answer.

1. $\frac{1}{6} + \frac{2}{5} =$

2. $\frac{3}{4} + \frac{4}{5} =$

3. $\frac{3}{5} + \frac{2}{3} =$

Use prime factors to find the LCM. Solve. Simplify the answer.

4. $\frac{1}{6} + \frac{3}{8} =$

5. $\frac{3}{10} + \frac{1}{4} =$

6. $\frac{3}{12} + \frac{1}{8} =$

Solve. (You may use either method to find common denominators.) Simplify the answer.

7. $\frac{5}{6}$
   $+ \frac{3}{8}$
   $\overline{\qquad}$

8. $\frac{7}{15}$
   $+ \frac{2}{9}$
   $\overline{\qquad}$

9. $\frac{2}{3}$
   $+ \frac{1}{10}$
   $\overline{\qquad}$

10. $\frac{5}{8}$
    $+ \frac{1}{3}$
    $\overline{\qquad}$

Application

Write an equation for each word problem. Solve. Simplify and label the answer.

11. The airport gift shop sold $\frac{1}{2}$ of their hats in June. They sold $\frac{1}{8}$ of their hats in July. What part of the hats were sold in the two months?

12. Amber works part-time in her father's store. On Saturday she spent $\frac{2}{6}$ of her working time dusting shelves in the gift shop. She spent $\frac{1}{4}$ of her time vacuuming. What part of her working time did Amber spend doing these two tasks?

13. Justin saved some money to take on his vacation. He spent $\frac{3}{4}$ of his money on souvenirs and $\frac{1}{5}$ of his money on snacks. How much of his money did he spend on souvenirs and snacks?

Adding Unlike Fractions and Mixed Numbers

To add mixed numbers, rename the fractions so they have a common denominator. Two methods for finding a common denominator are finding the LCM or multiplying the denominators together.

$$1\tfrac{3}{8} + 2\tfrac{5}{6} =$$

> The denominators are unrelated and not prime; so I will use factor trees to find the LCM.

Steps for Finding the LCM

1. Factor each number.
2. List the prime factors from least to greatest.
3. Circle the factors in the list they appear most.
4. Multiply the circled factors.

1. Find the LCM.

$$8 \\ 2 \times 4 \\ 2 \times 2 \times 2$$

$$6 \\ 2 \times 3$$

8: (2, 2, 2)
6: 2, (3)

$$2 \times 2 \times 2 \times 3 =$$
$$(2 \times 2) \times (2 \times 3) =$$
$$4 \quad \times \quad 6 \quad = 24$$

2. Rename both fractions, using the LCM as the least common denominator.

$$\frac{3 \times 3}{8 \times 3} = \frac{9}{24} \qquad \frac{5 \times 4}{6 \times 4} = \frac{20}{24}$$

3. Add; simplify if necessary.

$$\begin{array}{r} 1\tfrac{9}{24} \\ + \ 2\tfrac{20}{24} \\ \hline 3\tfrac{29}{24} = 4\tfrac{5}{24} \end{array}$$

Practice

Solve. Simplify the answer.

1. $\frac{5}{8} + \frac{1}{3} =$

2. $\frac{1}{6} + \frac{3}{4} =$

3. $\frac{5}{9} + \frac{1}{2} =$

4. $\begin{array}{r} \frac{3}{15} \\ + \frac{1}{2} \\ \hline \end{array}$

5. $\begin{array}{r} \frac{3}{4} \\ + \frac{1}{8} \\ \hline \end{array}$

6. $\begin{array}{r} \frac{1}{8} \\ + \frac{2}{3} \\ \hline \end{array}$

7. $\begin{array}{r} \frac{3}{4} \\ + \frac{1}{5} \\ \hline \end{array}$

8. $\begin{array}{r} 5\frac{2}{3} \\ + 4\frac{1}{5} \\ \hline \end{array}$

9. $\begin{array}{r} 7\frac{1}{8} \\ + 3\frac{5}{6} \\ \hline \end{array}$

10. $\begin{array}{r} 3\frac{3}{4} \\ + 2\frac{1}{2} \\ \hline \end{array}$

11. $\begin{array}{r} 3\frac{1}{4} \\ + 2\frac{1}{6} \\ \hline \end{array}$

Application

Write an equation for each word problem. Solve. Simplify and label the answer.

12. Mrs. Harper is making matching dresses for Lorinda and Heather. Lorinda's dress requires $4\frac{1}{2}$ yards of material. Heather's dress requires $3\frac{3}{8}$ yards. How much material must Mrs. Harper buy for both dresses?

13. Janiece purchased $\frac{3}{4}$ pounds of carrots and $\frac{2}{3}$ pounds of tomatoes. How many pounds of vegetables did she purchase in all?

14. Martine picked $\frac{7}{8}$ of a bushel of apples. Tom picked $\frac{5}{6}$ of a bushel. How many bushels of apples did they pick combined?

15. Melissa practiced the piano $1\frac{1}{4}$ hours on Monday and $\frac{2}{3}$ of an hour on Tuesday. How many hours did she practice on the two days together?

Subtracting Unlike Fractions

Steps for Subtracting Unlike, Unrelated Fractions

Fractions must have a common denominator before they can be subtracted. If the fractions are unrelated, you will need to find a common denominator by multiplying the denominators together or by finding the LCM.

$$\frac{7}{9} - \frac{9}{12} =$$

The denominators are unrelated and not prime; so I will use factor trees to find the LCM.

1. Find the LCM.

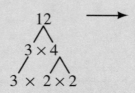

$$9: \enclose{circle}{3, 3}$$
$$12: \enclose{circle}{2, 2}\,3$$

$$2 \times 2 \times 3 \times 3 =$$
$$(2 \times 2) \times (3 \times 3) =$$
$$4 \quad \times \quad 9 \quad = 36$$

2. Rename both fractions, using the LCM as the least common denominator.

$$\frac{7 \times 4}{9 \times 4} = \frac{28}{36} \qquad \frac{9 \times 3}{12 \times 3} = \frac{27}{36}$$

3. Subtract; simplify if necessary.

$$\frac{28}{36} - \frac{27}{36} = \frac{1}{36} \qquad \frac{7}{9} - \frac{9}{12} = \frac{1}{36}$$

Steps for Subtracting Unlike, Related Fractions

If the fractions are related fractions (one denominator is a multiple of the other denominator), only one fraction needs to be renamed.

There was $\frac{7}{8}$ of a pizza in the box. Tony ate $\frac{1}{4}$ of the pizza. How much of the pizza was left?

8 is a multiple of 4.

$$\begin{array}{r} \frac{7}{8} \\ - \frac{1}{4} \end{array} = \frac{1 \times 2}{4 \times 2} = \begin{array}{r} \frac{7}{8} \\ - \frac{2}{8} \\ \hline \frac{5}{8} \end{array}$$

$$\frac{7}{8} - \frac{1}{4} = \frac{5}{8} \text{ of a pizza}$$

Practice

Solve. Simplify the answer.

1. $\dfrac{8}{9} - \dfrac{2}{3} =$ 2. $\dfrac{11}{18} - \dfrac{5}{12} =$ 3. $\dfrac{3}{4} - \dfrac{5}{12} =$ 4. $\dfrac{7}{18} - \dfrac{2}{6} =$

5. $\dfrac{4}{5} - \dfrac{3}{4} =$ 6. $\dfrac{7}{12} - \dfrac{4}{8} =$ 7. $\dfrac{3}{5} - \dfrac{3}{7} =$ 8. $\dfrac{3}{4} - \dfrac{4}{15} =$

9. $\begin{array}{r} \frac{9}{10} \\ -\frac{4}{5} \\ \hline \end{array}$ 10. $\begin{array}{r} \frac{7}{15} \\ -\frac{1}{6} \\ \hline \end{array}$

11. $\begin{array}{r} \frac{1}{2} \\ -\frac{1}{3} \\ \hline \end{array}$ 12. $\begin{array}{r} \frac{5}{9} \\ -\frac{3}{6} \\ \hline \end{array}$

Chapter 5 Review

Use rounding to estimate. Solve.

13. $\begin{array}{r} 8.9 \\ +6.7 \\ \hline \end{array}$ 14. $\begin{array}{r} \$1.05 \\ +3.94 \\ \hline \end{array}$ 15. $\begin{array}{r} 4.875 \\ +1.730 \\ \hline \end{array}$ 16. $\begin{array}{r} \$37.62 \\ +19.43 \\ \hline \end{array}$

Subtracting Unlike Fractions and Mixed Numbers

To subtract mixed numbers, rename the fractions so they have a common denominator. If the fraction in the subtrahend (second number) is greater than the fraction in the minuend (first number), rename 1 whole.

Zachary walked $4\frac{1}{3}$ miles. Andrew walked $1\frac{4}{5}$ miles. How much farther did Zachary walk than Andrew?

$$4\frac{1}{3} - 1\frac{4}{5} =$$

Step 1
Find the LCM.

$3 \times 5 = 15$

Both denominators are prime; so I can multiply them to find the LCM.

Step 2
Rename the fractions.

$4\frac{1}{3}$ $\frac{1 \times 5}{3 \times 5} = \frac{5}{15}$

$-1\frac{4}{5}$ $\frac{4 \times 3}{5 \times 3} = \frac{12}{15}$

Step 3
Rename 1 whole as a fraction if necessary.

$3\frac{15}{15}$
$\cancel{4}\frac{5}{15}$

$-1\frac{12}{15}$

Step 4
Subtract. Simplify if necessary.

$3\frac{20}{15}$
$-1\frac{12}{15}$
$\overline{2\frac{8}{15}}$

$$4\frac{1}{3} - 1\frac{4}{5} = 2\frac{8}{15} \text{ mi.}$$

If there is no fraction in the minuend, rename 1 whole as a fraction before subtracting.

Joy bought 2 yards of fabric. If a craft pattern calls for $1\frac{1}{3}$ yards, how much fabric will she have left?

$$2 - 1\frac{1}{3} =$$

Step 1
Find the LCM.

Step 2
Rename the fractions.

There is no fraction in the minuend. Go to step 3. →

Step 3
Rename 1 whole as a fraction.

$1\frac{3}{3}$
$\cancel{2}$

$-1\frac{1}{3}$

Step 4
Subtract. Simplify if necessary.

$1\frac{3}{3}$
$-1\frac{1}{3}$
$\overline{\frac{2}{3}}$

$$2 - 1\frac{1}{3} = \frac{2}{3} \text{ yd.}$$

Practice

Solve. Simplify the answer.

1. $\dfrac{7}{9} - \dfrac{1}{2} =$

2. $\dfrac{2}{3} - \dfrac{1}{8} =$

3. $\dfrac{7}{12} - \dfrac{3}{8} =$

4. $\begin{array}{r} 9\frac{2}{3} \\ -\ 3\frac{1}{6} \\ \hline \end{array}$

5. $\begin{array}{r} 4\frac{2}{3} \\ -\ 1\frac{1}{5} \\ \hline \end{array}$

6. $\begin{array}{r} 8 \\ -\ 5\frac{1}{5} \\ \hline \end{array}$

7. $\begin{array}{r} 5\frac{2}{3} \\ -\ 3\frac{4}{9} \\ \hline \end{array}$

8. $\begin{array}{r} 6 \\ -\ 2\frac{3}{4} \\ \hline \end{array}$

9. $\begin{array}{r} 5\frac{3}{8} \\ -\ 1\frac{2}{4} \\ \hline \end{array}$

10. $\begin{array}{r} 6\frac{5}{7} \\ -\ 4\frac{3}{4} \\ \hline \end{array}$

11. $\begin{array}{r} 9 \\ -\ 3\frac{5}{8} \\ \hline \end{array}$

Application

Write an equation for each word problem. Solve. Simplify and label the answer.

12. John had 5 pounds of plaster to make a volcano for science class. If he uses $2\frac{1}{4}$ pounds, how much plaster will he have left?

13. The base of John's volcano is a board that weighs $4\frac{1}{2}$ pounds. The completed project weighs $10\frac{5}{8}$ pounds. How much does the completed project weigh without the board?

Chapter 5 Review

Use rounding to estimate the sums. Solve.

14. $\begin{array}{r} \$14.16 \\ +\ 3.87 \\ \hline \end{array}$

15. $\begin{array}{r} 3.017 \\ +2.749 \\ \hline \end{array}$

16. $\begin{array}{r} 76.5 \\ +22.7 \\ \hline \end{array}$

17. $\begin{array}{r} \$37.04 \\ +\ 9.87 \\ \hline \end{array}$

Subtracting Mixed Numbers

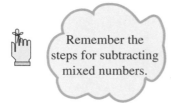

Remember the steps for subtracting mixed numbers.

1. Find the LCM.
2. Rename the fractions, using the LCM.
3. Rename 1 whole as a fractional name for 1, if needed.
4. Subtract; simplify if necessary.

Erin sold $2\frac{1}{3}$ cases of candy bars. Anne sold $1\frac{1}{2}$ cases. How much more candy did Erin sell?

$$2\frac{1}{3} - 1\frac{1}{2} =$$

Step 1
Find the LCM.

$$3 \times 2 = 6$$

Both denominators are prime; so I can multiply them to find the LCM.

Step 2
Rename the fractions.

$2\frac{1}{3}$ $\frac{1 \times 2}{3 \times 2} = \frac{2}{6}$

$- 1\frac{1}{2}$ $\frac{1 \times 3}{2 \times 3} = \frac{3}{6}$

Step 3
Rename 1 whole as a fraction.

$\overset{1\frac{6}{6}}{\cancel{2}\frac{2}{6}}$

$- 1\frac{3}{6}$

Step 4
Subtract. Simplify if necessary.

$1\frac{8}{6}$

$- 1\frac{3}{6}$

$\overline{\frac{5}{6}}$

$$2\frac{1}{3} - 1\frac{1}{2} = \frac{5}{6} \text{ of a case}$$

Tate's class received 7 cases of candy bars to sell. At the end of the week, they had sold $5\frac{3}{8}$ cases. How many cases did they have left?

$$7 - 5\frac{3}{8} =$$

Step 1
Find the LCM.

Step 2
Rename the fractions.

There is no fraction in the minuend. Go to step 3. ⟶

Step 3
Rename 1 whole as a fraction.

$\overset{6\frac{8}{8}}{\cancel{7}}$

$- 5\frac{3}{8}$

Step 4
Subtract. Simplify if necessary.

$6\frac{8}{8}$

$- 5\frac{3}{3}$

$\overline{1\frac{5}{8}}$

$$7 - 5\frac{3}{8} = 1\frac{5}{8} \text{ cases}$$

Practice

Solve. Simplify the answer.

1. $8\frac{1}{5}$ $-\ \ \frac{3}{4}$	2. $4\frac{1}{3}$ $-\ 4\frac{2}{9}$	3. $6\frac{2}{3}$ $-\ 1\frac{7}{12}$	4. 14 $-\ 9\frac{7}{10}$
5. $8\frac{7}{9}$ $-\ 5\frac{5}{6}$	6. 12 $-\ 1\frac{1}{6}$	7. $20\frac{1}{6}$ $-\ 11\frac{1}{4}$	8. $6\frac{2}{3}$ $-\ 1\frac{5}{8}$

Application

Write an equation for each word problem. Solve. Simplify and label the answer.

9. Jack has 2 cases of candy bars to sell. If he sells $\frac{2}{3}$ of a case to family members, how much more must he sell?

10. The twins, Megan and Regan, sold $1\frac{2}{3}$ cases on Tuesday and $\frac{5}{6}$ of a case on Wednesday. How much more did they sell on Tuesday?

Chapter 5 Review

Use rounding to estimate the sums. Solve.

11. $\$29.56$ $-\ \ \ 4.16$	12. 8.075 -2.59	13. 76 -29.4	14. 39.06 -14.709

+	−		5 ☐ 3 ☐ 2 ☐ 4 = 8						

You can multiply the numbers of possible choices of operations for each box to find how many possible combinations there are.

In the above problem there are 2 possible operations for each box.

$$2 \times 2 \times 2 = 8$$

There are 8 possible combinations.

5 + 3 + 2 + 4 = 14
5 − 3 − 2 − 4 = ⁻4
5 + 3 + 2 − 4 = 6
5 + 3 − 2 − 4 = 2
5 − 3 − 2 + 4 = 4
5 − 3 + 2 + 4 = 8
5 − 3 + 2 − 4 = 0
5 + 3 − 2 + 4 = 10

Write the equations with the correct signs.

1. ☐ × −
   6 ☒ 3 ☐ 4 = 14

2. ☐ + ÷
   8 ☐ 4 ☐ 3 ☐ 5 = 3

3. ☐ + ×
   5 ☐ 4 ☐ 2 ☐ 1 = 22

4. ☐ ÷ − +
   3 ☐ 5 ☐ 2 ☐ 3 = 2

Meet the Challenge!

Complete the puzzle using all four operations: + − × ÷

5.

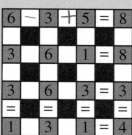

Fraction Word Problems

Write an equation for each problem. Solve and label. Simplify the answer.

1. It is $\frac{7}{10}$ of a mile from Jan's house to her school. She has already walked $\frac{3}{10}$ of a mile. What part of a mile does she need to walk to reach the school?

2. Craig practiced the piano $\frac{3}{4}$ of an hour on Monday and the same amount of time on Tuesday. How long did he practice on those two days?

3. Tasha used $\frac{2}{3}$ of a yard of green ribbon and $\frac{1}{6}$ of a yard of blue ribbon to make a bow for her mother. How many yards of ribbon did Tasha use?

4. Two months ago, Bill weighed $105\frac{1}{2}$ pounds. Now he weighs $112\frac{1}{4}$ pounds. How much weight has Bill gained?

5. Debbie rode her bike $3\frac{8}{10}$ miles on Monday, $1\frac{7}{10}$ miles on Tuesday, and $2\frac{1}{2}$ miles on Wednesday. How far did she ride altogether?

6. Cindy ate $\frac{3}{8}$ of a cheese pizza, and Trevor ate $\frac{3}{4}$ of a pepperoni pizza. How much more pizza did Trevor eat?

Flight Attendant

Dear Fifth Grade:

Just today I had another opportunity to use my math skills. On my New York to London flight, we offered the passengers two meal choices: chicken with rice or pork chops. I soon began to see that the chicken was the overwhelming favorite, and since we couldn't warm the meals fast enough, the passengers were having to wait for their dinner, which never makes them happy. When I tried to explain the delay, I was met with a few icy stares. My friend Gina, another flight attendant, was working the oven, and I was taking all the chicken dinners as fast as she could warm them up. The oven on this particular plane could only warm eight meals at a time, and Gina was warming up four of each kind of dinner each time. I suggested we could serve people faster if we warmed six chicken and two pork chop dinners each time, and we tried turning up the heat a few degrees to lessen the warming time. It was amazing what a difference it made! Passengers at the front of the plane were just finishing when I served the last meal at the back of the plane. I hope this letter helps you with your class project, and I wish you the best in your math efforts!

Yours very truly,

Kelly Winston

Kelly Winston

Pearson Airlines
228 Hargis Street
Richmond, Virginia 23220

Moore Christian School
334 Tara Lane
Mariposa, CA 95338

Copy and complete the number wheel. Add the center number to each number in the second ring. Write the answers in the third ring. Simplify if necessary in the outer ring. The first one has been done for you.

1.

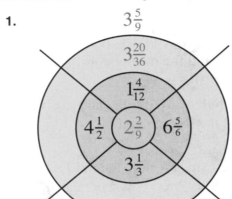

$3\frac{5}{9}$

$3\frac{20}{36}$

$1\frac{4}{12}$

$4\frac{1}{2}$ $2\frac{2}{9}$ $6\frac{5}{6}$

$3\frac{1}{3}$

Solve the addition problems. Simplify the answer.

2. $\frac{1}{6} + \frac{1}{6} =$

3. $\frac{3}{8} + \frac{1}{8} =$

4. $\frac{9}{10} + \frac{3}{10} + \frac{7}{10} =$

5. $\quad \frac{1}{3}$
$+ \frac{5}{6}$
———

6. $\quad \frac{5}{8}$
$+ \frac{7}{12}$
———

7. $\quad \frac{2}{9}$
$+ \frac{5}{6}$
———

8. $\quad 3\frac{1}{4}$
$+ 5\frac{2}{3}$
———

9. $\quad 5\frac{2}{3}$
$+ 4\frac{1}{5}$
———

Solve the subtraction problems. Simplify the answer.

10. $\frac{7}{10} - \frac{5}{10} =$

11. $\frac{13}{14} - \frac{3}{14} =$

12. $\frac{5}{8} - \frac{1}{8} =$

13. $\quad \frac{5}{6}$
$- \frac{1}{4}$
———

14. $\quad \frac{9}{10}$
$- \frac{2}{3}$
———

15. $\quad 8\frac{7}{8}$
$- 4\frac{2}{3}$
———

16. $\quad 3\frac{1}{6}$
$- 1\frac{1}{3}$
———

17. $\quad 7$
$- 2\frac{3}{5}$
———

Write an equation for each word problem. Solve and label.

18. Talia rode her bicycle $3\frac{4}{10}$ miles on Friday and $5\frac{1}{2}$ miles on Saturday. How much farther did she ride on Saturday?

19. Ethan cooked $\frac{3}{4}$ pounds of ground beef. After cooking, the meat weighed $\frac{1}{2}$ pound. How much less did the meat weigh after cooking?

20. Mrs. Felber walked $2\frac{3}{4}$ miles on Tuesday and $3\frac{1}{10}$ miles on Friday. How far did she walk in the 2 days combined?

21. Aleta baked 4 pans of brownies for the Parent-Teacher Fellowship. At the fellowship, $3\frac{2}{5}$ pans of brownies were eaten. What part of a pan of brownies was left?

Use the table to answer the questions.

22. How much farther did Mary walk on Friday than on Monday?

23. How far did Mary walk on Monday and Wednesday combined?

24. Which day did Mary walk the shortest distance?

25. How far did Mary walk on Tuesday and Thursday combined?

26. How much farther did Mary walk on Friday than on Thursday?

Mary's Walking

Day	Distance
Monday	$1\frac{1}{6}$
Tuesday	$1\frac{5}{8}$
Wednesday	$1\frac{3}{12}$
Thursday	$2\frac{1}{10}$
Friday	3

Cumulative Review

Write the letter of the correct answer.

1. Which sign will make the sentence true?

    $80,000 + 40 + 8 \bigcirc 80,048$

    a. >
    b. <
    c. =
    d. not given

2. Solve.

    $\begin{array}{r} 64,893 \\ -49,797 \end{array}$

    a. 10,100
    b. 13,900
    c. 14,906
    d. not given

3. Solve.

    $\begin{array}{r} 9,527 \\ \times\ \ \ 502 \end{array}$

    a. 4,782,554
    b. 4,800,782
    c. 5,280,504
    d. not given

4. What is the measure of the third angle?

    a. 30°
    b. 40°
    c. 50°
    d. 60°

5. Solve.

    $\begin{array}{r} 68 \\ +493.72 \end{array}$

    a. 435.72
    b. 561.72
    c. 575.72
    d. not given

6. Solve.

    $6\overline{)2,428}$

    a. 268 r2
    b. 342 r4
    c. 404 r4
    d. not given

7. What is the greatest common factor for 36 and 48?

    a. 1
    b. 3
    c. 6
    d. 12

8. Which measurement is not equivalent to 100 cm?

    a. 10 km
    b. 1 m
    c. 1000 mm
    d. not given

9. Solve.

    $44\overline{)399}$

    a. 7 r2
    b. 8 r2
    c. 9 r3
    d. not given

10. Solve.

    $\frac{6}{15} + \frac{2}{3} =$

    a. $\frac{8}{15}$
    b. $1\frac{1}{15}$
    c. $\frac{8}{3}$
    d. $1\frac{4}{5}$

11. The Cross family traveled 456 miles in 8 hours. What was their average speed in miles per hour?

    a. 54
    b. 55
    c. 56
    d. 57

12. Solve.

    $\begin{array}{r} 78.4 \\ -39.26 \end{array}$

    a. 39.14
    b. 117.66
    c. 38.86
    d. not given

Passenger Aircraft

The first real passenger aircraft were the German-designed zeppelins, invented before World War I. The zeppelins were dirigibles: huge balloons made out of heavy, wire-braced cotton material and propelled by an engine. People would fly short distances between cities, and as technology improved, zeppelins began shuttling people back and forth across the Atlantic. After the war some zeppelins were even flown as luxury airships. But when one of these airships burned upon landing, the public immediately lost faith in zeppelins as a means of passenger flight.

Aviation has come a long way since the days of the zeppelins. We now have large passenger airliners to transport us nearly anywhere we want to go—anyplace that has a runway long enough.

Passenger jets provide a fast, comfortable way to travel. The jet engine runs by means of action and reaction, in much the same way as if someone were letting air out of a balloon. As the air pushes out the mouth of the balloon, the balloon itself rushes forward. So as gases push backward out of a jet engine, the plane reacts in an opposite way—it speeds forward. The speeds at which jets can travel have been gradually increasing over the years. The supersonic jet is designed to travel faster than the speed of sound.

Flight in space has already been accomplished by astronauts in rocketships and space shuttles. Who knows? Sometime in the future we may have spacecraft that can take passengers on routine trips into space. Would you like to vacation on another planet? New discoveries may one day make that possible!

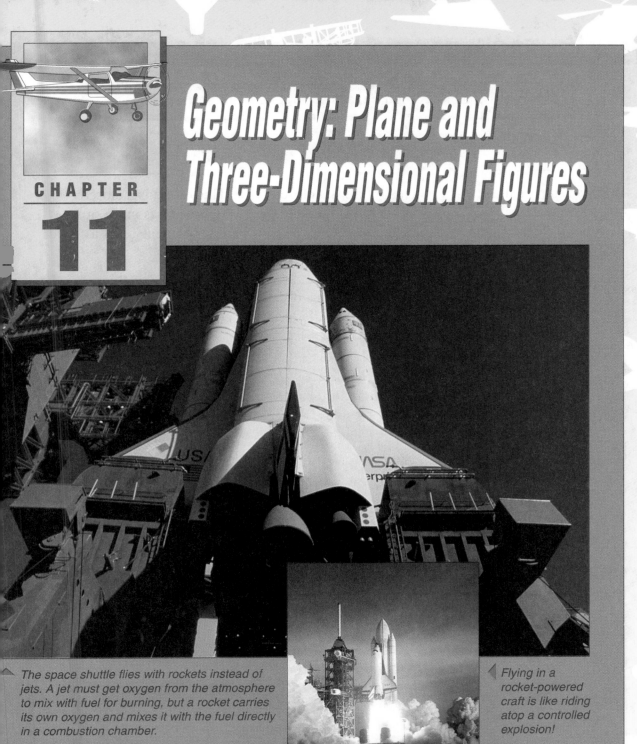

Geometry: Plane and Three-Dimensional Figures

The space shuttle flies with rockets instead of jets. A jet must get oxygen from the atmosphere to mix with fuel for burning, but a rocket carries its own oxygen and mixes it with the fuel directly in a combustion chamber.

Flying in a rocket-powered craft is like riding atop a controlled explosion!

Polygons

A **polygon** is a closed figure made of three or more line segments.

This figure is made of line segments but is not a closed figure.

This figure is a closed figure but is not made of line segments.

This figure is a closed figure and is made of line segments. It is a **polygon**.

These are polygons. Because they have sides of the same length (congruent sides), they are called **regular** polygons.

Triangle
3 sides
3 angles

Quadrilateral
4 sides
4 angles

Pentagon
5 sides
5 angles

Hexagon
6 sides
6 angles

Heptagon
7 sides
7 angles

Octagon
8 sides
8 angles

These are also polygons. Because they have sides of unequal lengths, they are called **irregular** polygons.

quadrilateral

pentagon

hexagon

octagon

Practice

Is the figure a polygon? Write *yes* or *no*.

1.
2.
3.
4.
5.

Identify the figure.

6.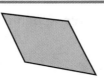
7.
8.
9.

10.
11.
12.
13.

Draw the polygon and write the number of sides and angles for each polygon.

Example: triangle   *3 sides, 3 angles*

14. octagon   15. quadrilateral   16. hexagon   17. pentagon

Language Link

18. Can a polygon be made with just 2 line segments? Explain why or why not.

Did you know . . .

Euclid, who lived about 300 years before Christ, was a Greek mathematician, known as the Father of Geometry. He wrote a 13-volume text on mathematics called *Elements*. He taught mathematics in Alexandria, Egypt.

Similar, Congruent, Symmetrical

Similar figures are exactly the same shape but not necessarily the same size. The symbol for similar is ~.

These triangles are similar. They have exactly the same shape because the corresponding angles are the same.

$$\triangle ABC \sim \triangle XYZ$$

Congruent figures are exactly the same size and shape. The symbol for congruent is $\cong$.

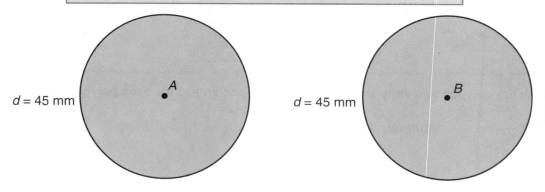

These circles are congruent. They both have diameters of 45 mm.

circle $A \cong$ circle B

Symmetrical figures can be folded along a line of symmetry so that the two halves match. A figure may have more than one line of symmetry.

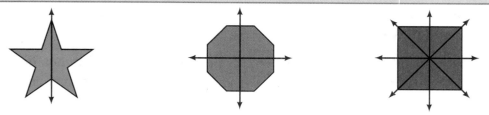

These figures are symmetrical.

Practice

Identify the similar pairs of figures. Write *yes* or *no*.

1.

2.

Write *similar*, *congruent*, or *neither* for each pair of figures.

3.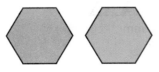

4.

5.

Trace the figure. Draw each line of symmetry.

6.

7.

8.

Trace the figure. Draw a similar figure.

9.

10.

Meet the Challenge!

11. This symmetrical word has been folded horizontally. What is the word?

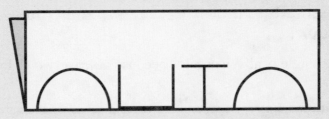

Classifying Triangles

You have learned that triangles can be classified by their angles (right, acute, obtuse). Triangles can also be classified by their sides.

When all three sides of a triangle are congruent (have equal lengths), it is an **equilateral triangle**.

32 mm   32 mm

32 mm

When at least two sides of a triangle are congruent (have equal lengths), it is an **isosceles triangle**.

39 mm   39 mm

21 mm

When all three sides of a triangle have different measurements, it is a **scalene triangle**.

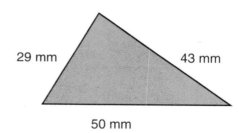

29 mm   43 mm

50 mm

Did you know . . .

An equilateral triangle is also isosceles because at least two of its sides are congruent.

Practice

Use the table to answer the questions.

1. What type of triangle did Jodie make?

2. What type of triangle did Mitchell make?

3. What type of triangle did Perry make?

Measure of Sides of Triangles

Name	Side 1	Side 2	Side 3
Jodie	36 mm	32 mm	51 mm
Mitchell	25 mm	25 mm	25 mm
Perry	19 mm	39 mm	39 mm

Measure each side to the nearest millimeter. Identify the type of triangle: *scalene, isosceles, equilateral.*

4.

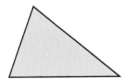

5.

6.

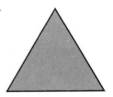

7. Can you make a right triangle that is scalene? isosceles? equilateral? Make drawings to prove your answers.

Chapter 8 Review

Complete each equation.

8. 39 mm = ____ cm ____ mm

9. 49 mm = _____ cm

10. 18 cm = _____ mm

11. 24 cm 5 mm= _____ mm

12. 503 mm = _____ cm

13. 97 cm = _____ mm

A **quadrilateral** is a polygon with four sides.

Rectangle
Opposite sides are parallel.
Opposite sides are congruent.
All angles are right angles.

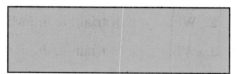

Square
Opposite sides are parallel.
All sides are congruent.
All angles are right angles.

Parallelogram
Opposite sides are parallel.
Opposite sides are congruent.
Opposite angles are congruent.

Rhombus
Opposite sides are parallel.
All sides are congruent.
Opposite angles are congruent.

Trapezoid
One pair of opposite
sides are parallel.

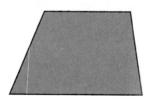

Practice

Identify each quadrilateral.

1.
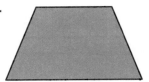

2.

3.
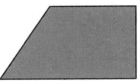

4.

5.
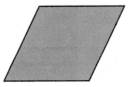

6.

Name the quadrilateral described.

7. four congruent sides, four right angles

8. one pair of opposite sides parallel

9. both pairs of opposite sides parallel, all four sides congruent, opposite angles congruent

Meet the Challenge!

Refer to the definitions on page 240 to answer the questions.

10. Is a square a rhombus?

11. Is a trapezoid a rectangle?

12. Is a square a parallelogram?

Perimeter

Perimeter is the distance around a figure.

Perimeter can be found by using this formula:
Perimeter = sum of the sides

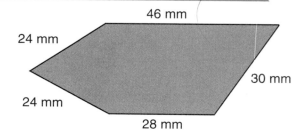

$P = s + s + s + s + s$
$P = 46 + 30 + 28 + 24 + 24$
$P = 152$ mm

The perimeter of a regular polygon (all sides congruent) can be found by using this formula:
Perimeter = number of sides × length of one side

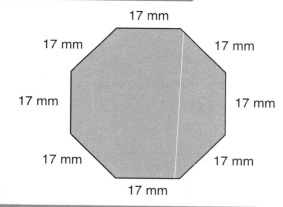

$P = n \times s$
$P = 8 \times 17$
$P = 136$ mm

The perimeter of a rectangle can be found by adding 2 times the length and 2 times the width.
$P = (2 \times l) + (2 \times w)$

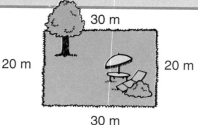

$P = (2 \times l) + (2 \times w)$
$P = (2 \times 30) + (2 \times 20)$
$P = 60 + 40$
$P = 100$ m

Practice

Write an equation to find the perimeter of each figure. Solve and label.

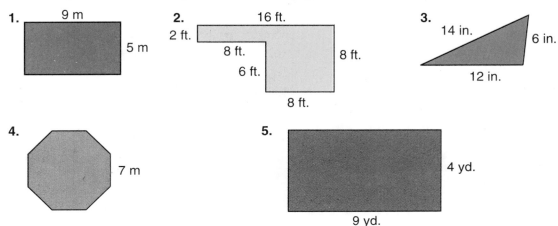

1. 9 m, 5 m

2. 16 ft., 2 ft., 8 ft., 6 ft., 8 ft., 8 ft.

3. 14 in., 6 in., 12 in.

4. 7 m

5. 4 yd., 9 yd.

Application

Write an equation for each word problem. Solve and label.

6. Sam's garden plot is a rectangle 5 meters long and 3 meters wide. How many meters of fence are needed to go all the way around the garden?

7. Connor drew a regular hexagon. Each of the sides measures 13 cm. What is the perimeter of the hexagon?

8. Paula is making a pillow in the shape of a pentagon. Each side is 12 inches long. How much cording is needed to edge the pillow?

9. Miss Mills jogged around the block. The length of the block is 0.3 miles, and the width is 0.2 miles. How far did Miss Mills jog?

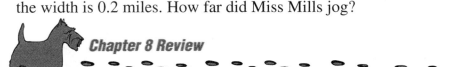

Chapter 8 Review

Write the more sensible temperature.

10. a cool autumn day   11. a child's fever   12. a hot oven

    14° C   45° C   39° C   100° C   94° C   200°C

Area

Area is the space within a region. It is measured in square units.
Area = length × width

Mr. and Mrs. Flint are putting new tile in their kitchen. Each tile has an area of 1 square foot.

It will take a long time to count all the squares. You can use a formula if you know the dimensions of the kitchen.

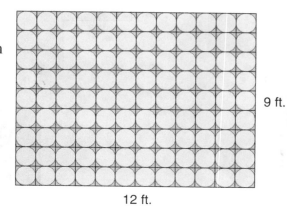

9 ft.

12 ft.

The area of a rectangle or square can be found by multiplying the length times the width.

$$A = l \times w$$
$$A = 12 \times 9$$
$$A = 108 \text{ ft.}^2$$

Sometimes you may need to divide a figure into two or more rectangles to find the area.

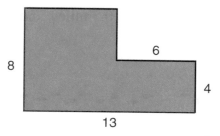

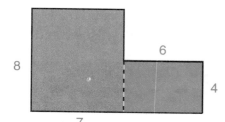

$$A = (7 \times 8) + (6 \times 4)$$
$$A = 56 + 24$$
$$A = 80 \text{ units}^2$$

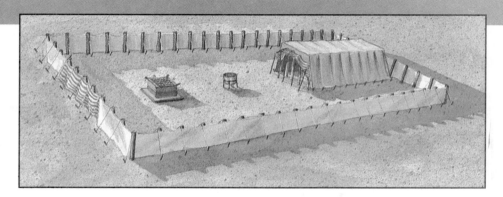

Practice

Write a multiplication equation to find the area of each figure. Solve and label.

1.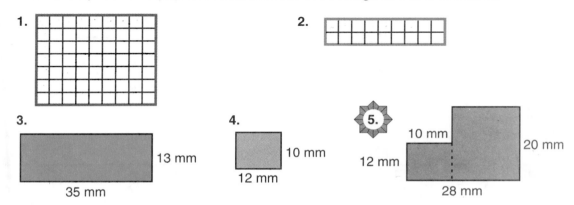

2.

3. 13 mm
   35 mm

4. 10 mm
   12 mm

5. 10 mm
   12 mm
   20 mm
   28 mm

Application

Write an equation for each word problem. Solve and label.

6. The mercy seat on the ark of the covenant was $2\frac{1}{2}$ cubits (45 inches) long and $1\frac{1}{2}$ cubits (27 inches) wide. What was the area of the mercy seat in square inches?

7. The table of shewbread in the holy place of the tabernacle was 2 cubits (36 inches) long and 1 cubit (18 inches) wide. What was the area of the table in square inches?

8. Each curtain in the tabernacle was 28 cubits (504 inches) long and 4 cubits (72 inches) wide. What was the area of each curtain in square inches?

9. There were 10 of the curtains described in problem 8 used in the tabernacle. What was the area in square inches of the 10 curtains combined?

Area of a Triangle

The area of a triangle is one-half the area of the related rectangle.

4 cm

5 cm

To find the area of the rectangle, multiply length times width.

$$A = 5 \times 4$$
$$A = 20 \text{ cm}^2$$

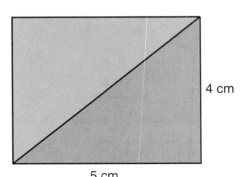

4 cm

5 cm

To find the area of the triangle, divide the area of the rectangle by 2.

$$A = 20 \div 2$$
$$A = 10 \text{ cm}^2$$

2 cm

6 cm

$$A = 6 \times 2$$
$$A = 12 \text{ cm}^2$$

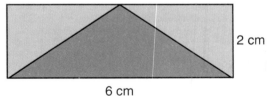

2 cm

6 cm

$$A = 12 \div 2$$
$$A = 6 \text{ cm}^2$$

Class Work

Find the area of each triangle.

1.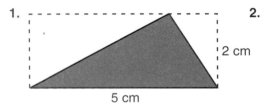

2 cm

5 cm

2.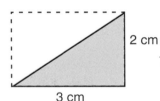

2 cm

3 cm

3.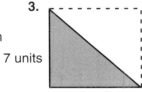

7 units

8 units

246

Chapter 11

Practice

Find the area of the colored figure. Write the equations you used.

1.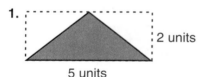

2 units
5 units

2.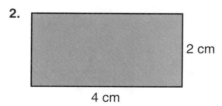

2 cm
4 cm

3.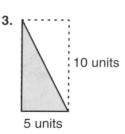

10 units
5 units

4.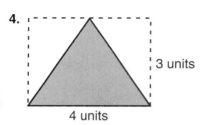

3 units
4 units

5.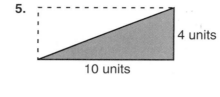

4 units
10 units

6.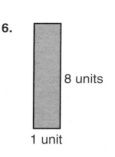

8 units
1 unit

Language Link

7. Explain why the area of a triangle is half the area of the related rectangle.

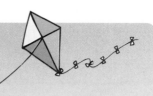

Did you know . . .

The kite was the earliest form of aircraft man designed. A kite can be thought of as 4 triangles. How could you find the area of a kite?

Three-Dimensional Figures

Three-dimensional figures have length, width, and height.

Each of these three-dimensional figures has one curved surface.

Sphere
1 curved surface

Cone
1 face
1 curved surface

Cylinder
2 faces
1 curved surface

Polyhedrons are three-dimensional figures whose faces are polygons. Polyhedrons do not have curved surfaces. Prisms and pyramids are polyhedrons.

Prisms
These figures are prisms. A prism has 2 congruent bases that are polygons. The other faces are parallelograms. A prism is named by the shape of its base.

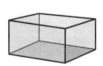

rectangular prism

square prism

triangular prism

Pyramids
These figures are pyramids. A pyramid has a base that is a polygon. The other faces are triangles that meet at a common vertex. A pyramid is named by the shape of its base.

rectangular pyramid

square pyramid

triangular pyramid

Practice

Is the figure a polyhedron? Write yes or no.

1.
2.
3.
4.

Write the number of flat and curved surfaces for each figure.

5.
6.
7.
8.

Identify each figure: *sphere, cylinder, cone, rectangular prism, triangular prism, square prism, rectangular pyramid, triangular pyramid, square pyramid.*

9.
10.
11.

12.
13.
14.

Copy and complete the table.

Polyhedron	Faces	Edges	Vertices
rectangular prism			
cube (square prism)			
triangular prism			
square pyramid			
triangular pyramid			

 Chapter 3 Review

Write the first five multiples of each number.

21. 4   22. 5   23. 7   24. 8   25. 9

Volume

> **Volume** is the number of cubic units within a closed three-dimensional figure.

> The volume of a rectangular prism can be found using the formula:
> Volume = length × width × height

> Volume is measured in cubic units:
> cm^3 (cubic centimeters), m^3 (cubic meters), $in.^3$ (cubic inches), $ft.^3$ (cubic feet).

Mr. Garcia has a shipment of books to make. He calculated the total size of the boxes he will use and found that he needs space for 4,000 ft.^{3} If he uses the boxcar shown, will he have enough room for his shipment?

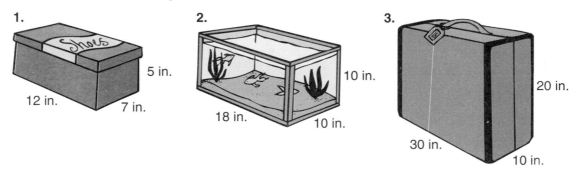

$50 \times 9 \times 11 = 4,950$ ft.^{3}
Yes, he has enough room.

Class Work

Find the volume of each figure.

1. 5 in. 12 in. 7 in.

2. 10 in. 18 in. 10 in.

3. 20 in. 30 in. 10 in.

Praise ye him, sun and moon: praise him, all ye stars of light.

Psalm 148:3

Practice

Write a multiplication equation to find the volume of each figure. Solve and label.

1.

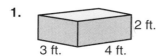

2 ft.

3 ft.   4 ft.

2.

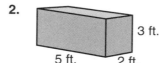

3 ft.

5 ft.   2 ft.

3.

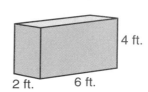

4 ft.

2 ft.   6 ft.

Application

Write an equation for each word problem. Solve and label.

4. Mrs. Davenport wants to kill the bugs in her pantry. The pantry is 3 feet wide, 4 feet long, and 7 feet high. The label on the bug bomb warns that it should not be used in a space with less than 100 ft.^{3} Is the pantry large enough for Mrs. Davenport to set off a bug bomb?

5. The bug bomb is effective for a volume of up to 6,000 ft.^{3} The Kwok's apartment is 31 feet long and 42 feet wide. The ceiling is 9 feet from the floor. How many bug bombs does Mr. Kwok need to buy?

6. Mrs. Kaminski has a window box planter that is 24 inches long, 8 inches wide, and 8 inches high. Will a bag containing 1 cubic foot (1,728 in.^{3}) of potting soil be enough to fill the planter completely?

Chapter 3 Review

Solve.

7. $70 \times 40 =$ 8. $8 \times 500 =$ 9. $60 \times 90 =$ 10. $30 \times 200 =$

Perimeter of a Rectangle

Perimeter = length + width + length + width

$$P = (2 \times l) + (2 \times w)$$

The LET statement tells the computer how much the letter is worth.

Use the following program to solve the word problem.

```
10 PRINT "PERIMETER OF A RECTANGLE"
20 PRINT
30 PRINT "ENTER THE LENGTH AND WIDTH"
40 PRINT "SEPARATED BY A COMMA"
50 INPUT L, W
60 LET P=(2*L)+(2*W)
70 PRINT
80 PRINT "THE PERIMETER IS"; P
90 END
```

1. Mrs. Hill's classroom bulletin board is 10 feet long and 3 feet wide. How much border will she need to go all the way around?

2. The softball league wants to fence the softball field. It is 150 feet by 100 feet. How many feet of fencing will be needed?

3. The distance between bases on the softball field is 65 feet. How far will a player run if he hits a home run and runs around all the bases?

4. How many feet of molding will be put around the living room window? The window measures 3 feet by 6.5 feet.

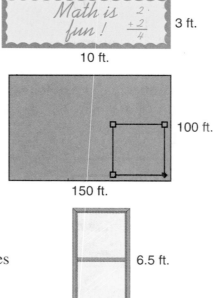

Math is fun!

2
+ 2
4

3 ft.

10 ft.

100 ft.

150 ft.

6.5 ft.

3 ft.

Geometry in Word Problems

**Use the diagram to solve the word problems. Write the equations you used.
Your teacher may allow you to use a calculator.**

1. Dr. Chen would like to put in a new lawn in his back yard. What will the area of the new lawn be?

2. A 10-lb. bag of grass seed will cover approximately 850 ft.^{2} How many of these bags does Dr. Chen need to buy to seed the new lawn in the back yard?

3. Each bag of grass seed costs $14.53. How much will Dr. Chen spend on grass seed in all for the new back lawn?

4. Dr. Chen would like to hire a cement contractor to pour a new driveway. What is the area of the driveway?

5. What is the perimeter of the front yard?

6. How many begonias will Mrs. Chen purchase if she plans to plant a row of begonias 8 inches apart in the front yard along the street?

7. Mrs. Chen has 2 planters. Each planter is 32 inches long, 18 inches wide, and 10 inches deep. How many bags of potting soil does she need to buy to fill both planters? Each bag contains 1 cubic foot (1,728 in.^{3}).

Diagram: BACK YARD 70 ft. / 90 ft., GARAGE, HOUSE 48 ft. / 30 ft., 10 ft., DRIVEWAY 12 ft., FRONT YARD 80 ft. / 110 ft. / 58 ft., MAGNOLIA AVENUE

Is the figure a polygon? Write *yes* or *no*.

1.

2.

3.

4.

Identify each three-dimensional figure.

5.

6.

7.

8.

9.

10.

Write *congruent, similar,* or *neither* for each pair of figures.

11.

12.

13.

14.

Determine whether a line of symmetry has been drawn. Write *yes* or *no*.

15.

16.

17.

Find the perimeter and area of each figure. Write the equations you use.

18.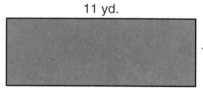

11 yd.

4 yd.

19.

8 ft.

Find the volume of each figure. Write the equations you use.

20.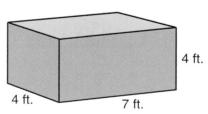

4 ft.

4 ft.

7 ft.

21.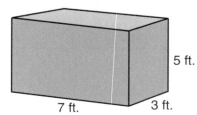

5 ft.

7 ft.

3 ft.

Identify the type of triangle: *equilateral, isosceles, scalene.*

22.

23.

24.

Identify the type of quadrilateral: *square, rectangle, parallelogram, rhombus, trapezoid.*

25.

26.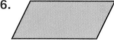

27.

28.

Write the letter of the correct figure.

29. eight-sided polygon

30. three-dimensional figure with one curved surface and no faces

31. quadrilateral with one pair of parallel sides

32. pyramid with a triangle base

33. five-sided polygon

a. trapezoid
b. pentagon
c. octagon
d. triangular pyramid
e. sphere

Write an equation for each word problem. Solve and label.

34. Lori made an afghan that measured 48 inches long and 45 inches wide. What was the area of the afghan?

35. What was the perimeter of Lori's afghan?

36. Chris bought a cooler that is 34 inches long, 20 inches wide, and 22 inches high. What is the volume of the cooler?

Five-Pointed Star

F̲ollow the instructions to cut out a five-pointed star. You will need a 5 in. × 5 in. piece of paper and a pair of scissors. Measure accurately.

Step 1
Fold the paper in half.

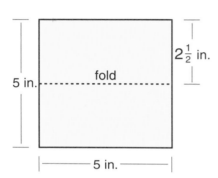

Step 2
Pinch in the center.

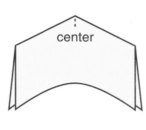

Step 3
Fold right-hand side down to form a 36° angle at the top.

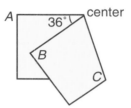

Step 4
Fold point C to point B. Turn paper completely over.

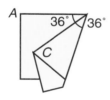

Step 5
Fold down point A to point D.

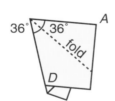

Step 6
Cut from point A to point E.

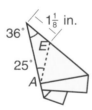

Step 7
Unfold the star!

Cumulative Review

Write the letter of the correct answer.

1. Round 885,689,873 to the nearest hundred million.
   - a. 900,000
   - b. 900,000,000
   - c. 980,000,000
   - d. not given

2. Solve.

   $$\begin{array}{r} 18,308 \\ 7,697 \\ + 1,283 \end{array}$$

   - a. 27,288
   - b. 28,279
   - c. 29,166
   - d. not given

3. Mrs. Whalen bought 15 flower arrangements for $15.50 each for the church banquet. How much did the arrangements cost in all?
   - a. $112.50
   - b. $222.50
   - c. $232.50
   - d. not given

4. Juan's Mexican sombrero needs some decorative trim around the brim. If the diameter of the sombrero is 22 in., about how much trim is needed?
   - a. 60 in.
   - b. 70 in.
   - c. 80 in.
   - d. 90 in.

5. Which sign will make the sentence true?

   $$7.75 \bigcirc 7.7$$

   - a. >
   - b. <
   - c. =
   - d. not given

6. Solve for n.
   $$n \times 2 = 92$$
   - a. $n = 45$
   - b. $n = 46$
   - c. $n = 47$
   - d. $n = 4$

7. What is the least common multiple of 6 and 8?
   - a. 8
   - b. 12
   - c. 24
   - d. 48

8. Milly drank 600 ml of juice. How many liters did she drink?
   - a. 0.6 L
   - b. 6 L
   - c. 60 L
   - d. 600 L

9. Solve.

   $$72\overline{)74,683}$$

   - a. 1,027 r 20
   - b. 1,037 r 19
   - c. 1,327
   - d. not given

10. Solve.
    $$5\frac{2}{8} + 3\frac{6}{8} =$$
    - a. 9
    - b. $9\frac{3}{8}$
    - c. $9\frac{1}{2}$
    - d. not given

11. Solve.

    $$\begin{array}{r} 0.654 \\ + 4.539 \end{array}$$

    - a. 4.193
    - b. 5.183
    - c. 5.193
    - d. not given

Aircraft in Meteorology

Meteorologists use airplanes to predict and track violent storms. In areas prone to hurricanes, the U.S. Air Force sends Weather Reconnaissance Squadrons into hurricanes to collect important information. These pilots fly their planes directly through the storm clouds into the eye, or the calm place in the center of a hurricane. They can then inform meteorologists of the eye's exact location and can measure the storm's wind speed, direction, and air pressure. The planes they use are equipped with computers that can transfer data into computers at the National Hurricane Center in Miami, Florida. Sometimes the planes drop special instruments called dropsondes into the heart of the hurricane to take readings at lower altitudes.

Weather scientists have also used planes in attempts to tame and prevent storms. In a process called cloud seeding, pilots fly into storms and drop silver iodide into the clouds. The silver iodide particles act as artificial freezing nuclei. The droplets in the water vapor will not freeze unless they have something to freeze onto. When the silver iodide particles enter the cloud, the water particles freeze onto them and produce larger ice crystals which eventually become heavy enough to fall from the cloud. Once started, the rain or snow continues to fall. In a project called Stormfury in 1961, scientists decided to try this procedure with hurricane clouds to lessen the power of these storms. They seeded four hurricanes over the next ten years, but no significant effects came from the seeding. Scientists are still researching new ways to predict and tame violent storms.

Decimal Fractions: Multiplication and Division

The eye of hurricane Esther. Hurricanes are named alphabetically, so the first hurricane of the season will have a name that begins with A, the second with B, and so on. What does that tell you about this hurricane?

Hurricane Ellen over the Atlantic in September 1973 as viewed from Skylab.

Multiplication: Whole Number Times a Decimal

Decimals are multiplied in the same way as whole numbers. Estimate to decide where to place the decimal point.

$$3 \times 2.3 =$$

Step 1
Estimate by rounding to the nearest whole number.

$$3 \times 2 = 6$$

Step 2
Multiply the same way whole numbers are multiplied.

$$\begin{array}{r} 2.3 \\ \times\ \ 3 \\ \hline 69 \end{array}$$

Step 3
Look at the estimate to place the decimal point.

6

$$\begin{array}{r} 2.3 \\ \times\ \ 3 \\ \hline 6.9 \end{array}$$

The answer is close to the estimate: 6 is close to 6.9.

Follow the steps to solve the word problem.

Monica walks 3.4 miles each day. How far does she walk in 5 days?

Step 1
Estimate.

$$5 \times 3 = 15$$

Step 2
Multiply.

$$\begin{array}{r} 3.4 \\ \times\ \ 5 \\ \hline 170 \end{array}$$

Step 3
Place the decimal point.

$$\begin{array}{r} 3.4 \\ \times\ \ 5 \\ \hline 17.0 \end{array}$$

$$5 \times 3.4 = 17 \text{ miles}$$

Class Work

Use rounding to estimate the product. Solve.

1.
$$\begin{array}{r} 0.6 \\ \times\ \ 3 \\ \hline \end{array}$$

2.
$$\begin{array}{r} 1.25 \\ \times\ \ 7 \\ \hline \end{array}$$

3.
$$\begin{array}{r} 6.032 \\ \times\ \ 4 \\ \hline \end{array}$$

Practice

Use rounding to estimate the product. Solve.

$$\text{Example:} \quad \boxed{32} \quad \begin{array}{r} 7.6 \\ \times\ 4 \\ \hline 30.4 \end{array}$$

1. $\begin{array}{r} 3.4 \\ \times\ 6 \\ \hline \end{array}$

2. $\begin{array}{r} \$2.04 \\ \times\quad 8 \\ \hline \end{array}$

3. $\begin{array}{r} 0.3 \\ \times\ 2 \\ \hline \end{array}$

4. $\begin{array}{r} 9.2 \\ \times\ 7 \\ \hline \end{array}$

5. $\begin{array}{r} 7.3 \\ \times\ 8 \\ \hline \end{array}$

6. $\begin{array}{r} 0.18 \\ \times\quad 5 \\ \hline \end{array}$

7. $\begin{array}{r} 5.371 \\ \times\qquad 4 \\ \hline \end{array}$

8. $\begin{array}{r} \$8.32 \\ \times\quad 5 \\ \hline \end{array}$

Application

Write an equation for each word problem. Solve and label. (You may need to estimate your answer before placing the decimal point.)

9. Dan read the label on a soft drink bottle. He noticed that the bottle contained 2 liters or 67.6 fluid ounces. How many fluid ounces would be in 3 of these bottles?

10. Mrs. Wooster wants to put a border all the way around her bulletin board. The bulletin board is 1.5 meters high and 2.8 meters wide. How many meters of border does she need?

11. Sarah rides the school bus 6.8 miles each day. How far does she ride in 5 days?

12. Jon took $5.00 to the store. He spent $3.25. How much did he have left?

Chapter 9 Review

Solve.

13. $90\overline{)900}$ 14. $40\overline{)360}$ 15. $50\overline{)150}$ 16. $70\overline{)420}$ 17. $80\overline{)640}$

Multiplication: Decimal by a Decimal

The number sentence 0.5×0.7 is to be read "0.5 of 0.7."

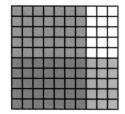

This grid shows 0.7. Seven-tenths of the grid is colored.

This grid shows five-tenths colored pink and seven-tenths colored blue. Thirty-five hundredths (0.35) is colored purple.

$$0.5 \times 0.7 = 0.35$$

Step 1
Multiply in the same way whole numbers are multiplied.

$$\begin{array}{r} 0.7 \\ \times 0.5 \\ \hline 35 \end{array}$$

Step 2
Place the decimal point.

$$\begin{array}{r} 0.7 \\ \times 0.5 \\ \hline .35 \end{array}$$

Step 3
Place a 0 in the Ones place if necessary.

$$\begin{array}{r} 0.7 \\ \times 0.5 \\ \hline 0.35 \end{array}$$

When multiplying with decimals, you do not need to line up the decimal points.

 The number of decimal places in the product is the same as the number of decimal places in the factors combined.

It is sometimes necessary to insert zeros in the product so that there will be enough decimal places.

$$\begin{array}{r} 1.25 \\ \times 0.05 \\ \hline 0.0625 \end{array}$$

There are 4 decimal places in the factors combined; so there will be 4 decimal places in the answer.

Insert 0 to make 4 decimal places.

Place a 0 in the Ones place.

Practice

Solve.

1. 0.1
   × 0.2

2. 0.45
   × 0.5

3. 0.23
   × 0.4

4. 0.5
   × 0.5

5. 0.03
   × 0.7

6. 2.14
   × 0.7

7. 7.14
   × 0.9

8. 2.52
   × 0.8

9. 3.6
   × 0.5

10. 1.11
    × 0.9

Application

Solve and label.

11. In February Fred purchased 8 gallons of gas. Each gallon cost $0.95. How much did he pay?

12. In March Fred purchased 8 gallons of gas at $1.01 per gallon. How much more did Fred pay for gas in March than in February?

13. Marti bought 6 items at $1.00 each. What was her total after the $0.05 per dollar sales tax was added?

14. Marti gave the cashier $10.00. How much change did she receive?

Meet the Challenge!

15. Sasha bought a hanging plant that was priced at $8.99. She lives in a state that charges 7% sales tax. What was the total cost of the plant?

More Multiplication with Decimals

> ### Steps for Multiplying Decimals
>
> 1. Multiply in the same way whole numbers are multiplied.
> 2. Place the decimal point.

$$2.5 \times 3.1 =$$

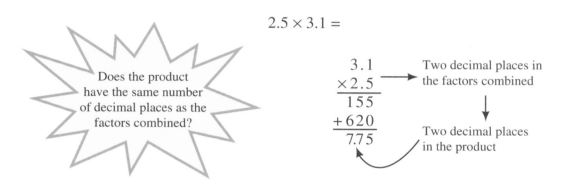

Does the product have the same number of decimal places as the factors combined?

$$
\begin{array}{r}
3.1 \\
\times 2.5 \\
\hline
155 \\
+620 \\
\hline
7.75
\end{array}
$$

Two decimal places in the factors combined

Two decimal places in the product

The Davis family drives to Grandma's house once a month. Each trip takes 4.5 gallons of gas. How much gas would be used after 2.5 of these trips?

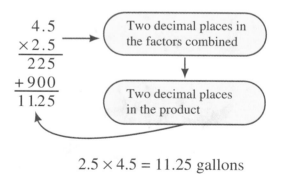

$$
\begin{array}{r}
4.5 \\
\times 2.5 \\
\hline
225 \\
+900 \\
\hline
11.25
\end{array}
$$

Two decimal places in the factors combined

Two decimal places in the product

$$2.5 \times 4.5 = 11.25 \text{ gallons}$$

He causeth the vapours to ascend from the ends of the earth; he maketh lightnings for the rain; he bringeth the wind out of his treasuries.

Psalm 135:7

Practice

Estimate the products. Solve.

1. $\begin{array}{r} 3.7 \\ \times\,1.8 \\ \hline \end{array}$

2. $\begin{array}{r} 4.2 \\ \times\,6.8 \\ \hline \end{array}$

3. $\begin{array}{r} 7.18 \\ \times\,2.9 \\ \hline \end{array}$

4. $\begin{array}{r} 1.65 \\ \times\,3.2 \\ \hline \end{array}$

5. $\begin{array}{r} 3.2 \\ \times\,5.8 \\ \hline \end{array}$

6. $\begin{array}{r} 4.4 \\ \times\,5.8 \\ \hline \end{array}$

7. $\begin{array}{r} 6.25 \\ \times\,4.9 \\ \hline \end{array}$

8. $\begin{array}{r} 21.2 \\ \times\,2.6 \\ \hline \end{array}$

Application

Write an equation for each word problem. Solve and label.

9. Each plastic cup holds 6.4 ounces. How many ounces will there be in 4 plastic cups?

10. Molly purchased a craft kit for $3.45. How much would 2 of these kits cost?

11. Ice cream is on sale at Foodville Grocery for $1.89 a half gallon. What is the price for 6 half gallons?

12. Each box contains 3.2 ounces of raisins. Joanne ate 4.5 boxes of raisins. How many ounces of raisins were eaten?

Write a word problem for the equation. Solve and label.

13. $1.5 \times 3.7 =$

 Ideas: boxes of cereal, bags of chips, relay race

Division: Decimal by a One-Digit Divisor

Decimals can be divided the same way as whole numbers.

Modified Traditional Form (with zeros)

$$2\overline{)4.6}$$

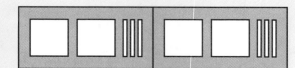

Divide the ones.
Multiply and subtract.

$$
\begin{array}{r}
2 \\
2\overline{)4.6} \\
-4.0 \\
\hline
6
\end{array}
$$

Write the decimal point in the quotient.

$$
\begin{array}{r}
2. \\
2\overline{)4.6} \\
-4.0 \\
\hline
6
\end{array}
$$

Divide the tenths.
Multiply and subtract.

$$
\begin{array}{r}
2.3 \\
2\overline{)4.6} \\
-4.0 \\
\hline
6 \\
-6 \\
\hline
0
\end{array}
$$

Traditional Form (without zeros)
Write the decimal point only in the quotient.

$$8\overline{)17.28}$$

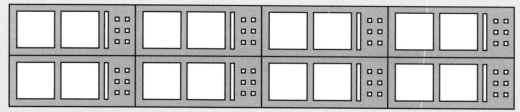

Divide the ones.
Multiply and subtract.
Write the decimal point.
Combine the tenths.

$$
\begin{array}{r}
2. \\
8\overline{)17.28} \\
-16 \\
\hline
12
\end{array}
$$

Divide the tenths.
Multiply and subtract.
Combine the hundredths.

$$
\begin{array}{r}
2.1 \\
8\overline{)17.28} \\
-16 \\
\hline
12 \\
-8 \\
\hline
48
\end{array}
$$

Divide the hundredths.
Multiply and subtract.

$$
\begin{array}{r}
2.16 \\
8\overline{)17.28} \\
-16 \\
\hline
12 \\
-8 \\
\hline
48 \\
-48 \\
\hline
0
\end{array}
$$

Practice

Solve.

1. $4\overline{)21.6}$

2. $8\overline{)74.4}$

3. $2\overline{)4.24}$

4. $4\overline{)37.2}$

5. $7\overline{)16.31}$

6. $4\overline{)19.2}$

7. $6\overline{)47.22}$

8. $8\overline{)9.76}$

Application

Write an equation for each word problem. Solve and label.

9. Mr. Henry had 60.88 meters of copper wire. He wanted to make 8 equal pieces from it. How long will each piece be?

10. Mrs. Hiebert spent $6.72 to make 6 identical Christmas tree ornaments. How much did it cost to make each ornament?

11. Mrs. Hiebert decided she wants 10 identical Christmas tree ornaments. How much would it cost her to make 4 more ornaments?

12. Mrs. Jones made 4 hamburgers from 1.28 pounds of meat. How much did each hamburger weigh?

13. The 3 turkeys that Mrs. Jones bought weighed 14.53 lb., 21.08 lb., and 19.37 lb. What is the total weight of the 3 turkeys combined?

14. How much more did the largest turkey weigh than the smallest?

Division: Zero in the Quotient

> When there are not enough tenths or hundredths to divide,
> write a 0 in that place in the quotient.

Sam and his two brothers saved $9.18 to buy an anniversary gift for their parents. If each boy earned an equal amount of money, how much did each earn?

> There are enough ones to divide. The quotient will not be less than 1.

$$
\begin{array}{r}
\$3.06 \\
3\overline{)\$9.18} \\
-900 \\
\hline
18 \\
-18 \\
\hline
0
\end{array}
$$

$9.18 \div 3 = \$3.06$

> When there are not enough ones to divide, the quotient will be less than 1,
> and a 0 will be written in the Ones place.

$$
\begin{array}{r}
0.91 \\
7\overline{)6.37} \\
-630 \\
\hline
7 \\
-7 \\
\hline
0
\end{array}
$$

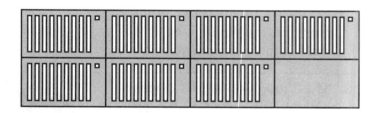

A 0 will not be written in the first place in the quotient if it is not the Ones place.

$$
\begin{array}{r}
\$\ 4.20 \\
4\overline{)\$16.80} \\
-16\downarrow \\
\hline
8 \\
-8\downarrow \\
\hline
0
\end{array}
$$

> Not enough tens to divide.

Sometimes a 0 must be annexed to help divide.

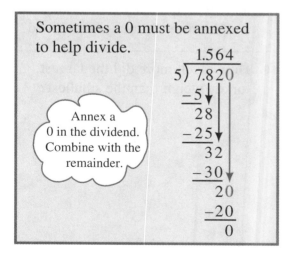

> Annex a 0 in the dividend. Combine with the remainder.

$$
\begin{array}{r}
1.564 \\
5\overline{)7.820} \\
-5\downarrow \\
\hline
28 \\
-25\downarrow \\
\hline
32 \\
-30\downarrow \\
\hline
20 \\
-20 \\
\hline
0
\end{array}
$$

Practice

Determine whether the quotient will be less than 1. Write *yes* or *no*.

1. $3\overline{)4.76}$ 2. $8\overline{)5.03}$ 3. $3\overline{)1.024}$ 4. $5\overline{)4.641}$

Solve.

5. $8\overline{)0.64}$ 6. $5\overline{)13.6}$ 7. $2\overline{)40.8}$

8. $3\overline{)\$18.60}$ 9. $9\overline{)\$18.81}$ 10. $6\overline{)0.42}$

11. $5\overline{)2.7}$ 12. $6\overline{)56.1}$ 13. $7\overline{)49.7}$

Write a word problem for the equation. Solve and label.

14. $\$2.16 \div 8 =$

   Ideas: gifts, snacks, buttons

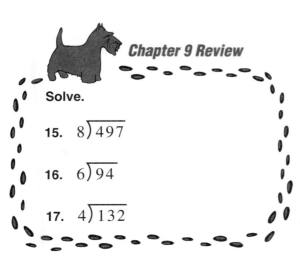

Chapter 9 Review

Solve.

15. $8\overline{)497}$

16. $6\overline{)94}$

17. $4\overline{)132}$

Division: Decimal Fraction in the Quotient

$2 \div 8 =$

$$\begin{array}{r} 0.25 \\ 8\overline{)\,2.00} \\ -16\!\downarrow \\ \hline 40 \\ -40 \\ \hline 0 \end{array}$$

1. When there are not enough ones to divide, write a 0 in the quotient in the Ones place.
2. Place a decimal point and annex a 0 to the dividend. Divide, multiply, and subtract.
3. Annex another 0 to the dividend if necessary. Divide, multiply, and subtract.

Repeating Decimal

A **repeating decimal** is not exact. It is a quotient in which one or more of the numbers in the decimal places keep repeating. A bar above the thousandths digit indicates that the decimal repeats.

$$\begin{array}{r} 0.44\overline{4} \\ 9\overline{)\,4.0000} \\ -36\!\downarrow \\ \hline 40 \\ -36\!\downarrow \\ \hline 40 \\ -36\!\downarrow \\ \hline 40 \end{array}$$

Rounding Decimal Fractions

Round a decimal fraction in the same way you round whole numbers.
1. Find the rounding place.
2. Look at the digit to the right of the rounding place. If the digit to the right of the rounding place is 5 or greater, increase the rounding place by 1. If the digit to the right of the rounding place is less than 5, the rounding place stays the same.

The symbol $\approx$ is read "is approximately equal to."

Decimal fractions are often rounded to the nearest thousandth.

$$\begin{array}{r} 0.666\overline{6} \\ 3\overline{)\,2.0000} \end{array} \approx 0.667 \qquad \begin{array}{r} 0.5714 \\ 7\overline{)\,4.0000} \end{array} \approx 0.571$$

Practice

Determine whether the quotient will be less than 1. Write *yes* or *no*.

1. $5\overline{)3.5}$ **2.** $4\overline{)2.03}$ **3.** $6\overline{)9.1}$ **4.** $3\overline{)5}$

Solve. Place a bar over the thousandths digit if the quotient repeats. If the quotient does not repeat, round to the Thousandths place when necessary.

5. $9\overline{)3}$ **6.** $6\overline{)4}$ **7.** $9\overline{)2}$ **8.** $8\overline{)15}$

9. $9\overline{)50}$ **10.** $3\overline{)30}$ **11.** $9\overline{)8}$ **12.** $7\overline{)33}$

13. $4\overline{)17}$ **14.** $6\overline{)5}$ **15.** $7\overline{)13}$ **16.** $3\overline{)1}$

Application

Write an equation for each word problem. Solve and label.

17. Susan had 1.25 meters of blue ribbon, 2.89 meters of pink ribbon, and 3.20 meters of white ribbon. How much ribbon did she have altogether?

18. If Susan cut the blue ribbon into 5 equal sections, how long would each blue ribbon be?

19. If Susan cut the white ribbon into 4 equal sections, how long would each white ribbon be?

20. How much more white ribbon does Susan have than pink ribbon?

21. Susan bought 3 pieces of ribbon that are each 2.56 meters long. What is the total length of the ribbons?

More Division with Decimals

Divide the same way whole numbers are divided. Place a decimal point in the quotient.

$$\begin{array}{r} 2.9 \\ 9\overline{)26.1} \\ -18 \\ \hline 81 \\ -81 \\ \hline 0 \end{array}$$

If there are not enough ones to divide, write a 0 in the quotient in the Ones place.

$3 \div 8 =$

$$\begin{array}{r} 0.375 \\ 8\overline{)3.000} \\ -24 \\ \hline 60 \\ -56 \\ \hline 40 \\ -40 \\ \hline 0 \end{array}$$

Annex zeros as needed.

If there are not enough tenths to divide, write a 0 in the quotient in the Tenths place.

$$\begin{array}{r} 3.04 \\ 5\overline{)15.20} \\ -15 \\ \hline 20 \\ -20 \\ \hline 0 \end{array}$$

Put a bar over the digit in the One Thousandths place if it is a repeating decimal.

$4 \div 6 =$

$$\begin{array}{r} 0.66\overline{6} \\ 6\overline{)4.0000} \\ -36 \\ \hline 40 \\ -36 \\ \hline 40 \\ -36 \\ \hline 40 \end{array}$$

Annex zeros as needed.

Practice

Solve. Place a bar over the thousandths digit if the quotient repeats. If the quotient does not repeat, round to the Thousandths place when necessary.

1. $5\overline{)4.75}$ 2. $4\overline{)12.48}$ 3. $3\overline{)\$8.46}$ 4. $4\overline{)1.28}$

5. $5\overline{)\$5.30}$ 6. $9\overline{)8.01}$ 7. $2\overline{)12.69}$ 8. $8\overline{)9}$

9. $7\overline{)1}$ 10. $8\overline{)15.36}$ 11. $4\overline{)2}$ 12. $8\overline{)16.3}$

Application

Write an equation for each word problem. Solve and label.

13. The Martinez's car averages 24.7 miles per gallon of gas. How far can they drive on 4 gallons of gas?

14. The gas tank holds 14.5 gallons. Mr. Martinez filled it with 7.9 gallons. How much gas was already in the tank?

15. Sharla bought a package of 5 pens that cost $1.35. What was the price per pen?

16. Mary Ann checked prices of doughnuts. They were 6 for $1.59 at Barry's Bakery and $0.25 each at Doris's Donuts. Which shop had the lower price per doughnut?

Meet the Challenge!

Doughnuts are 6 for $1.59 at Barry's Bakery and $0.25 each at Doris's Donuts. What is the price of 2 dozen doughnuts at Barry's if there is a discount of $0.50 on the second dozen? What is the price at Doris's for 2 dozen doughnuts, if every doughnut in the second dozen costs $0.20?

$16.92 \div 12 =$

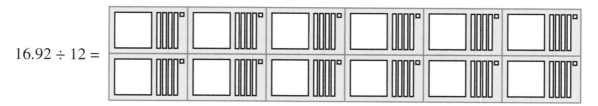

Divide the ones.
Multiply and subtract.

$$\begin{array}{r} 1. \\ 12\overline{)16.92} \\ -12.00 \\ \hline 4.92 \end{array}$$

Divide the tenths.
Multiply and subtract.

$$\begin{array}{r} 1.4 \\ 12\overline{)16.92} \\ -12.00 \\ \hline 4.92 \\ -4.80 \\ \hline 0.12 \end{array}$$

Divide the hundredths.
Multiply and subtract.

$$\begin{array}{r} 1.41 \\ 12\overline{)16.92} \\ -12.00 \\ \hline 4.92 \\ -4.80 \\ \hline 0.12 \\ -0.12 \\ \hline 0 \end{array}$$

Remember to annex a 0 in the dividend and in the remainder if necessary. Round the quotient to the nearest thousandth.

$$\begin{array}{r} 0.7307 \approx 0.731 \\ 26\overline{)19.0000} \\ -182 \\ \hline 80 \\ -78 \\ \hline 200 \\ -182 \\ \hline 18 \end{array}$$

$$\begin{array}{r} 0.53\overline{3} \\ 30\overline{)16.0000} \\ -150 \\ \hline 100 \\ -90 \\ \hline 100 \\ -90 \\ \hline 100 \end{array}$$

If the quotient is a repeating decimal, place a bar over the digit in the Thousandths place.

Practice

Solve. Place a bar over the thousandths digit if the quotient repeats. If the quotient does not repeat, round to the Thousandths place when necessary.

1. $8\overline{)57.6}$ 2. $15\overline{)8}$ 3. $3\overline{)47.22}$ 4. $15\overline{)95.4}$

5. $75\overline{)89.25}$ 6. $16\overline{)\$21.12}$ 7. $23\overline{)\$47.38}$ 8. $6\overline{)2.22}$

9. $8\overline{)12}$ 10. $7\overline{)6}$ 11. $8\overline{)9.43}$ 12. $5\overline{)1.462}$

Application

Write an equation for each word problem. Solve and label.

13. Mrs. Smith made 1.7 liters of lemonade. If the lemonade is shared equally among her 5 children, how much lemonade will each child receive?

14. Phoebe used 105 grams of sugar to make a lemonade recipe. How much sugar would be in 5 of these recipes?

15. If 8 children equally shared 2.32 liters of lemonade, how much lemonade did each child receive?

16. After dinner, 0.4 liters of lemonade was left. Mr. Burke drank 0.6 of it. How much did he drink?

Multiply or Divide a Decimal by a Multiple of 10

> Multiplying a decimal by 10 or a multiple of 10 can be done mentally when you remember that moving the decimal point one place to the right is the same as multiplying by 10.

 To multiply, move the decimal point one place to the right for each 0 in the factor. (Sometimes you may need to annex a 0.)

10 as a factor	100 as a factor	1,000 as a factor
$10 \times 8.75 = 87.5$	$100 \times 8.75 = 875$	$1,000 \times 8.75 = 8,750$
Think: 8.75	Think: 8.75	Think: 8.750

> Dividing a decimal by 10 or a multiple of 10 can be done mentally when you remember that moving the decimal point one place to the left is the same as dividing by 10.

 To divide, move the decimal point one place to the left for each 0 in the divisor. (Sometimes you may need to annex a 0.)

10 as the divisor	100 as the divisor	1,000 as the divisor
$89.4 \div 10 = 8.94$	$89.4 \div 100 = 0.894$	$89.4 \div 1,000 = 0.0894$
Think: 89.4	Think: 89.4	Think: 089.4

Practice

Mental Math: Write only the answer for each multiplication equation.

1. $10 \times 6.4 =$
2. $100 \times 6.4 =$
3. $1{,}000 \times 6.4 =$

4. $100 \times 0.77 =$
5. $10 \times 87.45 =$
6. $1{,}000 \times 3.87 =$

7. $100 \times 0.451 =$
8. $10 \times 1.01 =$
9. $100 \times 0.498 =$

10. $1{,}000 \times 1.479 =$
11. $10 \times 2.43 =$
12. $1{,}000 \times 3.78 =$

Write only the answer for each division equation.

13. $95.71 \div 10 =$
14. $95.71 \div 100 =$

15. $95.71 \div 1{,}000 =$
16. $8.55 \div 10 =$

17. $345.99 \div 100 =$
18. $0.88 \div 10 =$

19. $14.15 \div 1{,}000 =$
20. $388.05 \div 100 =$

21. $116.33 \div 10 =$
22. $8{,}008.7 \div 100 =$

23. $3{,}915 \div 1{,}000 =$
24. $6.75 \div 10 =$

Language Link

25. This problem can be solved by moving the decimal point. Explain where to move the decimal point and why this works.

    $62.5 \div 10 =$

Chapter 9 Review

Solve. (Write the answer with a remainder.)

26. $6\overline{)476}$
27. $14\overline{)971}$
28. $7\overline{)86}$
29. $22\overline{)306}$

Batting Champions

The batting average of a baseball player is a decimal fraction that indicates the percentage of at-bats in which the batter got a hit. A player with a batting average of .286 got a hit 286 times out of every 1,000 at-bats. You can calculate a player's batting average by dividing the number of hits by the number of at-bats.

| G = Games | AB = At-bats | H = Hits | HR = Home Runs | BA = Batting Average |

$$BA = H \div AB$$

Use a calculator to find the career batting average of each player.

Career Information

Player	G	AB	H	HR	BA
1. Ty Cobb	3,033	11,429	4,191	118	
2. Rogers Hornsby	2,259	8,173	2,930	301	
3. Babe Ruth	2,503	8,399	2,873	714	
4. Lou Gehrig	2,164	8,001	2,721	493	
5. Ted Williams	2,292	7,706	2,654	521	
6. Hank Aaron	3,298	12,364	3,771	755	

Use the table to find the answers.

7. Who had the highest career batting average?

8. Who played in the most games?

9. Who played in the least games?

10. Who had the highest number of career at-bats?

11. Who had the most hits during his career?

12. Who had more home runs than Babe Ruth?

Did you know . . .

The highest batting average for one year was .424, hit by Rogers Hornsby in 1924.

Hours, Minutes, Seconds

A stopwatch is used for accurate timing.

John ran a marathon in 2 hours 58 minutes 10 seconds. When John crossed the finish line, the stopwatch looked like this:

2:58:10

Practice

Write the following as time indicated on a stopwatch.

1. 1 hr. 45 min. 20 sec.

2. 3 hr. 35 min. 6 sec.

3. 4 hr. 3 min. 44 sec.

4. 2 hr. 11 min. 4 sec.

For further precision, time can be measured in hundredths of a second.

HR.	MIN.	SEC.	$\frac{1}{100}$
2:	36:	14	.75

Application

Write equations for the word problems. Solve and label.

5. Cinda and Anna ran a relay race against Nichole and Christie. Their times were 13.01 seconds, 12.90 seconds, 13.50 seconds, and 12.89 seconds respectively. Which team won the race? How much faster was the winning team?

6. The world's record for the men's 100-meter dash is 9.86 seconds. Stephen ran the 100-meter dash in 11.59 seconds. How much faster is the runner with the world's record?

7. The winning time of the men's 400-meter race in the 1908 Olympics was 50 seconds. In 1972, the winning time was 44.66 seconds. How much faster was the runner in 1972?

8. Jake competed in a local triathlon. He completed the swimming event in 1:14:58, the bicycling event in 2:29:36, and the running event in 3:49:15. What was his total time for the triathlon?

Meteorologist

Dear Fifth Grade:

If you watch the weather forecast on television, you often hear a meteorologist comparing the amount of rainfall this month with the amount last year during this month. Or he might say that the temperature on this day is a record high or the highest we have had for 50 years. Part of the work of a meterologist is keeping records. We keep records of things like temperatures, humidity, wind speeds, and rainfall for our area. Since weather often follows patterns, these records can help us make predictions about the upcoming weather. We can spot variations from normal patterns that could mean dramatic changes in the weather.

As for your question about how we meteorologists use math in our jobs, I can think of one pretty good example. Our computer calculates average rainfall. If we want to know the average rainfall for the month of April over the past 30 years, the computer adds the total amounts of rainfall over the last 30 years and divides by 30. If the average for April over the past 30 years has been 1 inch, we can expect about an inch of rain this April. If midway through April we have more than 1 inch already, we need to be concerned about flooding in low regions and take some precautions. Although we as humans have no control over the weather, we can at least give you an idea of what you can expect—and hopefully we're right more often than not!

Respectfully,

Patricia Booth
Patricia Booth

CHANNEL 19
Complete Weather Service

Moore Christian School
334 Tara Lane
Mariposa, CA 95338

Solve the multiplication problems.

1. 7.8
    × 4

2. 2.47
    × 3

3. 0.89
    × 5.2

4. $3.79
    × 8

5. 0.7
    ×0.4

6. 1.34
    ×0.23

7. 32.5
    ×4.02

8. 4.509
    × 0.7

Solve the division problems. Round to the nearest one thousandth if necessary. Place a bar over the digit in the One Thousandths place if the quotient is a repeating decimal.

9. 5)$20.25

10. 4)49.07

11. 8)50

12. 2)8

13. 12)6.39

14. 7)13

15. 9)1

16. 5)4.32

Mental Math: Write only the answers.

17. $62 \div 10 =$

18. $100 \times 49.07 =$

19. $1,000 \times 0.959 =$

20. $68.1 \div 10 =$

21. $897.65 \div 100 =$

22. $7,369.1 \div 1,000 =$

23. $10 \times 4.67 =$

24. $7.384 \times 100 =$

25. $0.3291 \times 100 =$

26. $1,000 \times 5.1 =$

27. $2.84 \div 10 =$

28. $25.46 \times 100 =$

Write an equation for each word problem. Solve and label.

29. On Friday 0.5 of a pizza was left. Jeffrey ate 0.5 of the remaining pizza. What part of the whole pizza did Jeffrey eat?

30. Mother made 3.5 liters of punch for the class party. There are 18 students in the class. If the punch is divided equally, how much punch will each student receive?

31. Mr. Hawkins pumped a total of 87.356 gallons of gas for 9 customers at the service station. What was the average amount of gas each customer bought?

32. The Torres family traveled 92.75 miles to Grandma's house in 2 hours. If they traveled at a constant speed, how many miles did they travel in each hour?

Use the chart to answer the questions. Write the equations you use.

Vehicle	Miles driven	Gallons of gas used
economy car	79.31	3
minivan	92.75	8
motor home	87.24	12

33. How many miles can the motor home drive for each gallon of gas?

34. How many miles can the minivan drive for each gallon of gas?

35. How many miles can the economy car drive for each gallon of gas?

Cumulative Review

Write the letter of the correct answer.

1. Use rounding to estimate the difference.

$$\begin{array}{r} 373 \\ -235 \\ \hline \end{array}$$

- a. 100
- b. 200
- c. 300
- d. 400

2. Solve.

$$\begin{array}{r} 4,607 \\ \times \quad 53 \\ \hline \end{array}$$

- a. 204,117
- b. 228,141
- c. 244,171
- d. not given

3. Which sentence is true for circle S?

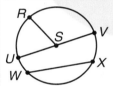

- a. $\overline{RS}$ is a radius.
- b. $\overline{UV}$ is a diameter.
- c. $\overline{WX}$ is a chord.
- d. all of the above

4. Round 6.478 to the nearest tenth.

- a. 6.4
- b. 6.5
- c. 6.48
- d. not given

5. Solve.

$$3\overline{)8,906}$$

- a. 2,968 r2
- b. 2,322 r3
- c. 3,698
- d. not given

6. Which sign will make the sentence true?

$$\frac{3}{9} \bigcirc \frac{18}{36}$$

- a. >
- b. <
- c. =
- d. not given

7. What is the mass of a 500 g soccer ball in kilograms?

- a. 0.5 kg
- b. 5 kg
- c. 50 kg
- d. 5000 kg

8. Solve.

$$23\overline{)482}$$

- a. 13 r32
- b. 20 r22
- c. 21 r2
- d. not given

9. What is the least common denominator for $\frac{5}{3}$, $\frac{5}{8}$, and $\frac{5}{6}$?

- a. 8
- b. 12
- c. 16
- d. 24

10. What is the name of the type of triangle with three congruent sides?

- a. isosceles
- b. equilateral
- c. scalene
- d. all of the above

11. Solve.

$$\begin{array}{r} 4 \text{ m } 14 \text{ cm} \\ +10 \text{ m } 87 \text{ cm} \\ \hline \end{array}$$

- a. 15 m 1 cm
- b. 15 m 100 cm
- c. 14 m 1 cm
- d. not given

12. Solve.

$$\begin{array}{r} 678,000 \\ -494,326 \\ \hline \end{array}$$

- a. 183,674
- b. 5,861,674
- c. 3,583,674
- d. not given

Helicopters

Maybe you've seen a helicopter circling overhead and heard the choppy sound it makes. Have you ever wondered what makes a helicopter different from an airplane?

A helicopter has vertical lift. It is designed in a special way that allows it to lift straight up off the ground, while an airplane must use a runway to pick up speed and take off at an angle.

The helicopter is also unique in its ability to hover. Hovering simply means being able to stop and hang in midair while in flight.

The helicopter flies by means of rotors, sets of rotating blades similar to propellers on airplanes. The large rotor on top of the helicopter serves as its wing, while the smaller rotor on the tail opposes the twisting force (torque) created by the main rotor.

If a helicopter loses its tail rotor (in battle, for example), the helicopter will start spinning around violently. But if the pilot disengages power to the main rotor, allowing it to spin freely, the helicopter will fall slowly. This is called autorotation.

Helicopters are used in searches for fugitives, crop spraying, fire fighting, aerial photography, and traffic direction and control. The military often uses helicopters for finding and destroying enemy submarines, carrying supplies to ships at sea, taking troops from sea to land, and lifting nuclear weapons. Since helicopters can hover and land in small spaces, they are ideal for rescue work. The Coast Guard has used helicopters to save thousands of lives in danger at sea or in flood conditions.

CHAPTER 13

Measurement: Customary

▲ This twin-rotor transport helicopter, now obsolete, was affectionately known as the "Flying Banana."

▲ A U.S. Air Force HH-53 "Super Jolly Green Giant."

The inch is the smallest unit of length in the customary measurement system. Rulers are often marked with half-inch, fourth-inch, eighth-inch, and sixteenth-inch markings.

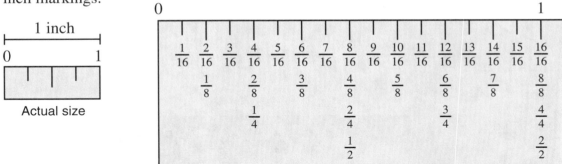

Enlarged to show detail

When measuring, remember to line up one end of the object with the ruler. Read the number of inches at the other end of the object.

To the nearest sixteenth of an inch, the turtle is $3\frac{9}{16}$ inches.

To the nearest fourth of an inch, the turtle is $3\frac{2}{4}$ inches.

To the nearest half of an inch, the turtle is $3\frac{1}{2}$ inches.

To the nearest inch, the turtle is 4 inches.

Practice

Estimate each object to the nearest inch. Measure to the nearest inch.

1.

2.

Measure each object to the nearest half inch.

3.

4.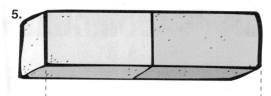

Measure each object to the nearest fourth inch.

5.

6.

Measure each line segment to the nearest sixteenth inch.

7. |————| **8.** |—————————| **9.** |————————————————|

Measure the inchworm to the nearest—

10. sixteenth inch.

11. fourth inch.

12. inch.

Customary linear measurement units are the inch (in.), foot (ft.), yard (yd.), and mile (mi.).

> The symbols for inch and foot are " (inch) and ' (foot).
> The other units do not have symbols.

A two-liter soft drink bottle is 1 foot tall.

$12'' = 1'$

The distance from your mother's nose to the end of her finger is about 1 yard.

$36'' = 1$ yd.
$3' = 1$ yd.

The length of 15 football fields, including the end zones, laid end to end, would be about 1 mile.

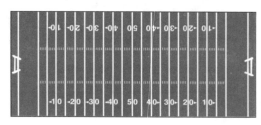

5,280 ft. = 1 mi.
1,760 yd. = 1 mi.

To rename larger units as smaller units, multiply.	To rename smaller units as larger units, divide.	Sometimes two units of measure are used.
Sarah made a comforter that was 3 yards long. How many inches long was the comforter?	Helen weeded a plot 48 inches long. How many feet long is the plot?	16 ft. = ___ yd. ___ ft.
3 yd. = ___ in.	48 in. = ___ ft.	$16 \div 3 = 5$ r1
Think 1 yd. = 36 in.	Think 12 in. = 1 ft.	16 ft. = 5 yd. 1 ft.
$3 \times 36 = 108$	$48 \div 12 = 4$	4 ft. 6 in. = ___ in.
3 yd. = 108 in.	48 in. = 4 ft.	$(4 \times 12) + 6$
		4 ft. 6 in. = 54 in.

Practice

Write the unit that would be used to measure each distance (*inch, foot, yard, mile*).

1. the distance a train travels in an hour

2. the length of a spoon

3. the width of a dollar bill

4. the material to make a dress

5. the length of a motorcycle

6. the distance from New York City to Los Angeles

Rename the units of length.

7. 12 in. = _____ ft.

8. 1 yd. = _____ ft.

9. 1 mi. = _____ ft.

10. 4 yd. = _____ in.

11. 3 mi. = _____ ft.

12. 72 in. = _____ yd.

13. 48 in. = _____ ft.

14. 5 yd. = _____ ft.

15. 180 ft. = _____ yd.

Rename the units of measure to complete each number sentence.

16. 21 in. = _____ ft. _____ in.

17. 6 ft. 4 in. = _____ in.

18. 60 in. = _____ yd. _____ in.

19. 7 yd. 9 in. = _____ in.

20. 6,000 ft. = _____ mi. _____ ft.

21. 1 mi. 300 ft. = _____ ft.

Complete each sentence, using *inches, feet, yards,* or *miles.*

22. A tall basketball player stands 7 _____ tall.

23. A shoestring measures 30 _____ long.

24. A football field with end zones is 120 _____ long.

25. A Navy helicopter may fly 400 _____ in a day.

Capacity and Temperature Measures

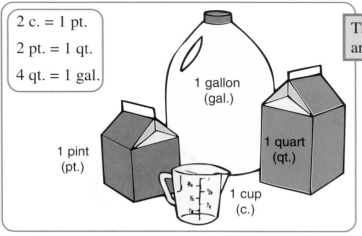

2 c. = 1 pt.

2 pt. = 1 qt.

4 qt. = 1 gal.

1 gallon (gal.)

1 pint (pt.)

1 quart (qt.)

1 cup (c.)

The cup, pint, quart, and gallon are customary units of capacity.

To rename larger units as smaller units, multiply.	To rename smaller units as larger units, divide.	Sometimes two units of measure are used.

70 gal. = _____ qt.

Think: 1 gal. = 4 qt.

70 × 4 = 280
70 gal. = 280 qt.

24 c. = _____ pt.

Think: 2 c. = 1 pt.

24 ÷ 2 = 12
24 c. = 12 pt.

19 qt. = _____ gal. _____ qt.

Think: 19 ÷ 4 = 4 r3

19 qt. = 4 gal. 3 qt.

Degrees Fahrenheit (°F) are used to measure temperature in the customary system.

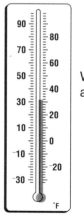

Water freezes at 32° F.

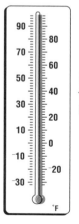

Normal body temperature is 98.6° F.

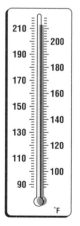

Water boils at 212° F.

Practice

Write the unit that would be used to measure each capacity (*cup, pint, quart, gallon*).

1. the water in a bathtub

2. the milk in a child's glass

3. a container of cream

4. a container of orange juice

Rename the units.

5. 1 gal. = ____ qt.

6. 1 qt. = ____ pt.

7. 2 c. = ____ pt.

8. 16 pt. = ____ c.

9. 10 pt. = ____ qt.

10. 20 qt. = ____ gal.

11. 12 qt. = ____ pt.

12. 16 gal. = ____ qt.

Rename the units of measure to complete each number sentence.

13. 3 gal. 2 qt. = ____ qt.

14. 9 qt. = ____ gal. ____ qt.

15. 3 pt. 1 c. = ____ c.

16. 35 c. = ____ pt. ____ c.

17. 10 gal. 3 qt. = ____ qt.

18. 25 pt. = ____ qt. ____ pt.

Choose the more sensible temperature.

19. hot chocolate

    20° F   110° F

20. boiling water

    100° F 212° F

21. inside a refrigerator

    65° F 40° F

Write the temperature.

22.
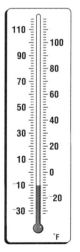

23.
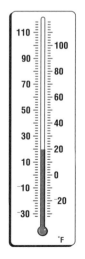

24.
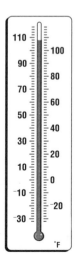

25.
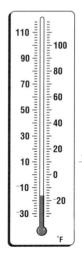

Weight Measurement

The units of customary measurement for weight are ounce, pound, and ton.

1 ounce (oz.)

1 pound (lb.)

1 ton (tn.)

$$1 \text{ lb.} = 16 \text{ oz.}$$

$$1 \text{ tn.} = 2{,}000 \text{ lb.}$$

To rename larger units as smaller units, multiply.

3 tn. = _____ lb.   (Think 1 tn. = 2,000 lb.) $3 \times 2{,}000 = 6{,}000$ 3 tn. = 6,000 lb.

To rename smaller units as larger units, divide.

128 oz. = _____ lb.   (Think 1 lb. = 16 oz.) $128 \div 16 = 8$ 128 oz. = 8 lb.

Sometimes two units of measure are used.

97 oz. = _____ lb. _____ oz.
97 ÷ 16 = 6 r1
    97 oz. = 6 lb. 1 oz.

2 lb. 6 oz. = _____ oz.
$(2 \times 16) + 6 =$
    $32 + 6 = 38$
2 lb. 6 oz. = 38 oz.

Did you know . . .

Our abbreviation for pound (lb.) comes from the word *libra*. The libra was a standard unit of weight in ancient Rome and was equivalent to approximately 12 ounces.

Practice

Write the abbreviation of the unit that would be used to measure each item: *oz.* (ounce), *lb.* (pound), *tn.* (ton).

1. bag of carrots
2. elephant
3. duck
4. jeep
5. seal
6. cotton balls
7. ship
8. oyster
9. handful of blueberries

Rename the units of weight.

10. 2 lb. = _____ oz.
11. 10 tn. = _____ lb.
12. 5 lb. = _____ oz.
13. 32 oz. = _____ lb.
14. 3 tn. = _____ lb.
15. 6 lb. = _____ oz.
16. 5 lb. 4 oz. = _____ oz.
17. 90 oz. = _____ lb. _____ oz.
18. 6 lb. 7 oz. = _____ oz.
19. 19 oz. = _____ lb. _____ oz.

Write the customary unit (from the box) that would be used to measure—

20. the amount of milk in a cake.
21. the length of the coast of California.
22. the height of the Statue of Liberty.
23. the width of a newspaper.
24. the weight of a fifth grade student.
25. the weight of a blue whale.
26. the weight of a tomato.
27. the amount of water in an aquarium.

gal.	ft.	mi.
c.	lb.	tn.
oz.	in.	yd.

Computing with Customary Measurements

Addition

Lelani bought 3 yd. 24 in. of lace and 2 yd. 12 in. of ribbon. How much trim did she buy in all?

Add the inches.
Add the yards.

$$\begin{array}{r} 3 \text{ yd. } 24 \text{ in.} \\ + 2 \text{ yd. } 12 \text{ in.} \\ \hline 5 \text{ yd. } 36 \text{ in.} \end{array}$$

Rename if necessary.

36 in. = 1 yd.

=   6 yd.

Subtraction

Carmen visited the aquarium. She saw a seahorse that measured 5 in. and a trumpetfish that measured 2 ft. 2 in. How much longer was the trumpetfish?

Rename if necessary.

12 + 2

$$\begin{array}{r} \overset{1}{\cancel{2}} \text{ ft. } \quad \cancel{2} \text{ in.} \\ - \qquad 5 \text{ in.} \\ \hline \end{array}$$

=

Subtract the inches.
Subtract the feet.

$$\begin{array}{r} 1 \text{ ft. } 14 \text{ in.} \\ - \qquad 5 \text{ in.} \\ \hline 1 \text{ ft. } \quad 9 \text{ in.} \end{array}$$

Multiplication

Coach Robbins's water jug holds 2 gal. 3 qt. He fills it with cold water for the team before each game. If the team plays 7 games in a season, how much water will Coach Robbins bring in all?

Multiply the quarts.
Multiply the gallons.

$$\begin{array}{r} 2 \text{ gal. } 3 \text{ qt.} \\ \times \qquad 7 \\ \hline 14 \text{ gal. } 21 \text{ qt.} \end{array}$$

Rename if necessary.

21 qt. = 5 gal. 1 qt.

=   19 gal. 1 qt.

Practice

Solve. Rename if necessary.

1. 5 ft. 2 in.
  + 6 ft. 9 in.

2. 7 yd. 4 in.
  + 12 yd. 6 in.

3. 6 lb. 15 oz.
  + 7 lb. 8 oz.

4. 4 gal. 2 qt.
  + 3 gal. 2 qt.

5. 14 lb. 13 oz.
  − 8 lb. 12 oz.

6. 7 gal. 1 qt.
  − 2 gal. 3 qt.

7. 4 tn.   620 lb.
  + 1 tn. 1,560 lb.

8. 3 ft. 6 in.
  − 1 ft. 9 in.

9. 6 ft. 8 in.
  ×   3

10. 3 lb. 13 oz.
  ×   2

11. 4 pt. 3 c.
  ×   3

12. 3 tn. 162 lb.
  ×   4

Application

Write an equation for each word problem. Solve and label.

13. Mrs. Erie plans to make dresses for 3 missionary children. Each dress requires 3 yd. 2 ft. of material. How many yards of material should Mrs. Erie buy?

14. Pastor Erie's daughter mailed a package weighing 8 lb. 9 oz. to a missionary friend in Brazil. Her brother mailed a package that weighed 13 lb. 5 oz. to a friend in Germany. How much more did the package to Germany weigh than the package to Brazil?

15. Mrs. Erie bought 3 packages of ground beef. Each package weighed 4 lb. 9 oz. How much meat did she purchase in all?

Chapter 10 Review

Solve.

16. $\dfrac{4}{5}$
  $+ \dfrac{4}{15}$

17. $\dfrac{7}{12}$
  $+ \dfrac{3}{16}$

18. $\dfrac{5}{9}$
  $+ \dfrac{5}{12}$

19. $\dfrac{11}{15}$
  $+ \dfrac{8}{10}$

Area of a Rectangle

$$\boxed{\text{Area} = \text{Length} \times \text{Width}}$$

$$A = L * W$$
$$\textbf{LET } A = L * W$$

```
10 PRINT "AREA OF A RECTANGLE"
20 PRINT "ENTER LENGTH, WIDTH"
30 INPUT L, W
40 LET A=L*W
50 PRINT "THE AREA IS"; A
60 END
```

RUN the program to help solve the problems below.

1. Joshua is selling fresh fruit. Each open box displayed on the table requires 4 ft.^{2} of space. The table is 12 ft. long and 8 ft. wide. How many boxes will fit on the table?

2. Mr. Myers will put a new roof on Mr. Cole's house. The front and back roof sections each measure 55 ft. in length and 25 ft. in width. What is the area of the entire roof?

3. Each package of shingles covers 33.5 ft.^{2} How many packages of shingles are needed to cover Mr. Cole's roof?

4. The kitchen floor is 14 ft. long and 12 ft. wide. What is the area of the kitchen floor? If each tile is 1 ft.^{2}, how many tiles are needed?

Measurement Word Problems

Application

Use the diagram to solve the problems. Write the equations you used.

1. What is the area of the soccer field?

2. A bag of grass seed will seed 85 yd.² How many bags of grass seed will be needed to seed the entire field?

3. What is the perimeter of the field?

4. It takes Mr. Amery 1 minute to chalk 8 yd. If he chalks the perimeter of the field, how long will it take?

5. What is the area of 1 penalty area and 1 goal area combined?

6. The diameter of the center circle is 20 yd. What is the circumference of this circle?

7. Garrett's soccer ball had a circumference of 25 in. What is the diameter of Garrett's ball?

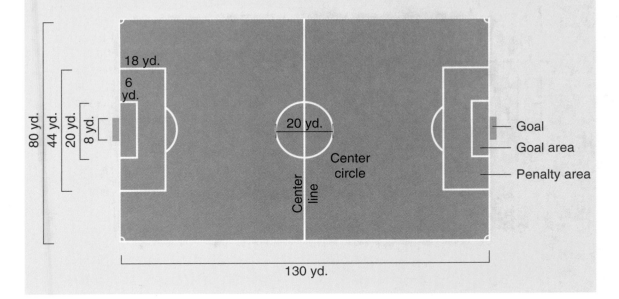

Landscape Planner

Dear Fifth Grade:

I was thrilled to learn of your interest in my career, and I think I can help you out with your project. A job like mine is both artistic and mathematical. When I design a landscape, I want the arrangement of trees, plants, shrubbery, and sidewalks to enhance a building and to please the eye. I like to group trees and flowers to create a look of naturalness but also an overall look of unity.

The first thing I need to know is how much room I have to work with; so the length of the building or the dimensions of the grounds I'm landscaping are important details. I begin at my drawing board with a scaled-down plan of the grounds. I go strictly by the scale to avoid design mistakes. I often use a scale of 1 inch = 10 feet. I then add my sketches of landscape details to the property.

One project I did recently was a front lawn and parking area for a church. I wanted a 100-foot-long tree-lined median in the center of the parking lot. First I measured the grounds in the plan to find the center point. Then I drew the median around that center point. I had to follow the scale to figure the length of the median on paper. Since an inch represented 10 feet, the 100-foot median was 10 inches long on paper. My greatest joy in my work is seeing a dream on paper become reality.

Cordially,

Luke Talbert

Luke Talbert

Talbert Landscaping
1253 McDoogan Lane
Steepleville, SC 29607

Moore Christian School
334 Tara Lane
Mariposa, CA 95338

USA 32

Measure the line segment to the nearest—

1. sixteenth inch. |————————|

2. eighth inch. |————————————————|

3. fourth inch. |——————|

4. half inch. |————————————|

5. inch. |——————————|

Solve. Rename if necessary.

6. 16 ft.   9 in.
    + 9 ft. 10 in.
    _____

7.   8 yd. 2 ft.
    + 3 yd. 1 ft.
    _____

8.   7 gal. 1 qt.
    + 5 gal. 3 qt.
    _____

9.   2 tn.
    − 1 tn. 600 lb.
    _____

10. 11 gal. 2 qt.
    − 6 gal. 3 qt.
    _____

11. 2 pt. 1 c.
    −   3 c.
    _____

12. 6 lb. 11 oz.
    ×   2
    _____

13. 3 ft. 5 in.
    ×   4
    _____

14. 5 gal. 2 qt.
    ×   5
    _____

Determine the appropriate customary unit to measure each amount.

15. height of a lighthouse	mi.	ft.	in.
16. width of a magazine	in.	yd.	ft.
17. height of Hoover Dam	mi.	in.	ft.
18. weight of a picnic basket	lb.	oz.	tn.
19. weight of a hippopotamus	oz.	tn.	lb.
20. cream in an carton	oz.	lb.	pt.
21. fuel in an airplane	c.	pt.	gal.
22. tea in a cup	pt.	oz.	lb.

Rename the units.

23. 2 yd. = _____ in.
24. 32 oz. = _____ lb.
25. 10 ft. = _____ in.

26. 4 lb. = _____ oz.
27. 4 c. = _____ pt.
28. 15 ft. = _____ yd.

29. 80 oz. = _____ lb.
30. 3 tn. = _____ lb.
31. 48 in. = _____ ft.

32. 4 lb. 4 oz. = _____ oz.
33. 83 oz. = _____ lb. _____ oz.

34. 5 yd. 1 ft. = _____ ft.
35. 22 ft. = _____ yd. _____ ft.

Write the temperature.

36.
37.
38.
39.

Write an equation for each word problem. Solve and label.

40. On Monday Margery painted 4 yd. 2 ft. of the fence. On Tuesday she painted 5 yd. of the fence. How much more fence did she paint on Tuesday than on Monday?

41. Kyle brought 3 gal. 3 qt. of punch to the school yard sale. Margo brought 4 gal. 1 qt. of punch. How much punch did they bring in all?

42. Mr. Richter bought 4 packages of chicken. Each package weighed 3 lb. 8 oz. What was the combined weight of the 4 packages?

Cumulative Review

Write the letter of the correct answer.

1. Which sentence is true?

   a. 13 is prime.
   b. 63 is composite.
   c. 43 is prime.
   d. all of the above

2. Which sentence is true?

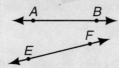

   a. $\overleftrightarrow{EF}$ and $\overleftrightarrow{AB}$ have endpoints.
   b. $\overleftrightarrow{EF}$ and $\overleftrightarrow{AB}$ are parallel lines.
   c. $\overleftrightarrow{EF}$ and $\overleftrightarrow{AB}$ are intersecting lines.
   d. all of the above

3. Dad drove 6.8 miles to church each Sunday. How many miles did Dad drive to church and back home again?

   a. 12.6 mi.   c. 14.6 mi.
   b. 13.6 mi.   d. not given

4. What is the average of 360, 888, and 240?

   a. 384   c. 495
   b. 486   d. not given

5. What is $\frac{36}{48}$ in lowest terms?

   a. $\frac{12}{24}$ c. $\frac{3}{4}$
   b. $\frac{9}{8}$ d. $\frac{4}{12}$

6. Which is sensible?

   a. Water freezes at $0°$ C.
   b. A cold day is $30°$ C.
   c. A very warm day is $^-30°$ C.
   d. all of the above

7. Which equation would you use to check $416 \div 13 = 38$ r2?

   a. $(3 \times 38) + 2$ c. $3 + (2 \times 126)$
   b. $2 + (3 \times 142)$ d. not given

8. $\frac{6}{15} + \frac{2}{5} =$

   a. $\frac{8}{15}$ c. $\frac{8}{5}$
   b. $\frac{4}{5}$ d. not given

9. Which three-dimensional figure does not have triangular faces that meet at a common vertex?

   a. rectangular pyramid
   b. square pyramid
   c. rectangular prism
   d. triangular pyramid

10. Solve.

$$\begin{array}{r} 9.3 \\ \times\ 6 \\ \hline \end{array}$$

   a. 53.8
   b. 54.9
   c. 55.8
   d. not given

Combat Aircraft

With the invention of airplanes, a whole new method of warfare came about. Airplanes began to play a significant part in combat in World War I. At the beginning, their main purpose was observation. Although very stable, these planes were slow and clumsy in the air. As the war went on, pilots realized they needed aircraft that were quick and easily maneuverable so that they could dodge enemy fire. Planes became weapons themselves. They could strike down enemy planes as well as make attacks on the ground from the air.

The world wars did much to speed up the development of the war airplane. Bombers started out as small planes that dropped hand grenades but gradually got larger and larger, dropping bigger and bigger bombs as World War I progressed. By the time World War II began, Germany had developed a powerful air force, the *Luftwaffe*. Their Junkers Ju 87 dive-bombers ruled the skies, launching heavy attacks on ground targets while the strong Messerschmitt fighters guarded them. Fighter pilots who shot down five enemy aircraft were called "aces."

As World War II went on, however, the Allies began building an arsenal of famous war planes. The Americans manufactured the Boeing B-17 Flying Fortress, the Boeing B-29 Superfortress, and the P-51 Mustang. The British contributed the Hawker Hurricane, the Vickers-Supermarine Spitfire, and the Avro Lancaster. The Allies' air might is what eventually helped them to defeat the Axis powers.

All four branches of the U.S. military use airplanes. Planes like the F-16 Fighting Falcon and the B-2 Stealth Bomber play important roles in combat. Top-secret research is still being done in stealth technology—making a plane radar proof.

CHAPTER

14

Common Fractions: Multiplication and Division

The American-made F-16 Fighting
Falcon is one of the most popular
fighters of all time and is used by air
forces all around the world. It is
renowned for its agility, ruggedness,
and maintainability.

This demonstra-
tion photo, taken
in 1911, shows
the first explosive
aerial bomb. It
was handheld.

Multiplying a Whole Number Times a Fraction

> Multiplication is the same as repeated addition.

Marcy had a pizza party on her birthday. Each of the six girls at the party ate three-eighths of a pizza. How many pizzas did they eat in all?

$$\frac{3}{8} + \frac{3}{8} + \frac{3}{8} + \frac{3}{8} + \frac{3}{8} + \frac{3}{8} = \frac{18}{8}$$

$$\frac{18}{8} = 2\frac{2}{8} = 2\frac{1}{4} \text{ pizzas}$$

or

6 groups of $\frac{3}{8} = 6 \times \frac{3}{8} = \frac{18}{8} = 2\frac{2}{8} = 2\frac{1}{4}$ pizzas

Jared ran $\frac{7}{10}$ of a mile each day for 5 days. How many miles did Jared run?

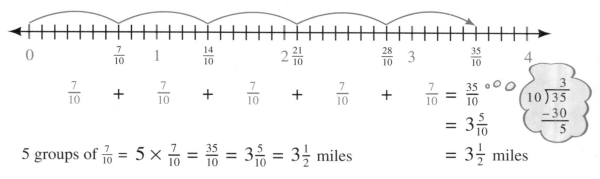

$$\frac{7}{10} + \frac{7}{10} + \frac{7}{10} + \frac{7}{10} + \frac{7}{10} = \frac{35}{10}$$

$$\begin{array}{r} 3 \\ 10\overline{)35} \\ -30 \\ \hline 5 \end{array}$$

$$= 3\frac{5}{10}$$

5 groups of $\frac{7}{10} = 5 \times \frac{7}{10} = \frac{35}{10} = 3\frac{5}{10} = 3\frac{1}{2}$ miles

$$= 3\frac{1}{2} \text{ miles}$$

Class Work

Write an equation for each word problem. Simplify and label.

1. Mom bought 3 blocks of cheese. Each block weighed $\frac{5}{8}$ pound. How much cheese did Mom buy?

2. Christine's kitten eats $\frac{1}{2}$ cup of kitten food each day. How much does the kitten eat in 7 days?

Practice

Use a fraction kit to multiply. Write only the answer in simplest form.

1. $3 \times \frac{2}{3} =$ **2.** $2 \times \frac{5}{12} =$ **3.** $4 \times \frac{2}{6} =$

Use a fraction number line to multiply. Write only the answer in simplest form.

4. $6 \times \frac{5}{8} =$ **5.** $8 \times \frac{1}{2} =$ **6.** $5 \times \frac{3}{4} =$

Write a repeated addition equation for each multiplication equation. Solve the problem and simplify the answer.

7. $7 \times \frac{3}{4} =$ **8.** $9 \times \frac{2}{3} =$ **9.** $5 \times \frac{3}{7} =$

Solve. Simplify the answer.

10. $7 \times \frac{4}{5} =$ **11.** $6 \times \frac{2}{3} =$ **12.** $4 \times \frac{3}{5} =$ **13.** $9 \times \frac{2}{9} =$

14. $2 \times \frac{7}{10} =$ **15.** $5 \times \frac{6}{8} =$ **16.** $3 \times \frac{3}{12} =$ **17.** $4 \times \frac{6}{10} =$

Application

Write an equation for each word problem. Solve. Simplify and label the answer.

18. Helen made 4 kites. She used $\frac{5}{8}$ of a yard of ribbon for the tail of each kite. How much ribbon did she use in all?

19. Michael spends $\frac{3}{4}$ of an hour working on his kite each day. If it takes him 8 days to finish the kite, how much time will he have spent?

Finding a Fraction of a Fraction

> **Steps for Multiplying Fractions**
> 1. Multiply the numerators.
> 2. Multiply the denominators.

Brannon and Camaryn share a small garden in the back yard. Each has $\frac{1}{2}$ of the garden to plant whatever he likes. Brannon planted potatoes in $\frac{1}{2}$ of his part. How much of the whole garden is planted with Brannon's potatoes?

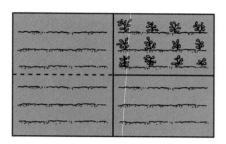

$$\frac{1}{2} \text{ of } \frac{1}{2} \text{ is written } \frac{1}{2} \times \frac{1}{2} = \frac{1}{4}$$

Brannon planted potatoes in $\frac{1}{4}$ of the garden.

There was two-thirds of a pan of brownies left, and Mother gave one-half of it to her children for dessert. What part of the whole pan of brownies did the children get?

$$\frac{1}{2} \text{ of } \frac{2}{3} \text{ is written } \frac{1}{2} \times \frac{2}{3} = \frac{2}{6} = \frac{1}{3}$$

The children ate $\frac{1}{3}$ of the pan of brownies.

Multiplication of fractions can be shown by folding paper.

$$\frac{1}{4} \times \frac{2}{3} = (\tfrac{1}{4} \text{ of } \tfrac{2}{3})$$

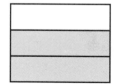

Fold the paper in thirds. Color two-thirds. Fold back the uncolored third.

Fold the paper in fourths. Color one-fourth.

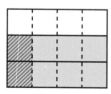

Unfold the paper. $\frac{2}{12}$ is doubly shaded.

$$\frac{1}{4} \times \frac{2}{3} = \frac{2}{12} = \frac{1}{6}$$

Practice

Write and solve a multiplication equation for each piece of paper.

Example:

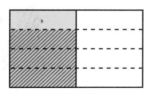

$$\frac{3}{4} \times \frac{1}{2} = \frac{3}{8}$$

1.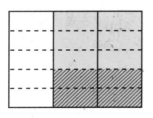

2.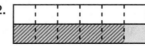

3.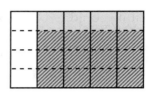

Solve. Write only the answer in simplest form.

4. $\frac{3}{4} \times \frac{1}{2} =$

5. $\frac{2}{3} \times \frac{3}{5} =$

6. $\frac{4}{5} \times \frac{2}{5} =$

7. $\frac{3}{8} \times \frac{1}{2} =$

8. $\frac{7}{10} \times \frac{3}{4} =$

9. $\frac{5}{8} \times \frac{1}{3} =$

10. $\frac{1}{2} \times \frac{2}{3} =$

11. $\frac{5}{8} \times \frac{3}{7} =$

Application

Write an equation for each word problem. Solve. Simplify and label the answer.

12. The soccer team practices $\frac{3}{4}$ of an hour each day. Half of that time is spent practicing dribbling and kicking. What part of an hour do they spend practicing these skills?

13. Jill ran halfway around the track. The track is $\frac{1}{4}$ of a mile long. How far did Jill run?

14. There was $\frac{1}{3}$ of a cake left over from dinner. Dad ate $\frac{4}{5}$ of the leftover cake for a snack. How much of the cake did Dad eat?

15. There was $\frac{4}{7}$ of the garden left to weed. Deanna weeded $\frac{2}{5}$ of it. How much of the garden did Deanna weed?

Finding a Fraction of a Whole Number

Finding a fraction of a whole number can be like finding a fraction of a fraction.

> 1. Rename the whole number as a fraction.
> 2. Multiply the numerators.
> 3. Multiply the denominators.

Trent had 20 baseball cards. He told Mark that he could have $\frac{1}{4}$ of them. Trent made 4 equal groups of the 20 cards and gave one of the groups to Mark. How many cards will Mark receive?

$\frac{1}{4}$ of 20 =

$\frac{1}{4} \times 20 =$

$\frac{1}{4} \times \frac{20}{1} = \frac{20}{4} = 5$ baseball cards

Trent found that he did not need to rename the whole number as a fraction. For the numerator in the answer, he will multiply the whole number by the numerator of the fraction. For the denominator, he will use the denominator of the fraction.

$$\frac{1}{4} \text{ of } 20 = \frac{1}{4} \times 20 = \frac{20}{4} = 5$$

Mother made 5 gallons of punch for the Women's Missionary Fellowship. Two-thirds of the punch was gone by the end of the meeting. How much punch did the ladies drink?

$\frac{2}{3}$ of 5 =

$\frac{2}{3} \times 5 =$

$\frac{2}{3} \times \frac{5}{1} = \frac{10}{3} = 3\frac{1}{3}$ gallons

Did you know . . .

An "ace" is a fighter pilot who shoots down at least 5 enemy aircraft. Manfred von Richtofen (the Red Baron) was a German ace who shot down 80 Allied planes during World War I. Eddie Rickenbacker, an American ace, shot down 22 enemy planes in only 6 months of the war.

Practice

Solve. Simplify the answer.

1. $\frac{1}{5} \times 20 =$ 2. $\frac{4}{7} \times 5 =$ 3. $\frac{5}{6} \times 8 =$ 4. $\frac{1}{4} \times 15 =$

5. $\frac{3}{8} \times 9 =$ 6. $\frac{2}{3} \times 10 =$ 7. $\frac{11}{12} \times 2 =$ 8. $\frac{7}{9} \times 6 =$

Write an equation for each problem. Solve. Simplify and label the answer.

9. How many inches are in $\frac{1}{2}$ yard?   10. How many inches are in $\frac{1}{3}$ yard?

11. How many inches are in $\frac{1}{4}$ yard?   12. How many inches are in $\frac{3}{4}$ yard?

13. How many hours are in $\frac{1}{4}$ day?   14. How many hours are in $\frac{3}{4}$ day?

Application

Write an equation for each word problem. Solve. Simplify and label the answer.

15. Mother had 16 eggs. She used $\frac{3}{4}$ of them to make pies. How many eggs did she use?

16. Mr. King bought a 25-pound bag of dog food. He used $\frac{2}{5}$ of it in one week. How many pounds of dog food were used that week?

17. Tracy wants to buy a sweater that costs $30.00. She has saved $\frac{2}{3}$ of that amount. How much has she saved?

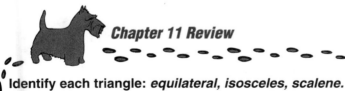

Chapter 11 Review

Identify each triangle: *equilateral, isosceles, scalene.*

18.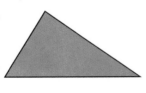

19.

20.

Diana is making a patchwork quilt. Her mother gave her $\frac{5}{8}$ of a yard of 3 different colors of material. How much material did Diana receive?

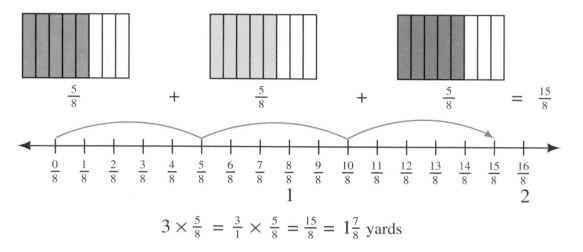

$$3 \times \frac{5}{8} = \frac{3}{1} \times \frac{5}{8} = \frac{15}{8} = 1\frac{7}{8} \text{ yards}$$

To multiply a whole number times a mixed number, use the Distributive Property of Multiplication *or* rename both factors as improper fractions before multiplying.

Keith runs $2\frac{1}{3}$ miles each day. How far does he run in 4 days?

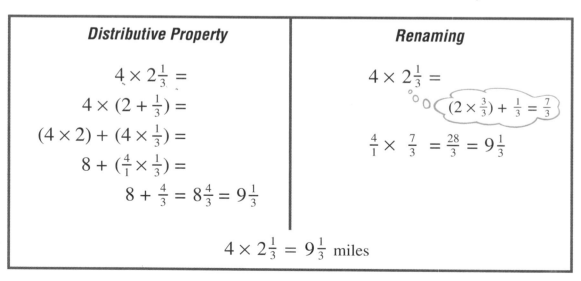

Practice

Solve the problems, using the Distributive Property of Multiplication. Simplify the answer.

1. $5 \times 1\frac{3}{4} =$ **2.** $4 \times 1\frac{5}{6} =$ **3.** $3 \times 2\frac{1}{3} =$ **4.** $2 \times 2\frac{2}{7} =$

Solve the problems by renaming as improper fractions. Simplify the answer.

5. $6 \times 2\frac{2}{3} =$ **6.** $3 \times 1\frac{1}{10} =$ **7.** $5 \times 1\frac{2}{5} =$ **8.** $4 \times 2\frac{8}{10} =$

Solve. Simplify the answer. (You may use either method.)

9. $8 \times 3\frac{1}{4} =$ **10.** $6 \times 4\frac{3}{10} =$ **11.** $3 \times 1\frac{2}{7} =$ **12.** $5 \times 2\frac{2}{9} =$

Application

Write an equation for each word problem. Solve. Simplify and label the answer.

13. Cynthia bought 4 packages of meat on sale. Each package weighed $2\frac{1}{8}$ pounds. How many pounds of meat did Cynthia buy?

14. Ellyson is making a ladder for his tree house. He will have 6 rungs on the ladder. If he makes each rung $1\frac{1}{2}$ feet wide, how many feet of board does he need for the ladder rungs?

Meet the Challenge!

15. Double the recipe to yield 6 dozen.

Nutmeg Crisps

$\frac{2}{3}$ c. butter   2 tsp. baking powder

$1\frac{1}{4}$ c. brown sugar $\frac{1}{4}$ tsp. salt

$1\frac{1}{2}$ tsp. vanilla extract   nutmeg

$\frac{1}{2}$ tsp. almond extract   1 egg white

$1\frac{3}{4}$ c. flour   2 tbsp. water

Cream first four ingredients. Add flour, baking powder, and salt. Pack mixture into empty 1-lb. butter carton. Chill. Remove from carton and slice lengthwise. Slice each section into $\frac{1}{8}$-inch-thick slices. Brush with water and egg white beaten together. Sprinkle with nutmeg. Bake at 375° F for 12 minutes until golden brown. Makes 3 dozen.

Multiplying Mixed Numbers

To multiply mixed numbers, use the Distributive Property *or* rename the mixed number as an improper fraction and multiply as usual.

Elaine is making cinnamon rolls. The recipe calls for $5\frac{1}{2}$ cups of flour. Elaine is making only one-half of the recipe. How many cups of flour should she use?

Distributive Property	**Renaming**
$\frac{1}{2} \times 5\frac{1}{2} =$	$\frac{1}{2} \times 5\frac{1}{2} =$
$(\frac{1}{2} \times 5) + (\frac{1}{2} \times \frac{1}{2}) =$	$\frac{1}{2} \times \frac{11}{2} = \frac{11}{4} = 2\frac{3}{4}$ cups
$(\frac{1}{2} \times \frac{5}{1}) + \frac{1}{4} =$	
$\frac{5}{2} + \frac{1}{4} =$	
$(\frac{5}{2} \times \frac{2}{2}) + \frac{1}{4} =$	
$\frac{10}{4} + \frac{1}{4} = \frac{11}{4} = 2\frac{3}{4}$ cups	

If both factors are mixed numbers, rename both factors as improper fractions before multiplying.

A book has dimensions of $4\frac{1}{2}$ inches by $7\frac{1}{3}$ inches. What is the area of the front cover?

Step 1	Step 2	Step 3
Rename mixed numbers as improper fractions by multiplying.	Multiply.	Simplify by dividing.
$4\frac{1}{2} \times 7\frac{1}{3} =$	$\frac{9}{2} \times \frac{22}{3} = \frac{198}{6}$	$\frac{198}{6} = 33$
$(4 \times \frac{2}{2}) + \frac{1}{2} = \frac{9}{2}$		
$(7 \times \frac{3}{3}) + \frac{1}{3} = \frac{22}{3}$		$4\frac{1}{2} \times 7\frac{1}{3} = 33$ in.^{2}

Practice

Solve. Simplify the answer.

1. $\frac{3}{4} \times \frac{5}{6} =$ **2.** $\frac{2}{3} \times \frac{7}{8} =$ **3.** $\frac{1}{6} \times \frac{2}{9} =$ **4.** $\frac{3}{8} \times \frac{8}{9} =$

Rename the mixed numbers as improper fractions to solve the problems. Simplify the answer.

5. $1\frac{2}{3} \times 3\frac{1}{4} =$ **6.** $3\frac{3}{4} \times 2\frac{1}{2} =$ **7.** $4\frac{3}{5} \times 2\frac{1}{3} =$

8. $2\frac{1}{9} \times 10\frac{1}{2} =$ **9.** $2\frac{1}{3} \times 8\frac{2}{3} =$ **10.** $6\frac{4}{5} \times 3\frac{2}{7} =$

Use the Distributive Property to solve the problems. Simplify the answer.

11. $\frac{1}{2} \times 5\frac{1}{4} =$ **12.** $\frac{3}{8} \times 2\frac{2}{3} =$ **13.** $6 \times 3\frac{1}{3} =$

14. $\frac{2}{5} \times 3\frac{1}{9} =$ **15.** $\frac{1}{4} \times 4\frac{8}{9} =$ **16.** $\frac{3}{5} \times 2\frac{1}{2} =$

Application

Write an equation for each word problem. Solve. Simplify and label the answer.

17. A box contains $2\frac{1}{2}$ pounds of cherries. Mrs. White has $3\frac{1}{3}$ boxes. How many pounds of cherries does Mrs. White have?

18. Troy's class spent $\frac{2}{3}$ of their school day taking achievement tests. The school day was $5\frac{1}{2}$ hours long. How many hours did they spend taking tests?

 Chapter 11 Review

Find the perimeter of each figure.

19.

9 cm

20.

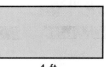

2 ft.

4 ft.

21.

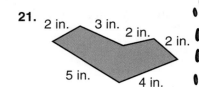

2 in. 3 in. 2 in.

5 in. 2 in.

4 in.

Dividing a Whole Number by a Fraction

Dividing a whole number by a fraction is similar to dividing whole numbers.

$12 \div 4$ can mean, "How many sets of 4 are in 12 or how many are in each of 4 sets?"

$3 \div \frac{3}{4}$ can mean, "How many sets of $\frac{3}{4}$ are in 3?"

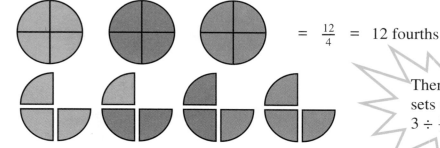

$= \frac{12}{4} = 12$ fourths

There are 4 sets of $\frac{3}{4}$ in 3.
$3 \div \frac{3}{4} = 4$

When the divisor is a proper fraction (less than 1), the quotient will be larger than the dividend.

How many servings can be made from 3 submarine sandwiches if a serving is $\frac{1}{2}$ of a sandwich?

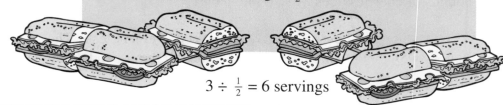

$3 \div \frac{1}{2} = 6$ servings

Sue and Caryn are making awards for a math contest. Each award is made from $\frac{2}{3}$ of a foot of ribbon. How many awards can they make from 4 feet of ribbon?

$4 \div \frac{2}{3} = 6$ awards

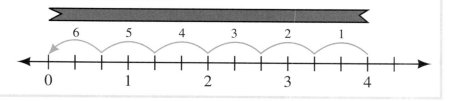

Practice

Use a fraction kit to solve the equations.

1. $4 \div \frac{2}{3} =$ 2. $3 \div \frac{3}{4} =$ 3. $3 \div \frac{1}{2} =$ 4. $2 \div \frac{8}{12} =$

Use a fraction number line to solve the equations.

5. $2 \div \frac{1}{6} =$ 6. $3 \div \frac{3}{8} =$ 7. $5 \div \frac{1}{2} =$ 8. $2 \div \frac{1}{4} =$

9. $6 \div \frac{3}{8} =$ 10. $4 \div \frac{2}{3} =$ 11. $7 \div \frac{1}{4} =$ 12. $5 \div \frac{2}{3} =$

Application

Write an equation for each word problem. Use a fraction kit or number line to solve the problem. Label.

13. Mother made 3 pies. The family will eat $\frac{3}{4}$ of a pie each night for dessert. How many nights will the pies last?

14. Beth has 2 large mint patties that she is going to share with friends. If she cuts each patty into thirds, how many pieces will she have?

Dividing a Fraction by a Fraction

Mr. Wooster has 10 double popsicles. If he gives each student $\frac{1}{2}$ of a popsicle, how many students can receive a popsicle?

$$10 \div \frac{1}{2} = 20 \text{ students}$$

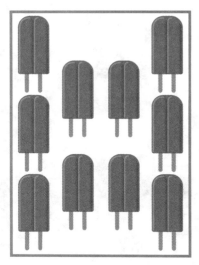 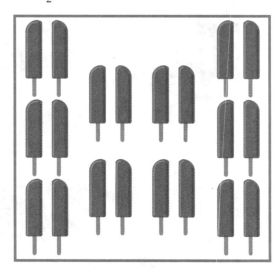

Joseph went to the park with $\frac{6}{8}$ lb. of birdseed. If he gives each friend $\frac{2}{8}$ lb., how many friends can feed the birds?

$$\frac{6}{8} \div \frac{2}{8} = \text{ "How many sets of } \frac{2}{8} \text{ are in } \frac{6}{8} \text{ ?"}$$

fraction kit

number line

repeated subtraction

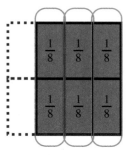

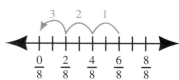

1. $\frac{6}{8} - \frac{2}{8} = \frac{4}{8}$

2. $\frac{4}{8} - \frac{2}{8} = \frac{2}{8}$

3. $\frac{2}{8} - \frac{2}{8} = \frac{0}{8} = 0$

$$\frac{6}{8} \div \frac{2}{8} = 3 \text{ friends}$$

Class Work

Use a fraction number line to solve the problems.

1. $\frac{6}{8} \div \frac{3}{8} =$ 2. $\frac{2}{4} \div \frac{1}{8} =$ 3. $\frac{4}{8} \div \frac{1}{4} =$ 4. $\frac{1}{2} \div \frac{2}{8} =$

Practice

Use a fraction kit to solve the problems.

1. $\frac{5}{8} \div \frac{1}{8} =$

2. $\frac{10}{12} \div \frac{2}{12} =$

3. $\frac{2}{3} \div \frac{1}{3} =$

4. $\frac{5}{6} \div \frac{1}{6} =$

5. $\frac{3}{4} \div \frac{1}{4} =$

6. $\frac{9}{12} \div \frac{3}{12} =$

Use a fraction number line to solve the problems.

7. $\frac{3}{4} \div \frac{3}{8} =$

8. $\frac{1}{2} \div \frac{1}{8} =$

9. $\frac{8}{8} \div \frac{1}{4} =$

Application

Write an equation for each word problem. Use a fraction number line or kit to solve the problem. Label.

10. Kimmie needed to carry a heavy box $\frac{3}{4}$ of a mile. Several of her friends volunteered to help carry it. If each can carry the box $\frac{1}{8}$ of a mile, how many friends need to help carry the box?

11. Lyndia has $\frac{6}{8}$ of a yard of elastic. She needs to cut pieces that are $\frac{1}{4}$ of a yard long. How many pieces will she be able to cut from the elastic?

Chapter 11 Review

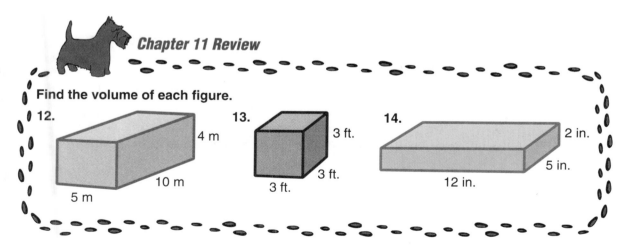

Find the volume of each figure.

12. 4 m, 10 m, 5 m

13. 3 ft., 3 ft., 3 ft.

14. 2 in., 5 in., 12 in.

Recipe

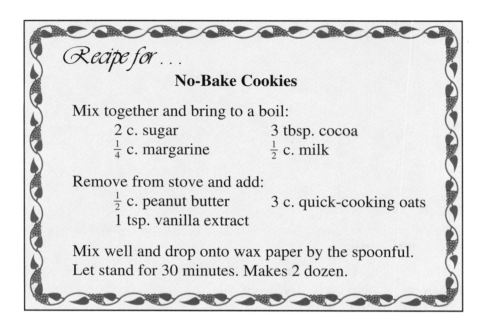

Recipe for . . .

No-Bake Cookies

Mix together and bring to a boil:

2 c. sugar	3 tbsp. cocoa
$\frac{1}{4}$ c. margarine	$\frac{1}{2}$ c. milk

Remove from stove and add:

$\frac{1}{2}$ c. peanut butter	3 c. quick-cooking oats
1 tsp. vanilla extract	

Mix well and drop onto wax paper by the spoonful.
Let stand for 30 minutes. Makes 2 dozen.

Use the recipe to solve the problems.

1. If you doubled the recipe, how many cups of peanut butter would you need?

2. If you wanted to make only half of the recipe, how much milk would you need?

3. If you had 1 cup of margarine, how many recipes of the cookies could you make?

4. If the only measuring cup you had was $\frac{1}{4}$ cup, how many times would you need to measure out the quick-cooking oats?

5. How many tablespoons of cocoa would you need if you made $1\frac{1}{2}$ recipes?

Fraction Word Problems

Solve. Simplify and label the answer.

1. Tom spent $\frac{3}{4}$ of an hour delivering papers each day. How much time did he spend in 6 days?

2. Ginger had a $\frac{1}{8}$-yard piece of material. She bought $\frac{3}{8}$ yard more. How many yards of material does Ginger have?

3. Laura had $2\frac{2}{3}$ yards of ribbon. She used $1\frac{1}{3}$ yards making barrettes for her sisters. How much ribbon does she have left?

4. Mrs. Anderson bought 3 packages of meat. Each package weighed $1\frac{3}{4}$ pounds. What was the total weight of the 3 packages of meat?

5. On Monday Caleb ran $\frac{7}{10}$ of a mile. He ran $\frac{9}{10}$ of a mile on Tuesday, and on Wednesday he ran $1\frac{1}{2}$ miles. How many miles did Caleb run in all?

6. How many square yards of carpet need to be purchased to cover a floor that is $7\frac{1}{2}$ yards long and $5\frac{1}{3}$ yards wide?

MY JESSIE

Solve. Simplify the answer if necessary.

1. $\frac{2}{5} \times \frac{2}{3} =$ **2.** $\frac{1}{4} \times \frac{1}{2} =$ **3.** $\frac{2}{9} \times \frac{3}{8} =$ **4.** $\frac{3}{7} \times \frac{3}{4} =$

5. $3 \times \frac{3}{4} =$ **6.** $5 \times \frac{2}{7} =$ **7.** $\frac{4}{5} \times 2 =$ **8.** $\frac{1}{3} \times 8 =$

Solve the problems using the Distributive Property of Multiplication. Simplify the answer.

9. $9 \times 1\frac{1}{3} =$ **10.** $3 \times 2\frac{2}{7} =$ **11.** $4 \times 3\frac{1}{5} =$ **12.** $5 \times 2\frac{1}{6} =$

Rename the mixed numbers as improper fractions to solve the problems. Simplify the answer.

13. $2\frac{2}{5} \times 2\frac{1}{2} =$ **14.** $2\frac{1}{4} \times 1\frac{1}{5} =$ **15.** $3 \times 2\frac{3}{4} =$ **16.** $3\frac{1}{6} \times 4 =$

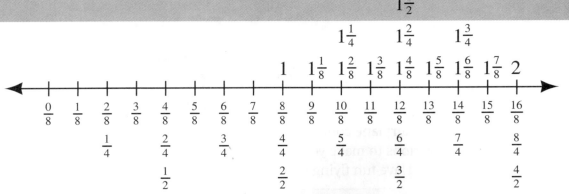

Use the number line to solve the problems.

17. $\frac{3}{4} \div \frac{1}{8} =$

18. $1\frac{1}{4} \div \frac{2}{4} =$

19. $\frac{6}{8} \div \frac{3}{8} =$

Solve the following word problems. Simplify the answer.

20. Alexandra needs $\frac{2}{3}$ of a cup of shortening to make a pie crust for 1 pie. How much shortening would she need to make pie crusts for 4 pies?

21. Jackson has a board that is 4 feet long. He wants to cut it into pieces measuring $\frac{3}{8}$ of a foot. How many pieces can he cut?

22. Jesse had 8 sons. Six-sixteenths of his sons went to battle against the Philistines. How many sons went to battle?

23. David took 10 cheeses to his brothers at the battle. If the brothers ate $\frac{3}{5}$ of the cheeses as soon as David arrived, how many cheeses were eaten?

Flying Machine

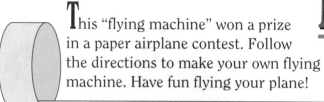

This "flying machine" won a prize in a paper airplane contest. Follow the directions to make your own flying machine. Have fun flying your plane!

1. Cut out pieces of construction paper with these measurements.

A ⸻ 1 in.

11 in.

B 1 in.   **C** $\frac{3}{4}$ in.

$6\frac{7}{16}$ in. $\frac{3}{16}$ in.   5 in. $\frac{3}{16}$ in.

2. Fold piece A in half down the center. Then fold in each half to the center.

3. Form a long triangular prism with piece A. Glue or tape together.

4. Make rings with pieces B and C by overlapping the ends. Glue or tape the rings. Glue or tape a ring to each end of piece A.

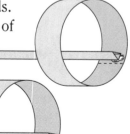

Cumulative Review

Write the letter of the correct answer.

1. Which is *not* a reasonable estimate for 672 − 381?

   a. 200 c. 300
   b. 290 d. not given

2. What fraction is in simplest form?

   a. $\frac{4}{8}$ c. $\frac{7}{11}$
   b. $\frac{16}{20}$ d. $\frac{32}{4}$

3. How many centimeters are in 2 meters?

   a. 2 cm c. 200 cm
   b. 20 cm d. 2000 cm

4. Solve.

   $$58\overline{)43.862}$$

   a. 756 r14
   b. 767 r24
   c. 676 r4
   d. not given

5. Solve.

   $$\frac{6}{10} + \frac{1}{2} =$$

   a. $1\frac{1}{5}$
   b. $\frac{6}{10}$
   c. $\frac{1}{10}$
   d. not given

6. Solve.

   $$\begin{array}{r} 9 \\ -\ 6\frac{3}{7} \\ \hline \end{array}$$

   a. $3\frac{3}{7}$
   b. $2\frac{2}{7}$
   c. $2\frac{4}{7}$
   d. not given

7. Which figure has one face and one point?

   a. cylinder c. sphere
   b. cone d. triangular prism

8. Solve.

   $$\begin{array}{r} 5.3 \\ \times\ 2.6 \\ \hline 318 \\ +\ 10\square \\ \hline 1\square.78 \end{array}$$

   a. 7, 8
   b. 1, 3
   c. 3, 8
   d. 6, 3

9. Solve.

   $$1{,}000 \times 0.052 =$$

   a. 52 c. 0.52
   b. 520 d. 5.02

10. Solve.

    $$23 \text{ ft.} =$$

    a. 8 yd. c. 7 yd. 2 ft.
    b. 6 yd. 1 ft. d. not given

11. The Yum Yum Shop sold 113 boxes of doughnuts for $4.20 each on Saturday morning. How much did the shop earn that morning?

    a. $374.50 c. $564.60
    b. $474.60 d. not given

12. Round 429.758 to the nearest hundredth.

    a. 429.76 c. 430.76
    b. 430.758 d. not given

Aerobatics

Have you ever seen a plane fly upside down? Or have you watched a group of planes fly in a beautiful formation? If so, you have seen a demonstration of aerobatics.

Aerobatics began with a sport called "barnstorming" in the early 1900s. Many barnstormers had been pilots in training for service in World War I, but the war ended before they could get to the battlefront. Rather than completely give up their dreams of flying, they purchased war surplus planes and flew out over the countryside in search of audiences for their exhibitions. In those days many small-town and country people had never seen an airplane. Their curiosity about flying led them to spend a fortune for a ride in a plane or a chance to see a pilot perform stunts in the air. Parachuting, wing-walking, and even changing planes in midair became popular feats as time went on. But eventually the war surplus planes deteriorated, and the novelty of the stunts wore off. Government officials became concerned about the safety of the sport. The Air Commerce Act in 1926 greatly limited barnstorming activity in the United States.

Today aerobatic sports are carefully restricted by the Federal Aviation Administration (FAA). But you can see some breathtaking maneuvers if you attend a performance of a specially trained aerobatic team. Teams such as the navy's Blue Angels and the air force's Thunderbirds demonstrate their dramatic formations in air shows to promote military service.

Statistics and Graphing

The Pitts Special is one of the most famous aerobatic aircraft in the world. Besides being great fun, a training course in aerobatics is a good way to improve a pilot's skill and safety in more conventional flying. Here you see the Royal Falcons, the aerobatics team of Jordan.

Statistics

Statistics is the mathematical study of the collection, organization, analysis, and interpretation of data (information).

Years	Tally	Frequency (number of tallies)
1	I I I I	4
2	I I I	3
3	I I	2
4	I I I	3
5	I I I I	4
6	I I I	3

The students in Miss Lee's class took a survey to find the average number of years the students have attended the school.

> The difference between the largest and smallest numbers in a set of data is the **range**.

What is the range of this survey?

The smallest number of years is 1.
The largest number of years is 6.
$6 - 1 = 5$ The range is 5 years.

> The typical number in a set of numbers is the **average** or **mean**.

The average (mean) is found by adding the quantities and dividing the total by the number of quantities.

What is the average number of years the students in Miss Lee's class have attended the school?

$(1 + 1 + 1 + 1) + (2 + 2 + 2) + (3 + 3) +$
$(4 + 4 + 4) + (5 + 5 + 5 + 5) + (6 + 6 + 6) = 66$

$66 \div 19 = 3.47 \approx 3.5$ years

> The **median** is the middle number in a sequential list of numbers.

The median can be found by crossing off the highest and lowest numbers from each side until the middle number is left.

What is the median for this survey?

~~1 1 1 1 2 2 2 3 3~~ (4) ~~4 4 5 5 5 5 6 6 6~~
The median is 4.

> If there is an even number of numbers in a list, two numbers will be left after the high and low numbers are crossed off. Add the two numbers together and divide by 2 to find the median.

~~1 1 1~~ 2 2 4 4 ~~4 6 7~~ $2 + 4 = 6$
The median is 3. $6 \div 2 = 3$

Practice

Use the gradebook page to answer the questions. Write the equations you used. Your teacher may allow you to use a calculator.

Teacher: Mr. Haas Subject: Heritage Studies			
Name	**Test 1**	**Test 2**	**Average**
Andrews, N.	85	95	
Bauder, O.	76	82	
Inglis, R.	100	100	
Lancaster, C.	87	95	
McCurdy, E.	85	96	
Rausch, M.	92	85	
Smythe, P.	94	82	
Yen, S.	85	85	

1. What is Bauder's average score?

2. What is Lancaster's average score?

3. What is Smythe's average score?

4. What is Yen's average score?

5. What is the class's average score for Test 1?

6. What is the class's average score for Test 2?

Copy the tally chart. Record the tallies and frequencies for Test 1. Use the tally chart to complete the sentences.

7. The range of the Test 1 score is _____ .

8. The median score is _____ .

Score	Tally	Frequency
100	I	1
94		
92		
87		
85		
76		

Bar Graph: Single, Double

> ### Steps for Making a Single Bar Graph
> 1. Round the numbers.
> 2. Decide on unit representation.
> 3. Decide on format (vertical or horizontal).
> 4. Draw the graph.
> 5. Label and title the graph.

Class Work

Make a bar graph, using the table of ocean depths. Answer the questions. Write any equations you use.

1. Which ocean has the greatest depth?

2. What is the range (difference between the greatest and least depth) for this chart?

3. What is the difference between the greatest depth of the Atlantic Ocean and the greatest depth of the Indian Ocean?

Ocean Depths

Ocean	Greatest depth (ft.)
Pacific	36,198
Atlantic	28,232
Indian	23,376
Arctic	17,881

The Lord is a great God . . .
in his hand are the deep
places of the earth.
Psalm 95:3-4

A double bar graph compares two sets of similar information on the same graph.

The double bar graph below shows the high and low temperatures for several cities on a January day. Use the graph to answer the questions.

Temperatures for January 11

	High	Low
Anchorage	27°	16°
Boston	36°	23°
Denver	43°	16°
Jacksonville	65°	42°
Los Angeles	67°	48°

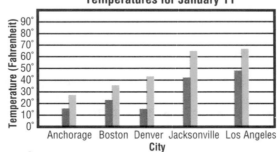

Temperatures for January 11

4. Which city had the highest temperature?

5. Which city had the least amount of temperature change?

6. What is the average high temperature for the graph?

7. What is the average low temperature for the graph?

8. What is the range of the high temperatures?

Practice

Mrs. Martin's class recorded the lunch count for one week. Use the bar graph to answer the questions. Write any equations you use.

1. On which day was there the greatest difference between hot lunch and bagged lunch?

2. On which day was there the smallest difference between hot lunch and bagged lunch?

3. What is the range for hot lunches?

4. What is the average number of hot lunches bought each day?

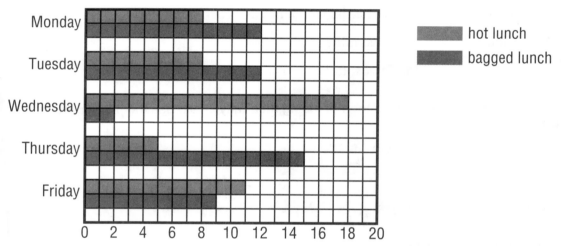

hot lunch
bagged lunch

Use the information in the table to make a single bar graph. Use graph paper. Answer the questions. Your teacher may allow you to use a calculator. (Hint: use 5,000 ft. as the unit.)

5. What is the range for the graph?

6. What is the average for the graph?

Highest Points of the Continents

Continent	Highest point (ft.)
Africa	19,340
Antarctica	16,864
Asia	29,028
Australia	7,310
Europe	15,771
North America	20,320
South America	22,834

Pictograph

A pictograph shows numerical data using pictures or symbols.

Miss Evans's class conducted
a survey to find the colors of the
cars in the school parking lot.
They made a tally chart
to record the colors.

Tally Chart

red	THL THL I
white	THL IIII
blue	THL THL THL III
green	II
brown	IIII
black	III
other	THL I

Class Work

1. Use the tally chart to write the frequency for each color.

2. Which color has the most tallies?

3. Which color has the fewest tallies?

Miss Evans's class made a pictograph using their tally chart. Use the pictograph to answer the questions.

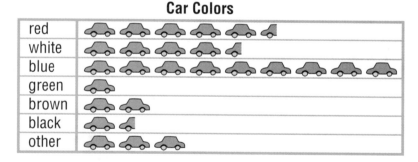

Car Colors

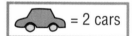

= 2 cars

4. How many blue cars were in the parking lot?

5. Are there more red or white cars in the lot?

6. Write an equation to show how many more blue cars there are than brown cars.

7. Write an equation to show the number of white and red cars combined.

Practice

Use the pictograph to answer the questions.

Camp Victory Attendance

Year	Campers
1975	🥾 🥾 🥾 🥾 🥾 🥾
1980	🥾 🥾 🥾 🥾 🥾 🥾 🥾
1985	🥾 🥾 🥾 🥾 🥾 🥾 🥾
1990	🥾 🥾 🥾 🥾 🥾 🥾 🥾 🥾
1995	🥾 🥾 🥾 🥾 🥾 🥾 🥾 🥾

🥾 = 50 campers

1. Which year had the most campers?

2. How many campers attended in 1980?

3. How many campers attended in 1990?

Use the information in the table to answer the questions.

4. Make a pictograph, using a to represent 10 campers.

5. How many campers attended during this week?

6. Which activity did most campers choose?

7. Did more campers choose to play basketball or go canoeing?

> Each camper can choose 1 activity.

Week 1 Free Time Activities

Activity	Number of campers
softball	45
basketball	15
canoeing	30
hiking	10

8. How many more campers chose to play softball rather than go hiking?

 Chapter 12 Review

Solve.

9. $4\overline{)9.46}$

10. $3\overline{)3.09}$

11. $6\overline{)\$15.84}$

12. $5\overline{)12.7}$

Circle Graph

A circle graph shows a whole divided into parts.

Jon's grandfather bought a new car and gave Jon his old one. Kristen borrowed money from a bank to purchase her car. The circle graphs show Kristen's and Jon's expenses for one year.

Kristen's Car Expenses

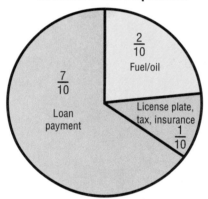

Jon's Car Expenses

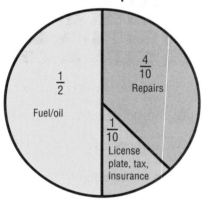

Total expenses: $4,348.00   Total expenses: $2,461.00

Remember: The **mode** is the number that occurs most frequently in a list.

The **median** is the middle number in a sequential set of data.

Jon recorded his fuel expenses for April. Then he found the mode, the median, and the average price paid.

Mode: $15.00

April Fuel Expenses

Date	Amount
4/4	$15.00
4/10	$15.00
4/16	$17.00
4/22	$18.00
4/30	$16.00

Median: $16.00

$15.00 $15.00 ($16.00) $17.00 $18.00

Average: $16.20

$15.00 + $15.00 + $17.00 + $18.00 + $16.00 = $81.00
$81.00 ÷ 5 = $16.20

Practice

The circle graph shows the type of fiction books preferred by fifth graders at a Christian school. Use the graph to answer the questions.

Fiction Favorites for Fifth Graders

1. What are the two favorite types of fiction?

2. Which category was chosen by more students: adventure or animal stories?

3. Did more students prefer mysteries or historical fiction?

4. What part of the students chose mysteries?

The librarian kept a record of the number of books checked out. Use the chart to answer the questions.

5. What is the mode?

6. What is the median?

7. What is the average (mean) number of books checked out each week?

8. Use the table below to make a circle graph of books bought at the book fair.

Books Checked Out	
week 1	225
week 2	200
week 3	250
week 4	250
week 5	185

Book Fair Purchases	
biographies	$\frac{1}{4}$
sports books	$\frac{1}{4}$
information books	$\frac{1}{2}$

$\longrightarrow$ **?**

Line Graphs: Single, Double

> A **line graph** is used to show how an amount changes over a period of time.

This line graph shows the growth of Karen's puppy. Each point can be described by an ordered pair of numbers. The first number tells the age of the puppy in weeks. The second number tells the weight of the puppy in pounds.

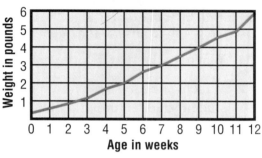

Class Work

1. Give the ordered pairs for weeks 5, 7, and 9.

2. What was the puppy's weight at 9 weeks?

3. How old was the puppy when it weighed $4\frac{1}{2}$ pounds?

4. During which week did the puppy gain the most weight?

5. About how many pounds did the puppy gain in the first 12 weeks?

> A *double line graph* compares how two amounts change over a period of time.

6. What is the average height of a girl at age 13?

7. What is the average height of a boy at age 13?

8. What is the average height of a girl at age 15?

9. What is the average height of a boy at age 15?

10. At what ages is the average girl taller than the average boy?

11. At what age does the average boy grow the most?

12. What is the range for the height of girls?

13. What is the range for the height of boys?

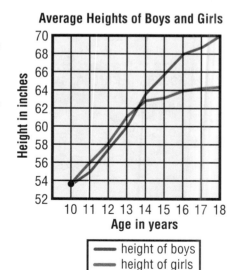

Practice

Use the graph to answer the questions.

1. What is the weight of an average 12-year-old boy?

2. What is the weight of an average 16-year-old girl?

3. At what age does the average boy gain the most weight?

4. At what age does the average girl gain the most weight?

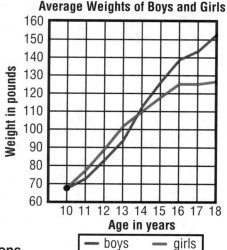

Average Weights of Boys and Girls

Weight in pounds / Age in years

— boys — girls

Use the table to make a line graph. Answer the questions.

5. What does the ordered pair (4, 100) mean for the graph?

6. Write an ordered pair of numbers to tell how tall Troy was when he was 3 years old.

7. Write an ordered pair of numbers to tell how tall Troy was when he was 10 years old.

Troy's Growth			
birth	50 cm	age 7	128 cm
age 1	70 cm	age 8	130 cm
age 2	86 cm	age 9	132 cm
age 3	90 cm	age 10	137 cm
age 4	100 cm	age 11	142 cm
age 5	110 cm	age 12	150 cm
age 6	120 cm		

Language Link

8. Did Troy grow the same amount each year? Explain your answer.

Chapter 12 Review

Mental Math: Write only the answer for each multiplication equation.

9. $100 \times 86.37 =$

10. $10 \times 9.24 =$

11. $1,000 \times 6.432 =$

Real Estate Agent

Peters Realtors
572 Shoaf Boulevard
Erie, Pennsylvania 16509

Moore Christian School
334 Tara Lane
Mariposa, CA 95338

USA 32

Dear Fifth Grade:

People fascinate me. I love to meet people, but even more so, I enjoy finding out what they like and dislike. My job is to sell new homes for a builder. Matching up a family with a home that fits their personalities and lifestyle is challenging. Houses vary in cost depending on what a buyer wants. Last week a buyer wanted some little extras for his family like a ceramic floor instead of linoleum, brass fixtures on the bathroom sink rather than chrome ones, and a three-car garage instead of a two-car one—all of these add to the cost of a home. So we totaled the costs for those extras and added them to the cost of the home to get the final price.

Probably the part of my job that most often calls for math skills is figuring out the amount for a loan. Hardly anyone can afford to buy a house all at once. So we allow people to pay only a portion of the price and borrow the rest. The amount of the loan is usually 80% or 90% of the price of the house. This buyer wanted an 80% loan. The loan officers at my company multiplied the total cost by 80% to determine the amount of money the buyer was going to borrow. The leftover amount is what the buyer paid right away—the down payment. After paying this amount, the buyer and his family started moving into their new home. Now they can enjoy their home while they gradually pay back the loan over several years. And their teen-age son can even park his car out of the rain!

Sincerely yours,

Sara Peters
Sara Peters

Use the table to copy and complete the tally chart. Answer the questions.

Hot Lunches Purchased

Monday	31
Tuesday	33
Wednesday	30
Thursday	28
Friday	33

1. **Tally Chart**

28	
29	
30	
31	
32	
33	

2. What is the mode?

3. What is the range?

4. What is the average number of hot lunches sold?

Identify the type of graph: *line graph, bar graph, circle graph.*

5.
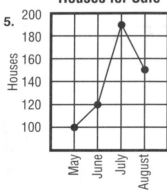
Newspaper Listings: Houses for Sale

6.
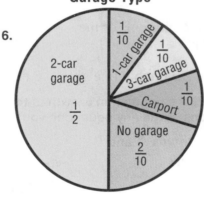
Garage Type

7.
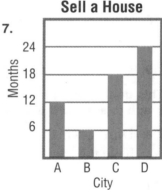
Average Time to Sell a House

Use the graphs above to answer the questions.

8. How many houses were listed for sale in May?

9. Which month had the most houses listed for sale?

10. In which month were 150 houses listed for sale?

11. Which is the most common type of garage for this survey?

12. Would a house be more likely to sell quickly in city A or city B?

13. In which city does it typically take the longest time to sell a home?

14. This table shows the number of bedrooms in houses of people surveyed.
Make a pictograph to show this
information.

Bedrooms in Houses

Number of bedrooms	Houses
1	11
2	27
3	89
4	38

⌂ = 10 houses

**This double line graph shows monthly precipitation. Use the graph to answer
the questions. Write any equations you use.**

15. Which year had more precipitation?

16. Which month had the most precipitation?

17. In which year did March have more
precipitation?

18. What is the average precipitation for the
months shown in 1990?

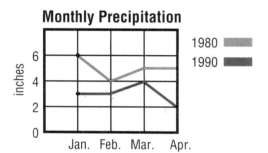

Monthly Precipitation

1980
1990

19. Use the information in the double line graph to make a double bar graph.

**This double bar graph shows the population growth of towns A and B. Use the
graph to answer the questions. Write any equations you use.**

20. During which year did towns A and B
have the same population?

21. During which year was the difference
in population greatest?

22. What is the range for town A?

23. What is the mode for town A?

24. In which year did town B match the
highest population of town A?

25. What is the combined total for the
populations of both towns for 1992?
for 1998?

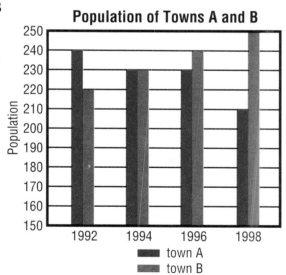

Population of Towns A and B

town A
town B

Cumulative Review

Write the letter of the correct answer.

1. What is the value of the 6 in 768,439,082?

   a. 60,000
   b. 6,000,000
   c. 600,000
   d. 60,000,000

2. Solve for *n*.
$$n \times 6 = 78$$

   a. $n = 13$
   b. $n = 14$
   c. $n = 15$
   d. $n = 16$

3. Which equation will *not* have a remainder of 3?

   a. $168 \div 11$
   b. $763 \div 95$
   c. $628 \div 74$
   d. not given

4. Shelly practiced piano each day for 35 minutes for a total of 210 minutes. How many days did she practice?

   a. 5 days
   b. 6 days
   c. 7 days
   d. not given

5. Solve.
$$4\frac{3}{5}$$
$$-1\frac{1}{3}$$

   a. $3\frac{4}{15}$
   b. $3\frac{2}{5}$
   c. $5\frac{4}{15}$
   d. not given

6. Which is *not* true about the figures?

   a. similar
   b. polygons
   c. congruent
   d. hexagons

7. Solve.
$$\begin{array}{r} \$16.25 \\ \times \quad 6 \\ \hline \end{array}$$

   a. $77.20
   b. $86.50
   c. $97.50
   d. not given

8. Solve.
$$\begin{array}{r} 6 \text{ yd. } 3 \text{ ft.} \\ +\ 4 \text{ yd. } 1 \text{ ft.} \\ \hline \end{array}$$

   a. 11 yd. 1 ft.
   b. 10 yd. 1 ft.
   c. 9 yd. 2 ft.
   d. not given

9. Solve.
$$5 \times \frac{3}{7} =$$

   a. $\frac{3}{35}$
   b. $\frac{11}{7}$
   c. $2\frac{1}{7}$
   d. not given

10. Kelly is making 8 flower baskets for some sick members of her church. If each basket requires $1\frac{1}{4}$ yards of ribbon, how much ribbon does she need?

    a. 7 yd.
    b. $8\frac{1}{4}$ yd.
    c. 9 yd.
    d. 10 yd.

Aircraft and Missions

Nate Saint took his first plane ride when he was seven years old. From that time on, he dreamed about flying. He wanted to be a military pilot, but a physical disability kept him from qualifying. Nate's dream had collapsed. Then the Lord opened another door for his flying skills—helping missionaries on foreign fields. In 1948 the Missionary Aviation Fellowship sent Nate to Ecuador. Stationed at Shell Mera, he was in a central location to fly supplies and medicines to missionaries at various posts throughout the jungle.

Several years later Nate joined four other missionaries in planning Operation Auca. The Auca Indian tribe was known for its violence and cruelty. Most white men were afraid to go near Auca settlements. But Jim Elliot, Pete Fleming, Ed McCully, and Roger Youderian believed that Nate's plane was the way to reach these Indians with the gospel.

From Nate's yellow Piper Cruiser, they lowered machetes, brightly colored buttons, and ribbons as gifts to the few Indians they could see on the ground. After making several low flights over the beach, Nate Saint landed his plane at the edge of the jungle. A few days passed. Then one morning they had a visit from three Aucas who seemed friendly. They sampled American food and examined the plane and the men. One Auca man even took a ride with Nate in the plane. Then the Indians disappeared into the jungle again. Two mornings later, a group of Auca Indians invaded the beach and killed the five missionaries.

Nate Saint's life was short, but his faith in God and his willingness to obey Him were strong. Inspired by the lives and deaths of these five missionaries, many other Christians have dedicated their lives to serve Christ in foreign countries.

CHAPTER
16

Ratio, Proportion, Percent

Small planes, like this Cessna 172, are used in missionary aviation because they can take off and land in small areas, and they are rugged and relatively easy to maintain.

A village in El Salvador, as a missionary pilot might see it on his way to a landing spot.

Ratios

A **ratio** is a comparison of the number or size of two different things. The comparisons can be part to part, part to whole, or whole to part.

The numbers of a ratio are called *terms*.

The ratio comparing the number of collies to the number of Scottish terriers can be written 3 ways. Each of these is read "two to three."

2 to 3   2:3 $\frac{2}{3}$

The first term is 2.   The second term is 3.

1. Part to part—apples to bananas   4 to 3   4:3 $\frac{4}{3}$

2. Part to whole—bananas to fruit   3 to 7   3:7 $\frac{3}{7}$

3. Whole to part—fruit to apples   7 to 4   7:4 $\frac{7}{4}$

Ratios can be used to compare numbers in a situation.
Use a ratio table to find equivalent ratios.

Lorna can buy a set of 4 books in a mystery series for $12.00. How much will 8 books cost? 12 books? 16 books?

Books	4	8	12	16
Cost	$12.00	$24.00	?	?

A set of books is purchased for every $12.00.

If 3 sets of books are purchased, then 3 × $12.00 = $36.00.
If 4 sets of books are purchased, then 4 × $12.00 = $48.00.

Practice

Write each ratio in 3 ways.

1. stars to smiley faces

2. smiley faces to stars

3. girls to boys

4. boys to children

Write each ratio in 3 ways.

5. Neal practices his trumpet 6 times in 7 days (practices:days).

6. Three pizzas can serve 5 people (pizzas:people).

7. There are 16 ounces in 1 pound (ounces:pounds).

8. You can receive 1 free gift for every product you buy (gifts:purchases).

Copy and complete each ratio table to answer the question.

9. An art teacher needs 3 bottles of glue for every 4 students. How many bottles does she need for 20 students?

Bottles	3	6	?	?	?
Students	4	8	12	16	20

10. Five plants cost $16.00. How much do 20 plants cost?

Plants	5	10	15	20	25
Cost	$16.00	?	?	?	?

Language Link

11. Do the ratios 2:7 and 7:2 describe the same thing? Why or why not? Draw a diagram to illustrate your answer.

Ratio Tables

> The first number in a ratio is called the *first term*.
> The second number in a ratio is called the *second term*.

> ### Comparing Ratios with Cross Multiplication
> 1. Multiply the second term in the second ratio times the first term in the first ratio.
> 2. Multiply the second term in the first ratio times the first term in the second ratio.

If 4 cans of water are mixed with 1 can of frozen lemonade, how many cans of water will be used with 2 cans of frozen lemonade? How many cans of water will be used with 4 cans of frozen lemonade?

Cans of frozen lemonade	1	2	3	4
Cans of water	4	8	12	16

Is 1:4 equal to 2:8, 3:12, and 4:16? Cross-multiply to find out.

⑧ ⑧   ⑫ ⑫   ⑯ ⑯

$\frac{1}{4} \times \frac{2}{8}$ $\frac{1}{4} \times \frac{3}{12}$ $\frac{1}{4} \times \frac{4}{16}$

1:4 = 2:8   1:4 = 3:12   1:4 = 4:16

Class Work

Cross-multiply to find out if the ratios are equal. Complete each number sentence using = or ≠.

1. $\frac{4}{5} \bigcirc \frac{12}{15}$ 2. $\frac{6}{9} \bigcirc \frac{4}{5}$

The symbol ≠ means "is not equal to."

Complete the tables.

3. For every 2 roses in her flower arrangement, Diane puts in 3 miniature carnations. How many roses does she need if she has 18 miniature carnations?

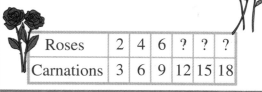

Roses	2	4	6	?	?	?
Carnations	3	6	9	12	15	18

4. With $20.00, Jason bought 3 small pizzas. How much would 12 pizzas cost?

Pizzas	3	6	9	12
Cost	$20.00	$40.00	?	?

Practice

Cross-multiply to find out if the two ratios are equal. Complete each number sentence, using a = or ≠.

1. $\frac{1}{7}$ ◯ $\frac{4}{12}$

2. $\frac{4}{5}$ ◯ $\frac{16}{20}$

3. $\frac{6}{8}$ ◯ $\frac{24}{30}$

4. $\frac{2}{8}$ ◯ $\frac{3}{8}$

5. $\frac{5}{50}$ ◯ $\frac{7}{70}$

6. $\frac{8}{37}$ ◯ $\frac{3}{14}$

Application

Make a ratio table to solve each word problem. Write and label the answer.

7. Mrs. Stegall mixes 2 cups of water with 6 cups of strawberries to make a sauce. How many cups of water will she need to use if she uses 18 cups of strawberries?

8. Shannon is making a fruit salad with 10 strawberries for every 2 bananas. She decided to use 10 bananas. How many strawberries will she use?

9. Going up in a hot air balloon for 20 minutes costs $15.00. At this rate, how long could you stay up in the balloon if you had $60.00?

10. Mr. Carlson can complete 3 projects in 14 days. How many days will it take him to complete 12 projects?

11. Two cheese crackers weigh 0.5 of an ounce. How many ounces do 10 crackers weigh?

Chapter 13 Review

Write the appropriate customary unit: *inches, feet, yards, miles.*

12. The length of a kitchen might be 18 _____ .

13. The distance from Atlanta to Cleveland is 670 _____ .

14. The width of a football field is 50 _____ .

15. The thickness of an unabridged dictionary might be 5 _____ .

Equal Ratios

> Equal ratios describe the same relationship.

You can find equal ratios by multiplying. The terms will be higher.

$$\frac{16 \text{ ounces}}{1 \text{ pound}} \longrightarrow \begin{array}{l} \frac{16 \times 2}{1 \times 2} = \frac{32}{2} \\ \frac{16 \times 3}{1 \times 3} = \frac{48}{3} \\ \frac{16 \times 4}{1 \times 4} = \frac{64}{4} \end{array} \longrightarrow \frac{16}{1} = \frac{32}{2} = \frac{48}{3} = \frac{64}{4}$$

In every instance, there are 16 ounces in every 1 pound.

You can also find equal ratios by dividing. The terms will be lower.

$$\frac{18 \text{ caramels}}{6 \text{ apples}} \longrightarrow \begin{array}{l} \frac{18 \div 2}{6 \div 2} = \frac{9}{3} \\ \frac{18 \div 3}{6 \div 3} = \frac{6}{2} \\ \frac{18 \div 6}{6 \div 6} = \frac{3}{1} \end{array} \longrightarrow \frac{18}{6} = \frac{9}{3} = \frac{6}{2} = \frac{3}{1}$$

In every instance, there are 3 caramels for every 1 apple.

Class Work

Make an equation with ratios for each word problem. Multiply or divide to solve the problems. Label the answers.

1. Mrs. Mills makes an orange crunch cake that serves 10 people. How many cakes does she need to make so she can serve 40 people?

$$\frac{1 \text{ cake}}{10 \text{ people}} = \frac{\square \text{ cakes}}{40 \text{ people}} \qquad \frac{1 \quad \times \quad ?}{10 \quad \times \quad ?} = \frac{\square}{40} \qquad \text{4 cakes}$$

2. There are 8 volleyballs for every 32 students. How many volleyballs will 16 students receive?

Practice

Find two equal ratios by multiplying.

1. $\frac{3}{7}$
2. $\frac{25}{1}$
3. $\frac{4}{60}$
4. $\frac{7}{11}$

Find two equal ratios by dividing.

5. $\frac{4}{32}$
6. $\frac{24}{16}$
7. $\frac{42}{6}$
8. $\frac{6}{42}$

Application

Make an equation with ratios for each word problem. Multiply or divide to solve the problems. Label the answer.

Example:

Mr. Horn can run around the track 2 times in 5 minutes. At this speed, how long will it take him to run around the track 8 times?

$$\frac{2\ times}{5\ minutes} = \frac{8\ times}{\Box\ minutes} \qquad \frac{2\times4}{5\times4} = \frac{8}{20} \qquad 20\ minutes$$

9. A large gear revolves 2 times in the same time that a smaller gear revolves 3 times. How many times will the small gear revolve if the large gear revolves 20 times?

10. Six fluid ounces of instant drink mix contain 80 calories. How many calories are in 3 ounces of instant drink mix?

11. Twenty-five formal envelopes can be purchased for $5.00. At this rate, how much do 50 envelopes cost?

12. Seventy pamphlets cost $28.00. At this rate, how much do 10 pamphlets cost?

13. Nine cans of corn cost $2.70. At this rate, how much do 3 cans of corn cost?

Scale Drawings

A **scale drawing** is a representational drawing of an actual object. It can be larger or smaller than the actual object.

This is a scale drawing of Katie's house.

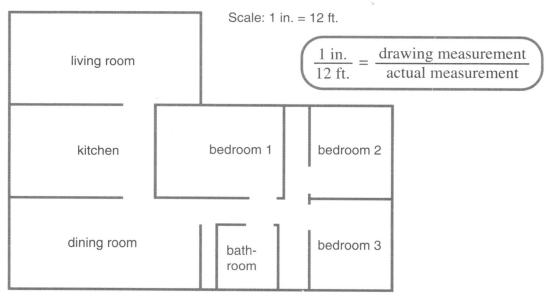

Scale: 1 in. = 12 ft.

$$\frac{1 \text{ in.}}{12 \text{ ft.}} = \frac{\text{drawing measurement}}{\text{actual measurement}}$$

Class Work

Make an equal ratio to solve each problem.

1. The length of the dining room is 2 inches. What is the actual length?

   $\frac{1}{12} = \frac{2}{\square}$ $\frac{1 \times 2}{12 \times 2} =$

2. The length of the outside wall from the dining room to bedroom 3 is actually 48 feet. What is the length on the drawing?

   $\frac{1}{12} = \frac{\square}{48}$ $\frac{1}{12} \times \frac{4}{4} =$

Practice

Multiply to find two equal ratios.

1. $\frac{3}{21}$
2. $\frac{9}{4}$
3. $\frac{5}{16}$
4. $\frac{25}{7}$

Divide to find two equal ratios.

5. $\frac{48}{16}$
6. $\frac{63}{21}$
7. $\frac{8}{12}$
8. $\frac{60}{15}$

Application

Write an equation with ratios for each word problem. Multiply or divide the ratios to solve. Write and label the answer.

9. A nursing school employs 70 teachers. There are 420 students. How many students are there for every 10 teachers?

10. On a map, 1 centimeter represents 50 kilometers. How many kilometers will 4 centimeters represent?

11. A room in an office building is 10 meters long. On a scale drawing with a scale of 1 cm = 5 m, how long will this room be?

Use the scale and the drawing to answer the questions. Write the equations you use.

12. The kitchen is really 20 feet long. Without using a ruler, find how long it is in the drawing.

13. What is the actual length of the outside wall from the bathroom to the kitchen?

14. The deck outside is 15 feet long. If it were in the drawing, how long would it be?

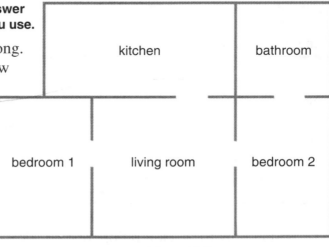

kitchen   bathroom

bedroom 1   living room   bedroom 2

1 in. = 10 ft.

Proportions

An homer of barley seed shall be valued at fifty shekels of silver.
Leviticus 27:16

An homer was equal to 58 gallons.
What was the worth of 29 gallons of barley seed?

$$\frac{58 \text{ gallons}}{50 \text{ shekels}} = \frac{29 \text{ gallons}}{\square \text{ shekels}} \qquad \frac{58 \div 2}{50 \div 2} = \frac{29}{25}$$

29 gallons of barley seed was worth 25 shekels.

> A **proportion** is an equation that states that two ratios are equal.

> Use an n in a proportion to solve word problems in which you cannot multiply or divide by a whole number to find an unknown term.

Step 1
Write a proportion.
$$\frac{\$5.00}{2 \text{ hours}} = \frac{n}{7 \text{ hours}}$$

Rachel was paid $5.00 for baby-sitting 2 hours. At this rate, how much would she earn if she baby-sat for 7 hours?

Step 2
Cross-multiply.
Multiply known factors.
$$7 \times \$5.00 = 2 \times n$$
$$\$35.00 = 2 \times n$$

Step 3
Write a division equation to find the missing factor.
$$\$35.00 \div 2 = n$$

Step 4
Solve for n.
$$\$17.50 = n$$

Step 5
Rewrite the proportion.
Substitute the answer for n.
$$\frac{\$5.00}{2 \text{ hours}} = \frac{\$17.50}{7 \text{ hours}}$$

Step 6
Cross-multiply to check if ratios are equivalent.

$$\widehat{\$35.00} \qquad \widehat{\$35.00}$$
$$\frac{\$5.00}{2 \text{ hours}} \times \frac{\$17.50}{7 \text{ hours}}$$

Practice

Complete the proportions using the steps from page 350.

1. $\frac{6}{21} = \frac{n}{70}$ 2. $\frac{10}{75} = \frac{n}{60}$ 3. $\frac{42}{18} = \frac{126}{n}$ 4. $\frac{8}{15} = \frac{n}{120}$

5. $\frac{20}{6} = \frac{50}{n}$ 6. $\frac{4}{18} = \frac{18}{n}$ 7. $\frac{192}{4} = \frac{n}{9}$ 8. $\frac{2}{38} = \frac{5}{n}$

Application

**Write a proportion for each word problem.
Solve for *n*. Label your answers.**

9. Paula can read 8 pages in 10 minutes. At that rate, how many pages can she read in 25 minutes?

10. Two stickers cost $0.40. At this price, what will the cost of 5 stickers be?

11. A pharmacist must prepare an ointment that has 9 grams of substance A and 12 grams of substance B. If she makes a larger amount of the ointment so that there are 21 grams of substance A, how many grams of substance B will the ointment contain?

Chapter 13 Review

Rename the units of weight.

12. 6,000 lb. = _____ tn.

13. 5 tn. = _____ lb.

14. 64 oz. = _____ lb.

15. 3 lb. = _____ oz.

Ratios and Percents

Joanna took a written test which had 100 questions. She answered 91 of the questions correctly.

Each of these 100 squares represents 1 of the 100 questions on Joanna's test. Ninety-one of the squares are green. These represent Joanna's correct answers.

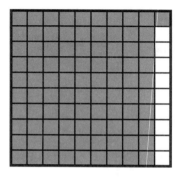

The ratio of green squares to total squares is 91 to 100. This can also be written 91:100 or $\frac{91}{100}$.

A ratio in which the second term is 100 can be written as a percent (*per* means "for each," and *cent* means "100"). The sign for percent is %.

Joanna answered 91% of the questions correctly.

A ratio can be written as a percent.

$$\frac{5}{100} = 5\%$$

$$\frac{40}{100} = 40\%$$

$$\frac{65}{100} = 65\%$$

You can write a percent as a ratio.

$$20\% = \frac{20}{100}$$

$$89\% = \frac{89}{100}$$

$$7\% = \frac{7}{100}$$

Practice

Write each ratio as a percent.

1. $\frac{45}{100}$ 2. $\frac{19}{100}$

3. $\frac{90}{100}$ 4. $\frac{8}{100}$

5. 11 per hundred

6. 38:100   7. $\frac{1}{100}$

8. 60:100

9. 100 out of 100

10. 97 for each 100

Write each percent as a ratio in fraction form.

11. 24%   12. 3%   13. 46%   14. 50%

15. 99%   16. 75%   17. 40%   18. 7%

19. 10%   20. 68%   21. 27%   22. 86%

Application

One hundred students were surveyed to find what flavor of ice cream they prefer. This square shows the number of students who preferred each flavor: chocolate (brown), vanilla (white), mint chocolate chip (green), or strawberry (red).

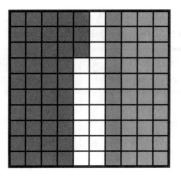

Using the survey information, write a ratio and a percent to compare the part to the whole.

23. chocolate   24. strawberry   25. vanilla   26. mint chocolate chip

Percents and Common Fractions

Percents can be written as common fractions, and fractions can be written as percents.

$\frac{14}{100}$ = 14 out of 100 or 14 per 100

$\frac{14}{100}$ = 14%

Changing a Percent to a Fraction in Lowest Terms

1. Rename the percent as a fraction with 100 as the denominator.
2. Rename in lowest terms by dividing by the greatest common factor (GCF).

$$28\% = \frac{28 \div 4}{100 \div 4} = \frac{7}{25}$$

Changing a Fraction to a Percent

1. Set up a proportion. $\frac{36}{40} = \frac{n}{100}$

or

2. Cross-multiply and divide.
$100 \times 36 = 40 \times n$
$3{,}600 = 40 \times n$
$3{,}600 \div 40 = n$
$90 = n$
$\frac{36}{40} = \frac{90}{100} = 90\%$

1. Set up a proportion. $\frac{7}{20} = \frac{n}{100}$

2. Multiply the fraction by a fractional name for 1 if the denominator is a factor of 100.

$$\frac{7 \times 5}{20 \times 5} = \frac{35}{100} = 35\%$$

Class Work

Copy and complete the chart.

Mr. Alexander's class surveyed 100 students to find their favorite Bible character. The table shows the results of the survey.

Bible character	Percentage of students	Percentage as a fraction	Divide or multiply	Fraction in lowest terms
Moses	16%	$\frac{16}{100}$	$\frac{16 \div 4}{100 \div 4} = \frac{4}{25}$	$\frac{4}{25}$
Esther	15%	$\frac{15}{100}$	$\frac{15 \div 5}{100 \div 5} =$	
David	30%	$\frac{30}{100}$		
Joseph	25%			
Daniel			$\frac{1 \times 10}{10 \times 10} = \frac{}{100}$	$\frac{1}{10}$
other				$\frac{1}{25}$

Practice

Write each percent as a fraction with 100 as the denominator.

1. 33%   2. 12%   3. 5%   4. 80%

5. 26%   6. 74%   7. 60%   8. 8%

Write each percent as a fraction. Rename in lowest terms if necessary.

9. 50%   10. 20%   11. 39%   12. 10%

13. 75%   14. 24%   15. 8%   16. 83%

Write each fraction as a percent.

17. $\frac{6}{10}$ 18. $\frac{1}{4}$ 19. $\frac{3}{5}$ 20. $\frac{11}{20}$ 21. $\frac{2}{25}$ 22. $\frac{4}{5}$

Percents and Decimal Fractions

Percents can be written as decimal fractions,
and decimal fractions can be written as percents.

This circle graph and table show the percent of earth's land contained in each of the seven continents.

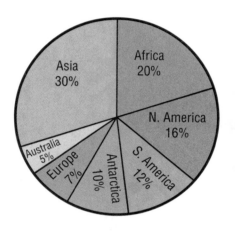

Continent	Percent	Common fraction	Decimal fraction
Asia	30%	$\frac{30}{100}$	0.30
Africa	20%	$\frac{20}{100}$	0.20
North America	16%	$\frac{16}{100}$	0.16
South America	12%	$\frac{12}{100}$	0.12
Antarctica	10%	$\frac{10}{100}$	0.10
Europe	7%	$\frac{7}{100}$	0.07
Australia	5%	$\frac{5}{100}$	0.05

This circle graph and table show the distribution of earth's water.

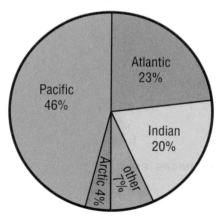

Earth's water	Decimal fraction	Common fraction	Percent
Pacific Ocean	0.46	$\frac{46}{100}$	46%
Atlantic Ocean	0.23	$\frac{23}{100}$	23%
Indian Ocean	0.20	$\frac{20}{100}$	20%
other	0.07	$\frac{7}{100}$	7%
Arctic Ocean	0.04	$\frac{4}{100}$	4%

Have ye not known? have ye not heard? hath it not been told you from the beginning? have ye not understood from the foundations of the earth? It is he that sitteth upon the circle of the earth.
Isaiah 40:21-22

Practice

Write each percent as a common fraction and as a decimal.

Example: $17\% = \frac{17}{100} = 0.17$

1. 32%
2. 50%
3. 67%
4. 9%
5. 24%
6. 1%
7. 10%
8. 40%

Write each decimal as a common fraction and a percent.

Example: $0.43 = \frac{43}{100} = 43\%$

9. 0.60
10. 0.11
11. 0.79
12. 0.06
13. 0.72
14. 0.03
15. 0.90
16. 0.44

Write each percent as a decimal and each decimal as a percent.

Example: $3\% = 0.03$ $0.87 = 87\%$

17. 2%
18. 0.99
19. 91%
20. 0.75
21. 0.54
22. 0.07
23. 89%
24. 33%

Chapter 9 Review

Solve.

25. $12\overline{)\$3.96}$

26. $25\overline{)\$30.75}$

27. $18\overline{)\$11.52}$

Percent of a Number

To find a percent of a number, solve a proportion *or* multiply the number by the decimal fraction (percent).

Proportion Method
Percent becomes a common fraction

20% of 475

$$\frac{20}{100} = \frac{n}{475}$$
$$475 \times 20 = 100 \times n$$
$$9{,}500 = 100 \times n$$
$$9{,}500 \div 100 = n$$
$$95 = n$$
20% of 475 = 95

Multiplication Method
Percent becomes a decimal fraction

$$
\begin{array}{ccc}
20\% & \text{of} & 475 \\
\downarrow & \downarrow & \downarrow \\
0.20 & \times & 475
\end{array}
= \longrightarrow
\begin{array}{r}
475 \\
\times 0.20 \\
\hline
95.00
\end{array}
$$

20% of 475 = 95

To find the price of a discounted item, find the amount of the discount and subtract it from the regular price.

Joel wants to buy a baseball. The regular price is \$3.80. The baseball is on sale for 15% off. What is the discounted price?

1. Find the amount of the discount. (Joel prefers the multiplication method.)

   15% of \$3.80 = 0.15 × \$3.80 $\longrightarrow$
   15% of \$3.80 = \$0.57

$$
\begin{array}{r}
\$3.80 \\
\times 0.15 \\
\hline
1900 \\
+3800 \\
\hline
\$0.5700
\end{array}
$$

2. Subtract the discount from the regular price.

   \$3.80 − \$0.57 = $\longrightarrow$

$$
\begin{array}{r}
\$3.80 \\
-0.57 \\
\hline
\$3.23
\end{array}
$$

   The baseball costs \$3.23.

Practice

Find the percent of a number using the proportion method.

1. 25% of 96   **2.** 18% of 50   **3.** 95% of 20   **4.** 15% of 80

Find the percent of a number using the multiplication method.

5. 30% of 80   **6.** 20% of 30   **7.** 4% of 50   **8.** 25% of 12

Application

Write an equation for each word problem. Solve and label.

9. Sixty percent of the students in Mrs. Simpson's class are boys. There are 30 students in the class. How many are boys?

10. A company employed 130 workers. Out of these, 30% worked on Saturday. How many employees worked on Saturday?

11. Janiece earned $175.00. She gave 12% of it to the church missionary fund. How much did she give?

12. Fly-In Airlines offered 30% off all flights during the summer. Julie wanted to buy a ticket that was regularly priced at $220.00. How much was taken off the regular price?

13. Jody's Bike Shop has 50 bicycles for sale. Seventy percent of these bikes are ten-speeds. How many of the bikes are ten-speeds?

14. Phil has a coupon for a 40% discount on hiking boots. If the boots regularly cost $67.00, how much will Phil pay?

25% of $10.00 is the same as 10% of $25.00. The discount is $2.50.

> ## Did you know . . .
>
> 80% of 45 is the same as 45% of 80 because multiplication is commutative.

Group Problem Solving: Probability

Problem: Predict the results of a probability experiment. Test your predictions by using the spinner to conduct a probability experiment. Record your results on a table.

Information: Look at the spinner. Predict the results of a probability experiment by answering the questions. Write the probability as a percent.

Use the diagram to predict the answers to the questions.

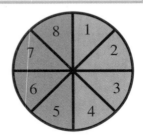

1. What is the probability that the spinner will land on red?

2. What is the probability that the spinner will land on an odd number?

3. What is the probability that the spinner will land on a blue even number?

Conduct a probability experiment to see if your predictions were correct.

Step 1   Make and color a spinner like the one above. Use your pencil and a paper clip for spinning.

Step 2   Make a tally chart like the one shown.

Step 3   Spin 100 times. Make a tally mark beside the number on the chart for each spin. (Your chart should have 100 tally marks on it.)

Step 4   Find the frequency for each number.

Number	Tallies	Frequency
1		
2		
3		
4		
5		
6		
7		
8		

Use the frequency table to answer the questions.

4. What is the total number of tallies for red numbers? Write this number as a ratio and a percent.

5. What is the total number of tallies for odd numbers? Write this number as a ratio and a percent.

6. What is the total number of tallies for a blue even number? Write this number as a ratio and a percent.

How do your findings compare with your predictions?

Follow the directions to perform a probability experiment.

1. Design your own spinner.
   - Use a compass to draw a circle.
   - Divide your circle into equal parts.
   - You may color the parts of the spinner any color.
   - You many also use numbers or letters.

2. Write your own questions for predicting the probability. Answer the questions by expressing the probability as a percent.

3. Test your predictions by conducting a probability experiment using the new spinner. Record the results of your experiment on a table using tally marks. (Your table should have 100 tally marks.)

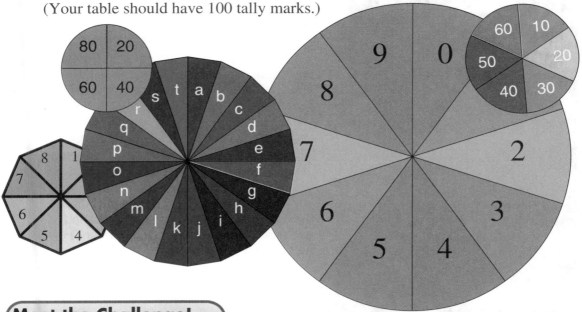

Meet the Challenge!

Use the spinner on page 360 to answer the problem.

4. If you spin twice, what is the probability that the 2 numbers you land on will add up to 10? (Hint: Multiply to find the number of possible combinations [Cartesian product] when you spin twice. Determine how many of the combinations add up to 10. Round your answer to the nearest whole number. Write the probability as a percent.)

Dear Fifth Grade:

When our Italian restaurant is catering a dinner party or a wedding reception, I need to get an estimate of how many people will be attending to make sure we have more than enough food. Last week we catered an anniversary dinner for a pastor and his wife. About four hundred people were expected. We always allow for unexpected guests and for those who might want seconds and thirds on salad or garlic bread. Sometimes we offer several different choices of entrees. That particular night we offered a choice of manicotti, lasagne, or chicken parmesana. I had to estimate the number of each entree I needed to bring. When we cater a dinner, our chef must know ahead of time how many entrees to prepare.

Finally, I added up our costs to determine how much to charge the church giving the dinner. Costs vary depending on how many people attend the dinner and which entrees are served. I multiply our food costs by 3.5 to determine how much to charge our customer. That will cover our labor, delivery, and setup costs and will allow us a profit. So you can see that my job involves a lot of counting, adding, and estimating. When my part in the preparation is finished, I like going to the location and overseeing the dinner. Watching everyone enjoy the meal gives me the good feeling that I've done my job well—almost like the feeling I get after solving a difficult math problem!

Yours truly,

Charissa Mace

Charissa Mace

Caterer

Giordano's
755 Tonkawa Road
Ponca City, OK 74601

Moore Christian School
334 Tara Lane
Mariposa, CA 95338

Chapter Review

Write each ratio in three ways.

Example: dogs to cats $3:1$ 3 to 1 $\frac{3}{1}$

1. circles to pentagons

2. pentagons to circles

3. shapes to circles

4. pentagons to shapes

5. red shapes to blue shapes

6. blue shapes to green shapes

7. green shapes to red shapes

8. red circles to red pentagons

Cross-multiply to find out if the two ratios are equal. Complete each number sentence using = or ≠.

9. $\frac{5}{16} \bigcirc \frac{2}{6}$

10. $\frac{9}{60} \bigcirc \frac{6}{40}$

11. $\frac{3}{12} \bigcirc \frac{9}{36}$

12. $\frac{3}{8} \bigcirc \frac{11}{24}$

13. $\frac{4}{14} \bigcirc \frac{10}{35}$

14. $\frac{15}{60} \bigcirc \frac{25}{100}$

Find two equal ratios by multiplying.

15. $\frac{12}{5}$

16. $\frac{2}{\$1.10}$

17. $\frac{5}{3}$

Find two equal ratios by dividing.

18. $\frac{120}{40}$

19. $\frac{\$70.00}{28}$

20. $\frac{50}{30}$

Write each percent as a ratio, common fraction, and decimal fraction for each percent.

21. 70%

22. 4%

23. 98%

24. 1%

Copy and complete the ratio table to answer the questions.

Roses	2	4	6	8
Cost	$3.00	?	?	?

25. How much do 6 roses cost?

26. How many roses can be purchased for $12.00?

Find the percent of a number by using the proportion method.

27. Twenty percent of Mrs. McCauley's students bought hot lunch. There are 25 students in the class. How many bought hot lunch?

28. Forty-five people came to the family reunion. Of these, 60% traveled to the reunion by airplane. How many people came by airplane?

Find the percent of a number by using the multiplication method.

29. 70% of 70   **30.** 30% of 80   **31.** 60% of 90

Write a proportion for each word problem. Solve for *n*. Label the answer.

32. If you travel at a rate of 94 miles in 2 hours, how many miles can you travel in 6 hours?

33. With $4.00 you can buy 30 invitations. At this rate, how many invitations can you buy with $6.00?

34. For every 18 students, a teacher needs 9 paint sets. How many students will use 5 paint sets?

35. A chicken costs $3.00 for 4 pounds. At this rate, how much will 10 pounds of chicken cost?

Cumulative Review

Write the letter of the correct answer.

1. Which is *not* a multiple of 8?

   a. 32   c. 56
   b. 24   d. 42

2. Rick ran 1 mile in 6.5 minutes. Bill ran the mile in 6.48 minutes. Who had the better time, and what was the difference in their times?

   a. Rick, 0.2 min.
   b. Bill, 0.02 min.
   c. Rick, 0.18 min.
   d. Bill, 0.18 min.

3. Solve.

   $$23\overline{)9,314}$$

   a. 404 r22   c. 268 r3
   b. 305 r20   d. not given

4. Which fraction is not simplified?

   a. $\frac{3}{7}$ c. $\frac{36}{18}$
   b. $\frac{11}{32}$ d. $\frac{7}{16}$

5. What is true about a parallelogram and a rhombus?

   a. quadrilaterals
   b. congruent
   c. similar
   d. all of the above

6. Which division equation does *not* have a repeating decimal?

   a. $5.6 \div 6$ c. $64 \div 8$
   b. $3 \div 9$ d. $2 \div 9$

7. Solve.

   43 oz. =

   a. 1 lb. 11 oz.   c. 2 lb. 1 oz.
   b. 1 lb. 12 oz.   d. not given

8. Solve.

   $$\frac{3}{9} \times \frac{2}{8} =$$

   a. $\frac{5}{17}$ c. $\frac{3}{72}$
   b. $\frac{4}{36}$ d. $\frac{1}{12}$

Kevin's Math Quiz Scores

quiz	1	2	3	4	5	6	7	8	9	10
Kevin	90	95	85	86	98	95	96	95	93	90

9. What is the mode for Kevin's quiz scores?

   a. 90   c. 96
   b. 95   d. 98

10. What is the median for Kevin's quiz scores?

    a. 85   c. 94
    b. 91   d. 95

Test Flying

Before an airplane can be sold, it must be tested to make sure it is in proper working order. The only way to truly test a plane is to fly it.

Of course, every possible precaution is taken before a plane ever leaves the ground. Test pilots, more than any other type of pilot, must be careful and thorough in doing their preflight inspections.

There are several different types of test flying occupations. Test pilots are needed in airplane manufacturing firms to test newly assembled planes before they can be sold. Airlines also hire test pilots to test newly purchased airplanes or airplanes that have just been overhauled. Experimental pilots test new designs of aircraft or test planes to see how they will react in various condi-

tions. Many times pilots who test fly experimental planes have experience in engineering so that they are very familiar with how the plane works.

Once a plane is in the air, pilots must test the different instruments to see that they are functioning properly. Sometimes they must also take the plane through difficult maneuvers in the air to test its reaction to stress. Often planes have to be flown under adverse conditions, and test pilots must practice dives, high-speed landings, and aborted takeoffs.

Test flying can be a hazardous occupation. A test pilot must be willing to risk his own safety to make a plane safe for others.

CHAPTER
17

Time and Money: Consumer Applications

Sometimes a person who builds from a kit his own airplane, like this Berkut, will hire a test pilot to make sure it meets the expected safety and performance standards before he starts flying it himself.

Telling and Renaming Time

Knowing how to tell time is an important skill. You need to know when it is time to get up, to go to school, to go to church, to ride to soccer practice, to go to your music lesson, to go home for dinner, or to get ready for bed. Parents and teachers need to know when to go to work and when to pick up their children from school. We need to know what time it is for most activities in our lives.

The 24 hours of each day are divided into A.M. times and P.M. times.

midnight		noon		midnight

$$\underset{12 \text{ hours}}{\text{A.M.}} \quad + \quad \underset{12 \text{ hours}}{\text{P.M.}} \quad = \quad 24 \text{ hours} \quad = \quad 1 \text{ day}$$

Class Work

Tell the time.

1.

2.

3.

Remember!   1 minute (min.) = 60 seconds (sec.)
1 hour (hr.) = 60 min.
1 day = 24 hr.

Multiply to rename larger units as smaller units.

4 hours = _____ minutes

Think: 1 hr. = 60 min.
$4 \times 60 = 240$

4 hours = 240 minutes

Divide to rename smaller units as larger units.

48 hours = _____ days

Think: 24 hr. = 1 day
$48 \div 24 = 2$

48 hours = 2 days

Practice

Write the time.

Example: 10:50;

1. 2. 3. 4.

Write A.M. or P.M. for each activity.

5. Joanne played throughout the day until 7:00.

6. After supper, Micah read a book until 6:00.

7. Stephen slept until 8:40.

8. Annette watched the sun rise at 5:25.

Complete the number sentences.

9. 1 minute = _____ seconds

10. 4 minutes = _____ seconds

11. 1 hour = _____ minutes

12. 180 seconds = _____ minutes

13. 1 day = _____ hours

14. 48 hours = _____ days

15. 2 minutes = _____ seconds

16. 5 hours = _____ minutes

17. 420 minutes = _____ hours

18. 3 days = _____ hours

 Chapter 14 Review

Solve. Simplify in lowest terms.

19. $5 \times \frac{3}{5} =$

20. $7 \times \frac{4}{9} =$

21. $3 \times \frac{1}{6} =$

22. $4 \times \frac{4}{6} =$

Add or Subtract Time

Addition

If the number of minutes is 60 or more, rename as hours.

Mrs. Hansen pays Sandra to rake leaves. On Friday Sandra raked for 1 hr. 55 min. On Saturday she raked for 1 hr. 37 min. How long did she rake in the 2 days together?

Add the minutes.   Rename if necessary.
Add the hours.

```
  1 hr. 55 min.     2 hr. 92 min. = 3 hr. 32 min.
+ 1 hr. 37 min.
  2 hr. 92 min.
```

Subtraction

If there are not enough minutes in the minuend, rename 1 hour as 60 minutes.

Chad spent 3 hr. 15 min. at the zoo. He spent 1 hr. 40 min. in the reptile house, his favorite part of the zoo. How much time did he spend in the other parts of the zoo?

3 hr. 15 min. – 1 hr. 40 min. =

Rename if necessary.
Subtract the minutes, then the hours.

```
    2   75
  3 hr. 15 min.
- 1 hr. 40 min.
  1 hr. 35 min.
```

Practice

Add or subtract the time.

1. 2 hr. 55 min.
     +   26 min.

2. 2 hr. 37 min.
     – 1 hr. 55 min.

3. 4 hr. 25 min.
     – 1 hr. 44 min.

4. 2 hr. 40 min.
     + 2 hr. 35 min.

There are 24 time zones around the world. Six of these time zones are in the United States. When you travel from east to west, the time moves back one hour each time you cross a time zone boundary.

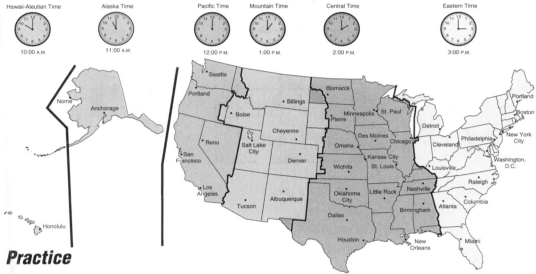

Practice

Complete the sentences. Write A.M. or P.M. (Hint: Subtract when traveling west; add when traveling east.)

1. If it is 5:00 P.M. in Nome, Alaska, it is _____ in Pierre, S. Dak.

2. If it is 8:00 P.M. in Boston, Mass., it is _____ in Tucson, Ariz.

To find out how much time has elapsed, count the elapsed hours first, then count the remaining time in minutes.

Irene began working in the yard at 2:10 P.M. and completed the job at 4:45 P.M. How long did Irene work in the yard?

2:10 to 3:10 = 1 hr.   3:10 to 4:10 = 1 hr.   4:10 to 4:45 = 35 min.
Irene worked 2 hr. 35 min.

Write the amount of time that has elapsed or the time that is described.

3. 2:00 P.M. to 4:57 P.M.

4. 9:15 P.M. to 12:35 A.M.

5. 11:25 A.M. to 2:50 P.M.

6. 1 hr. 15 min. before 4:30 P.M.

7. 4 hr. 38 min. after 10:02 A.M.

8. 5 hr. 40 min. after 9:30 P.M.

Calendar

January, March, May, July, August, October, and December have 31 days.
April, June, September, and November have 30 days.
February has 28 days, except in leap years, when it has 29 days.

♥	February	♥				
S	M	T	W	Th	F	S
	1	2	3	4	5	
6	7	8	9	10	11	12
13	14	15	16	17	18	19
20	21	22	23	24	25	26
27	28					

March						
S	M	T	W	Th	F	S
	1	2	3	4	5	
6	7	8	9	10	11	12
13	14	15	16	17	18	19
20	21	22	23	24	25	26
27	28	29	30	31		

April						
S	M	T	W	Th	F	S
					1	2
3	4	5	6	7	8	9
10	11	12	13	14	15	16
17	18	19	20	21	22	23
24	25	26	27	28	29	30

*While the earth remaineth, seedtime and
harvest, and cold and heat, and summer and
winter, and day and night shall not cease.*
Genesis 8:22

Practice

Use the calendars above to answer the questions.

1. Are these months from a leap year calendar?

2. What is the fourth Monday in April?

3. Which day of the week is March 24?

4. How many Tuesdays are in February?

Dates can be written in number form.

June 30, 2009 ⟶ 6/30/09
(6th month) (30th day) (last two digits of year)

Write these dates in number form.

5. May 6, 1996

6. August 31, 1999

7. January 1, 1998

8. September 9, 2004

9. July 18, 2012

10. December 13, 2008

Time Line

Remember the basic units of time.

1 week = 7 days	1 decade = 10 years
1 year = 365 days, 52 weeks, or 12 months	1 century = 100 years
1 leap year = 366 days	1 millennium = 1,000 years

Complete the number sentences.

1. 8 weeks = _____ days

2. 48 months = _____ years

3. 6 years = _____ months

4. 2 decades = _____ years

5. 3 years = _____ weeks

6. 3 centuries = _____ years

7. 21 days = _____ weeks

8. 260 weeks = _____ years

9. 4 millennia = _____ years

10. $1\frac{1}{2}$ years = _____ months

A time line shows the chronological sequence of events. This time line shows information about two famous musicians.

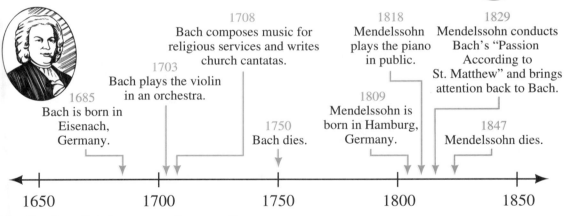

1708
Bach composes music for religious services and writes church cantatas.

1818
Mendelssohn plays the piano in public.

1829
Mendelssohn conducts Bach's "Passion According to St. Matthew" and brings attention back to Bach.

1703
Bach plays the violin in an orchestra.

1685
Bach is born in Eisenach, Germany.

1750
Bach dies.

1809
Mendelssohn is born in Hamburg, Germany.

1847
Mendelssohn dies.

1650   1700   1750   1800   1850

Use the time line to answer the questions.

11. How old was Mendelssohn when he died?

12. How many years elapsed between Bach's beginning to compose religious music and Mendelssohn's conducting "Passion According to St. Matthew"?

13. How many years before Mendelssohn's birth was Bach born?

14. How many years have elapsed since Bach's death?

Checking Account

Checks can be used instead of cash to make payments. When your mom or dad writes a check to the church for their tithe, the church deposits it into its bank account. Then the bank transfers the money from your parents' account to the church's account. It is important for anyone writing a check to keep very careful records of checks written!

Parts of a check

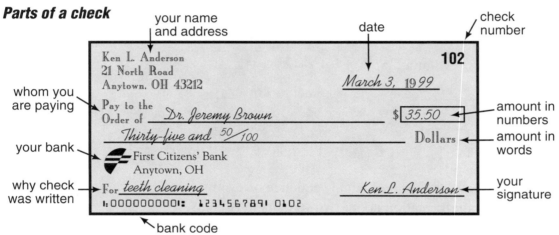

Check register

1999 Date	Check Number	Checks Issued to or Deposits Received From	Amount of Deposit		Amount of Check		Balance	
							571	15
2-21	101	Calvary Church			25	75	545	40
2-26		Paycheck	210	53			755	93
3-1		Birthday present	40	50			796	43
3-3	102	Dr. Jeremy Brown			35	50	760	93

Class Work

Use the check and register above to answer the questions.

1. On what date did Mr. Anderson pay Dr. Brown?

2. What was the amount of Mr. Anderson's paycheck?

3. Why did Mr. Anderson visit the dentist?

4. What was the number of the check written to the church?

5. What was Mr. Anderson's bank balance on February 26?

Practice

Use the information given to complete the checking account register and checks given to you by your teacher.

1. Start a checking account by depositing $624.55 in the bank on March 1, 1999.

2. On March 15 write your first check to Hadley & Co. for car insurance. The check will be $65.00.

3. On March 17 write a check for $95.66 to Paisley Power for your electric bill.

4. You receive a $5.95 refund by mail from Pierson's Products. You deposit it on March 18.

5. At Mr. Clipper's, the hair styling shop, you pay $8.05 for a haircut on March 21.

6. On March 25 write a check to pay your veterinarian, Dr. Panosian, $57.24 for your dog Whisker's visit.

7. You deposit your paycheck on March 26. The paycheck is $220.97.

8. On March 31, you deposit your federal tax refund of $213.86.

Chapter 14 Review

Solve. Simplify in lowest terms.

9. $4 \times 1\frac{2}{5} =$

10. $5 \times 2\frac{3}{8} =$

11. $6 \times 4\frac{1}{2} =$

12. $8 \times 2\frac{4}{7} =$

Sales Tax

Sales tax is the amount of money a customer pays to the state for each item he buys. Businesses add the tax on to the price of the item and then send the sales tax to the state. Most states collect sales taxes. A state with a 5% sales tax collects 5 cents in tax for each dollar spent. Does your state collect sales tax? What is the percentage rate?

This table shows the amount of tax that would be paid in a state that charges a 5% sales tax.

5% Sales Tax Table

Price Range	Tax
$ 0.10 –$ 0.29	$ 0.01
0.30 – 0.49	0.02
0.50 – 0.69	0.03
0.70 – 0.89	0.04
0.90 – 1.09	0.05
1.10 – 1.29	0.06
1.30 – 1.49	0.07
1.50 – 1.69	0.08
1.70 – 1.89	0.09
1.90 – 2.09	0.10
2.10 – 2.29	0.11
2.30 – 2.49	0.12
2.50 – 2.69	0.13
2.70 – 2.89	0.14
2.90 – 3.09	0.15
3.10 – 3.29	0.16
3.30 – 3.49	0.17
3.50 – 3.69	0.18

Steps for Finding the Total Cost

1. Find the subtotal.
2. Find the sales tax.
3. Add the subtotal and the sales tax.

SAVE–A–BUNCH
GROCERY

Tasty toothpaste .97
Softouch tissue .99
Cleano detergent .87

$$\begin{array}{r} \$0.97 \\ 0.99 \\ +0.87 \\ \hline \$2.83 \end{array} \text{ subtotal}$$

$$\begin{array}{r} +0.14 \\ \hline \$2.97 \end{array} \begin{array}{l} \text{tax} \\ \text{total} \end{array}$$

If you do not have a tax table, find the sales tax by renaming the percentage rate to a decimal fraction and multiplying the percentage rate (decimal fraction) times the subtotal. Round to the nearest hundredth (penny).

Marcy bought a teddy bear for $4.68 in a state that charges 4% sales tax. What is the total cost of the bear?

$$\begin{array}{r} \$4.68 \\ \times 0.04 \\ \hline 0.1872 \end{array}$$

round to $0.19

$$\begin{array}{r} \$4.68 \\ +0.19 \\ \hline \$4.87 \end{array}$$

The total cost of the bear is $4.87.

Practice

Use the tax table to find the sales tax for each item.

1. $1.25

2. $5.25

3.  Deluxe $8.99 CHESS game set

4.  $6.67

5.  $0.78

6.  CHOCOLATE CHIP COOKIES $2.49

Use the tax table to find the total price (subtotal plus tax) of each group of items.

7. mug, ruler, shampoo

8. cookies, mug

9. chess set, ruler

Find the sales tax for each item. (Notice the different sales tax rates before calculating.) Write the equations you used.

10.

$10.57 (7% tax)

11. My Memories

$7.64 (6%)

12. Unsalted CRACKERS

$2.49 (4%)

13.

$3.95 (8%)

14.

$39.95 (3%)

15. Student Dictionary

$8.87 (5%)

6% Sales Tax Table	
Price Range	Tax
$ 0.10 – $0.24	$ 0.01
0.25 – 0.41	0.02
0.42 – 0.58	0.03
0.59 – 0.74	0.04
0.75 – 0.91	0.05
0.92 – 1.08	0.06
1.09 – 1.24	0.07
1.25 – 1.41	0.08
1.42 – 1.58	0.09
1.59 – 1.74	0.10
1.75 – 1.91	0.11
1.92 – 2.08	0.12
2.09 – 2.24	0.13
2.25 – 2.41	0.14
2.42 – 2.58	0.15
2.59 – 2.74	0.16
2.75 – 2.91	0.17
2.92 – 3.08	0.18
3.09 – 3.24	0.19
3.25 – 3.41	0.20
3.42 – 3.58	0.21
3.59 – 3.74	0.22
3.75 – 3.91	0.23
3.92 – 4.08	0.24
4.09 – 4.24	0.25
4.25 – 4.41	0.26
4.42 – 4.58	0.27
4.59 – 4.74	0.28
4.75 – 4.91	0.29
4.92 – 5.08	0.30
5.09 – 5.24	0.31
5.25 – 5.41	0.32
5.42 – 5.58	0.33
5.59 – 5.74	0.34
5.75 – 5.91	0.35
5.92 – 6.08	0.36
6.09 – 6.24	0.37
6.25 – 6.41	0.38
6.42 – 6.58	0.39
6.59 – 6.74	0.40
6.75 – 6.91	0.41
6.92 – 7.08	0.42
7.09 – 7.24	0.43
7.25 – 7.41	0.44
7.42 – 7.58	0.45
7.59 – 7.74	0.46
7.75 – 7.91	0.47
7.92 – 8.08	0.48
8.09 – 8.24	0.49
8.25 – 8.41	0.50
8.42 – 8.58	0.51
8.59 – 8.74	0.52
8.75 – 8.91	0.53
8.92 – 9.08	0.54
9.09 – 9.24	0.55
9.25 – 9.41	0.56
9.42 – 9.58	0.57
9.59 – 9.74	0.58
9.75 – 9.91	0.59
9.92 – 10.08	0.60

Money deposited into a savings account will earn interest. Many banks will credit interest to a savings account every quarter (3 months). The percent varies among banks, but it is advertised at a yearly rate.

Heather opened a savings account at the Trust Savings Bank on July 10, 1998, with a deposit of $265.41. On August 19 she deposited $302.48. On October 8 the bank credited Heather's account with $5.83 interest. On October 14 she withdrew $45.00 from her account.

This is how Heather recorded her transactions in her savings account register.

Date	Withdrawal		Deposit		Interest		Balance	
7-10-98			265	41			265	41
8-19-98			302	48			567	89
10-8-98					5	83	573	72
10-14-98	45	00					528	72

Marcus's account earns 5.4% interest. If his average balance for the year is $500.00, how much interest will Marcus earn in a year?

Follow these steps to find how much interest Marcus will earn in a year.

1. Rename the percentage rate to a decimal fraction (divide the rate by 100).

$$5.4\% \div 100 = 0.054$$

2. Multiply the percentage rate (decimal fraction) times the balance.

$0.054 \times \$500.00 = \longrightarrow$

$$
\begin{array}{r}
\$500.00 \\
\times\ 0.054 \\
\hline
200000 \\
2500000 \\
\hline
\$27.00000
\end{array}
$$

Marcus will earn $27.00 in interest.

Practice

Find the amount of annual interest each principal (savings) would earn in one year. Then find the balance for the end of the year. Your teacher may allow you to use a calculator.

Example: $375.00 at 6.2%

$$\begin{array}{r} \$375 \\ \times\,0.062 \\ \hline 750 \\ +22500 \\ \hline \$23.250 \end{array}$$

$$\begin{array}{r} \$375.00 \\ +\quad 23.25 \\ \hline \$398.25 \end{array}$$

1. $123.00 at 2.4%

2. $200.00 at 5%

3. $565.00 at 4.5%

4. $430.00 at 3.9%

5. $644.00 at 7.8%

6. $1,000.00 at 5.6%

Use the information given to complete a savings account register. Use the register given to you by your teacher.

7. On August 15, 1998, you opened a savings account by depositing $157.00.

8. On August 15, 1999, $4.71 interest was credited to your account.

9. On September 12, 1999, you withdrew $15.00.

10. On September 25, 1999, you deposited $193.50.

11. What is your balance on September 25?

Meet the Challenge!

12. Harry kept $450.00 in a savings account for 5 years. The interest rate on his account was 3.6%. What was his balance after 5 years? (Hint: Interest is added to Harry's account yearly.)

Problem: Suppose you wanted to buy a mountain bike to help you deliver newspapers on your weekend newspaper route. The cost of the bike, including tax, is $280.00. Decide which method to use to pay for the mountain bike.

Information:

Credit Card (18% yearly interest rate)
- You pay the minimum payment of $20.00 per month.
- It will take you 17 months to pay the balance on your credit card.

Installment Plan (8% yearly interest rate)
- You make a $50.00 down payment.
- You will make monthly payments of $39.23 for 6 months to pay the balance.

Bank Loan (11% yearly interest rate)
- You take out a 12-month loan for $300.00
- You make monthly payments of $26.51.

Use the information on page 380 to answer the questions.

1. How much would you pay for your new mountain bike using each payment plan?

2. Which method of payment did you choose to pay for the mountain bike? Why?

3. How much more than $280.00 did you pay? Why do you think you had to pay more?

4. List other ways to pay for the mountain bike. Compare these methods of payment to paying by credit card, installment plan, and bank loan.

Church Treasurer

COMMUNITY
BAPTIST CHURCH
817 West Main Street
Madison Heights, IN 46227

Moore Christian School
334 Tara Lane
Mariposa, CA 95338

Dear Fifth Grade:

As a church treasurer, I use math just about all the time, especially the kind of math relating to money. Part of my job is to keep records for the church. I do this on a computerized spreadsheet—it looks a lot like a checkbook register. The spreadsheet has columns for me to place figures in. In the credit column I key in the amounts of money the church receives as income, such as gifts and offerings. In the debit column I place the amounts of money that the church pays out for various expenses. Then in the third column the computer keeps a running total, which means it adds the credits to the total and subtracts the debits from the total as I go along. I also write and sign the checks when the church pays expenses or bills.

Another important part of my job is to work on the church budget with the pastor and board members. The budget tells how much money the church has to spend for various things. If at a board meeting we decide we would like to give a gift of a certain amount of money to each missionary we support, I calculate the total and the amount available in the missionary fund to determine if we can give the proposed amount. The most important thing about my work is being accurate. Double-checking my figures takes time, but it saves time, hassle, and maybe even money later on.

Sincerely,

Bradley Davis

Bradley Davis

Write the time.

1.

2.

Write the date in number form.

3. April 7, 1998

4. July 24, 2009

Write A.M. or P.M. for each activity.

5. After dinner, Dad washed dishes until 6:30.

6. Neil ran to meet the school bus at 7:15.

7. Rochelle ate lunch at 12:35.

8. Mom made coffee for breakfast at 6:45.

Add or subtract the time.

9. 2 hr. 25 min.
   −   45 min.

10. 10 hr. 45 min.
    + 5 hr. 47 min.

11. 6 hr. 13 min.
    +7 hr. 29 min.

12. 7 hr. 11 min.
    −3 hr. 30 min.

Write the elapsed time or the time that is described.

13. 8:00 P.M. to 1:30 A.M.

14. 5:45 P.M. to 10:20 P.M.

15. 6:00 A.M. to 2:15 P.M.

16. 2 hr. 25 min. before 9:30 P.M.

17. 7 hr. 15 min. after 6:45 A.M.

18. 3 hr. 20 min. before 10:00 A.M.

Complete the number sentences.

19. 10 minutes = _____ seconds

20. 1 year = _____ days

21. 2 days = _____ hours

22. 48 months = _____ years

23. 72 hours = _____ days

24. 1 leap year = _____ days

25. 1 century = _____ years

26. 1 millennium = _____ years

27. 5 minutes = _____ seconds

28. 2 minutes = _____ seconds

29. 2 centuries = _____ years

30. 3 days = _____ hours

Find the total price (including sales tax) for each item.

31. $14.75

3% tax

32. $12.25

5% tax

33. $2.97

7% tax

Use the check to answer the questions.

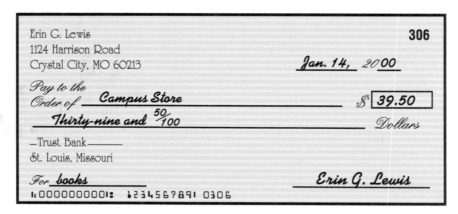

34. On what day was the check written?

35. Who was the check written to?

36. Who wrote the check?

37. For what reason was the check written?

38. What is the number of the check?

Find the elapsed time.

39. Emily started raking leaves at 3:15 P.M. She raked for 1 hr. 20 min. What time did Emily finish raking?

40. Tamiko went home from Grandma's house at 6:15 P.M. She had been at Grandma's for 2 hr. 30 min. What time did she arrive at Grandma's?

Cumulative Review

Write the letter of the correct answer.

1. What is the measurement of the third angle?

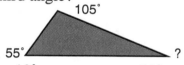

a. 10°   c. 30°

b. 20°   d. 40°

2. Solve.

$$62\overline{)72,672}$$

a. 1,172 r8

b. 1,163

c. 1,278 r2

d. not given

3. What is the volume of the cube?

4 ft.

a. 12 cubic feet   c. 64 cubic feet

b. 16 cubic feet   d. not given

4. Solve.

$$\begin{array}{r} 13 \\ -\ 1\frac{1}{6} \\ \hline \end{array}$$

a. $11\frac{1}{6}$

b. $11\frac{5}{6}$

c. $12\frac{1}{6}$

d. not given

5. What is the perimeter of the figure?

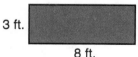

3 ft.

8 ft.

a. 22 ft.   c. 11 ft.

b. 14 ft.   d. 5 ft.

6. Solve.

$$21.15 \div 6 =$$

a. 35.15

b. 32.5

c. 15.2

d. 3.525

7. Solve.

$$\begin{array}{r} 15 \text{ ft. } 8 \text{ in.} \\ +\ 8 \text{ ft. } 9 \text{ in.} \\ \hline \end{array}$$

a. 22 ft. 1 in.

b. 23 ft. 5 in.

c. 24 ft. 5 in.

d. not given

8. Caleb needs $\frac{1}{3}$ of a cup of shortening to make one batch of cookies. How much shortening would he need for 3 batches?

a. $\frac{1}{3}$ c.   c. 1 c.

b. $\frac{2}{3}$ c.   d. $1\frac{1}{3}$ c.

9. What ratio is not equal to $\frac{7}{11}$?

a. $\frac{14}{22}$ c. $\frac{21}{33}$

b. $\frac{17}{44}$ d. $\frac{28}{44}$

10. Will began raking leaves at 9:20 A.M. He raked for 45 min. What time did he finish raking?

a. 9:50 A.M.   c. 10:00 A.M.

b. 9:55 A.M.   d. 10:05 A.M.

Experimental Aircraft

Every summer thousands of aircraft fly to a huge airfield in Oshkosh, Wisconsin. Their owners go to see one of the greatest aviation events in the world, the annual Fly-In Convention, sponsored by the Experimental Aircraft Association (EAA). Approximately 15,000 aircraft come and go during the week-long event, and many come from foreign countries. Throughout the convention the airfield is crowded with planes of all shapes and sizes and with the people who build them, fly them, or simply like to look at them. Some visitors bring their families and camp out in tents next to their airplanes.

Children enjoy doing many different things at the Fly-In. They can sit in the cockpits of various types of aircraft. They can meet and talk with the people who built the planes. They can see everything from the Goodyear blimp to a supersonic Concorde jet that flies at speeds of up to 1,550 miles an hour. They can watch the Parade of Nations featuring the flags of all the countries represented at the convention. Sometimes they can hear speeches by people who have done great things in the history of aviation.

Perhaps the most exciting part is the air shows by international teams. Planes flying in formations, skywriters, aerobatic teams, and parachutists all contribute to the thrills. At the end of the week, people get back in their planes and return home, having made new friends and obtained new ideas for future experimentation.

CHAPTER
18

Pre-Algebra

The Goodyear blimp America *serves as a steady camera platform at sporting events and other public gatherings.*

Aircraft built at home are classi-fied as experi-mental.

Comparing and Ordering Positive and Negative Numbers

On a number line, the values of the numbers increase as you move to the right. The values of the numbers decrease as you move to the left.

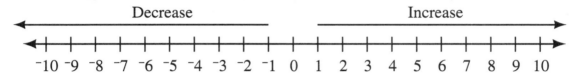

Decrease   Increase

$^{-}10$ $^{-}9$ $^{-}8$ $^{-}7$ $^{-}6$ $^{-}5$ $^{-}4$ $^{-}3$ $^{-}2$ $^{-}1$ 0 1 2 3 4 5 6 7 8 9 10

The value of a negative number will always be less than the value of a positive number.

$1 > {}^{-}7$ $^{-}7 < 3$ $4 > {}^{-}4$

The values of negative numbers continue to decrease as you move to the left on a number line.

$^{-}15 < {}^{-}7$ $^{-}7 < {}^{-}5$ $^{-}3 > {}^{-}4$

These numbers are written in order from least to greatest.
$^{-}17, {}^{-}14, {}^{-}3, 1, 4, 7, 10$

Class Work

Complete each number sentence using a > or <.

1. $^{-}7 \bigcirc 9$ 2. $3 \bigcirc {}^{-}5$

3. $^{-}6 \bigcirc {}^{-}9$ 4. $^{-}4 \bigcirc 4$

Practice

Copy and complete each number sentence using a < or >.

1. $7 \bigcirc {}^-4$
2. ${}^-12 \bigcirc {}^-8$
3. $8 \bigcirc {}^-10$

4. ${}^-4 \bigcirc {}^-5$
5. ${}^-3 \bigcirc 0$
6. $0 \bigcirc {}^-2$

7. ${}^-6 \bigcirc 6$
8. ${}^-8 \bigcirc {}^-4$
9. ${}^-7 \bigcirc 6$

Order the negative and positive numbers from least to greatest.

10. $4, {}^-4, 0, 7$
11. $3, 7, {}^-8, {}^-18$

12. $10, {}^-5, 3, {}^-1$
13. $0, {}^-1, {}^-2, {}^-5$

14. ${}^-16, 8, {}^-5, 5$
15. ${}^-10, {}^-12, 9, 0$

Chapter 3 Review

Solve.

16.
$$\begin{array}{r} 1,842 \\ \times \quad 5 \\ \hline \end{array}$$

17.
$$\begin{array}{r} 901 \\ \times \quad 7 \\ \hline \end{array}$$

18.
$$\begin{array}{r} 3,655 \\ \times \quad 6 \\ \hline \end{array}$$

19.
$$\begin{array}{r} 751 \\ \times \quad 4 \\ \hline \end{array}$$

Adding Positive and Negative Numbers

The Zero Principle

A number may be renamed by adding or subtracting 0,
or a form of 0, without changing the value of that number.

Steps for Adding Positive and Negative Numbers on a Number Line

1. Start at the first addend.
2. To add a positive number, take jumps to the right.
   or
   To add a negative number, take jumps to the left.

It is ⁻6° F outside. If the temperature warms by 4°, what will the temperature be?

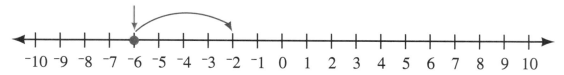

Step 1
Start at the first addend.

Step 2
Take a jump the amount of the
second addend.

$$^-6 + 4 = {^-2}° \text{ F}$$

The Zero Principle can be applied to addition when using the algebra mats
by subtracting the same number of counters from each side of the mat.

Put on the addends.   Apply the Zero Principle.   The answer remains.
$^-6 + 4 =$ $^-6 + 4 = {^-2}$

Practice

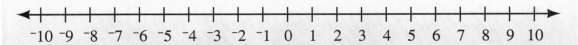

Copy and complete each equation using the number line.

1. $5 + {}^-6 =$
2. ${}^-1 + {}^-8 =$
3. $9 + {}^-7 =$
4. $2 + 8 =$
5. $8 + {}^-8 =$
6. $7 + {}^-9 =$
7. ${}^-4 + 4 =$
8. ${}^-4 + 6 =$
9. ${}^-9 + 16 =$

Use an algebra mat and counters to solve the problems.

10. $5 + {}^-3 =$
11. ${}^-4 + 5 =$
12. $8 + {}^-2 =$
13. ${}^-10 + 12 =$
14. ${}^-3 + {}^-1 =$
15. ${}^-6 + 6 =$
16. $5 + {}^-8 =$
17. ${}^-7 + {}^-2 =$
18. $6 + 3 =$

Application

Write an addition equation for each word problem. Use the number line to solve the problems. Write and label the answer.

19. A team receives 1 point for each correct answer and loses 1 point for every incorrect answer. Mr. Cook's team answered 5 questions correctly and then 7 questions incorrectly. What was the team's final score?

20. Mrs. Hall's team answered 8 questions incorrectly and then 10 questions correctly. What was the team's final score?

Meet the Challenge!

21. Mr. Smith's bank charges $5.00 for each day that his account is overdrawn. Mr. Smith's balance was ${}^-\$8.00$ on Monday. What was his balance on Friday after he deposited $75.00?

Number Lines and Manipulatives

Steps for Adding Positive and Negative Numbers on a Number Line
1. Start at the first addend.
2. To add a positive number, take jumps to the right.
   or
   To add a negative number, take jumps to the left.

$^-4 + 9 = 5$

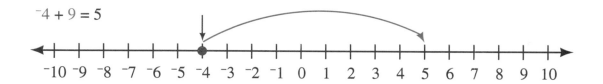

$3 + {}^-7 = {}^-4$

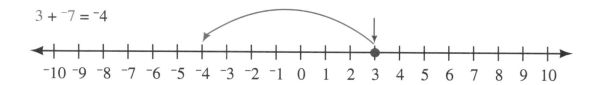

Steps for Adding Positive and Negative Numbers Using an Algebra Mat
1. Put on the first addend.
2. Put on the second addend.
3. Rename if necessary by subtracting 0. (Subtract 0 by removing an equal number of counters from each side of the mat.) The answer remains.

$^-6 + {}^-4 = {}^-10$
No renaming necessary

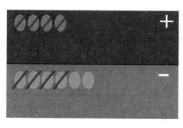

$^-6 + 4 = {}^-2$

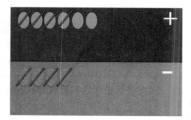

$6 + {}^-4 = 2$

Practice

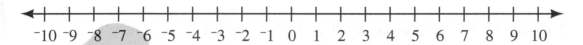

$$-10 \quad -9 \quad -8 \quad -7 \quad -6 \quad -5 \quad -4 \quad -3 \quad -2 \quad -1 \quad 0 \quad 1 \quad 2 \quad 3 \quad 4 \quad 5 \quad 6 \quad 7 \quad 8 \quad 9 \quad 10$$

Use the number line to solve the problems.

1. $7 + {}^-7 =$
2. $5 + {}^-10 =$
3. ${}^-6 + 14 =$
4. ${}^-7 + {}^-2 =$
5. $8 + {}^-14 =$
6. ${}^-10 + 5 =$
7. ${}^-5 + {}^-6 =$
8. $4 + {}^-9 =$
9. ${}^-2 + 4 =$

Use an algebra mat and counters to solve the problems.

10. $6 + {}^-2 =$
11. $7 + {}^-1 =$
12. $8 + {}^-9 =$
13. ${}^-2 + {}^-4 =$
14. ${}^-10 + 3 =$
15. ${}^-2 + 2 =$
16. ${}^-8 + 12 =$
17. ${}^-1 + 10 =$
18. ${}^-6 + {}^-5 =$

Application

Write an addition equation for each word problem. Use an algebra mat and counters to solve the problem. Label the answer.

19. In a game in which each team receives 1 point for each correct answer and loses 1 point for each incorrect answer, Sharon's team answered 8 questions correctly and 2 questions incorrectly. What was the team's final score?

20. Kyle's team answered 3 questions incorrectly and 4 questions correctly. If each question was worth 1 point, what was the team's score?

21. Mr. Adams's team had a score of ${}^-6$ points. The team gained 3 points consecutively. What was the team's final score?

22. At midnight the temperature was ${}^-4°$ F. The weatherman predicted the temperature would rise 10 degrees by morning. What will the temperature be if the weatherman's prediction is correct?

Subtracting Positive and Negative Numbers

> **Steps for Subtracting Positive and Negative Numbers Using an Algebra Mat**
> 1. Put on the minuend (first number).
> 2. Rename if necessary by adding 0. (Add 0 by placing an equal number of counters on each side of the mat until there are enough counters to subtract the subtrahend, the second number.)
> 3. Subtract the subtrahend (second number). The answer remains.

Positive – Positive   7 – 2 = 5

 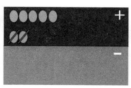 

Negative – Negative   ⁻7 – ⁻2 = ⁻5

Positive – Negative   7 – ⁻2 = 9

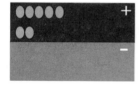  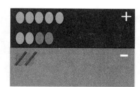 

Negative – Positive   ⁻7 – 2 = ⁻9

Chapter 18

Practice

Use an algebra mat and counters to solve the problems.

1. $3 - 2 =$ 2. $^-9 - 2 =$ 3. $10 - {}^-4 =$

4. $^-5 - {}^-1 =$ 5. $^-4 - 3 =$ 6. $^-2 - 6 =$

7. $8 - {}^-4 =$ 8. $^-6 - {}^-6 =$ 9. $^-3 - {}^-7 =$

10. $^-8 - 1 =$ 11. $8 - 3 =$ 12. $^-3 - {}^-4 =$

13. $^-10 - {}^-4 =$ 14. $^-5 - 2 =$ 15. $^-7 - 3 =$

Application

Write a subtraction equation for each word problem. Use an algebra mat and counters to solve the problem. Label the answer.

16. At 9:30, the temperature was 15° F. By 12:00, the temperature had dropped 18°. What was the temperature then?

17. The weatherman predicted the temperature would rise to 7° F. If the temperature is $^-4$° F, how many degrees must the temperature rise to make the prediction true?

18. John's score was 5 points. Jamie's score was $^-10$ points. Compare the scores to find out the difference between John's score and Jamie's score.

19. Bryan's score is $^-8$ points. How many points must he score consecutively to reach a final score of 0?

Chapter 3 Review

Solve.

20. $\begin{array}{r} 4{,}201 \\ \times\ \ \ \ 36 \\ \hline \end{array}$ 21. $\begin{array}{r} 647 \\ \times\ 25 \\ \hline \end{array}$ 22. $\begin{array}{r} 1{,}203 \\ \times\ \ \ \ 18 \\ \hline \end{array}$ 23. $\begin{array}{r} 935 \\ \times\ 64 \\ \hline \end{array}$

Adding and Subtracting Using Manipulatives

Addition

1. Put on the first addend.
2. **Put on the second addend.**
3. **Rename if necessary by subtracting 0. (Subtract 0 by removing an equal number of counters from each side of the mat.) The answer remains.**

$$5 + {}^-10 = {}^-5$$

$${}^-4 + 7 = 3$$

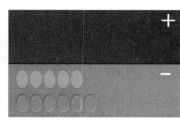

$${}^-5 + {}^-6 = {}^-11$$

Subtraction

1. Put on the minuend (first number).
2. **Rename if necessary by adding 0. (Add 0 by placing an equal number of counters on each side of the mat until there are enough counters to subtract the subtrahend, the second number.)**
3. **Subtract the subtrahend (second number). The answer remains.**

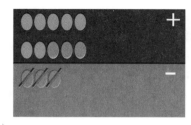

$$7 - {}^-3 = 10$$

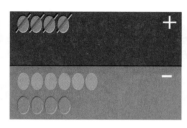

$${}^-6 - 4 = {}^-10$$

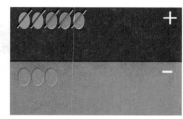

$$2 - 5 = {}^-3$$

Practice

Use an algebra mat and counters to solve the problems.

1. $7 + {}^-3 =$

2. $2 - {}^-2 =$

3. $10 + {}^-3 =$

4. $4 - {}^-1 =$

5. $3 - 8 =$

6. $1 + {}^-6 =$

7. ${}^-3 + 1 =$

8. ${}^-5 - 3 =$

9. $4 - {}^-7 =$

Complete the addition equations.

10. $6 + {}^-5 =$

11. ${}^-2 + {}^-5 =$

12. ${}^-3 + 2 =$

13. $4 + {}^-9 =$

14. ${}^-7 + 3 =$

15. $5 + {}^-7 =$

Complete the subtraction equations.

16. ${}^-5 - 7 =$

17. ${}^-4 - {}^-5 =$

18. $7 - 9 =$

19. $6 - {}^-3 =$

20. $7 - 11 =$

21. ${}^-6 - 5 =$

Application

Write an equation for each word problem. Solve the problem using an algebra mat and counters. Label the answer.

22. Meredith's team had a score of 5 points. Her team lost 6 consecutive points. What is the team's final score?

23. Miss Garland's team has a score of ${}^-3$ points. Mrs. Berry's team has a score of 7 points. Compare the scores to find out the difference between the scores.

24. The temperature was $9°$ F at 3:00. It dropped $12°$ overnight. What was the temperature then?

25. When school started the temperature was ${}^-4°$ F. By noon the temperature had risen 8 degrees. What was the temperature at noon?

26. Mrs. Simmons overdrew her bank account and had a balance of ${}^-\$11.00$. If her bank charges a $7.00 fee for overdrawing, what is her balance after the charge has been made?

27. How much more money should Mrs. Simmons deposit to have a balance of $25.00?

Lesson 164

397

Chapter Review

Complete each number sentence using a > or <.

1. $^-3 \bigcirc ^-7$
2. $^-10 \bigcirc 4$
3. $7 \bigcirc 11$

4. $6 \bigcirc 9$
5. $^-5 \bigcirc ^-4$
6. $^-7 \bigcirc ^-11$

7. $5 \bigcirc ^-5$
8. $3 \bigcirc ^-5$
9. $^-16 \bigcirc ^-6$

Write the numbers in order from least to greatest.

10. $3, ^-5, ^-10, 0$
11. $6, 8, ^-4, ^-7$

12. $^-1, ^-4, ^-7, ^-2$
13. $8, ^-8, 4, ^-4$

Solve the addition problems using the number line.

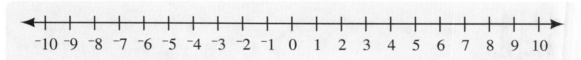

14. $3 + ^-8 =$
15. $9 + ^-1 =$
16. $^-7 + 2 =$
17. $^-2 + ^-4 =$

Use an algebra mat and counters to solve the problems.

18. $5 + ^-5 =$

19. $^-2 + ^-4 =$

20. $4 + ^-11 =$

21. $^-9 + 7 =$

22. $7 - 11 =$

23. $7 - ^-3 =$

24. $^-7 + 2 =$

25. $^-4 - 6 =$

26. $^-3 - ^-5 =$

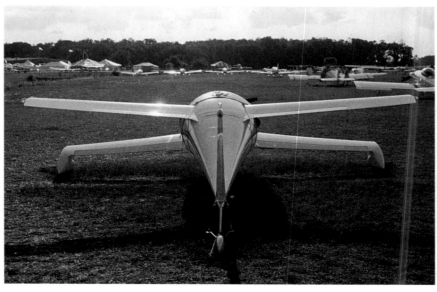

Write an equation for each word problem. Use the number line or an algebra mat and counters to solve the problems. Write and label the answer.

27. The temperature was ⁻6° at 7:00. By 9:00, the temperature had risen 9°. What was the temperature then?

28. At 4:00, the temperature was 5°. By 8:30, the temperature had fallen 8°. What was the temperature then?

29. A team receives 1 point for every correct answer and loses 1 point for every incorrect answer. Maxine's team answered 5 questions correctly and 7 questions incorrectly. What was the final score?

30. Claire's team answered 11 questions incorrectly and then 7 questions correctly. What was the final score?

31. Bobby's checkbook balance was $6.00. He wrote a check for $9.00. What is his current balance?

32. The football team lost 7 yards on the first down and gained 3 yards on the second down. What was the total yardage for the plays?

THURSDAY

Last day of school!!

June 7

Did you know . . .

A normal school year is 180 days. That means you go to school 5 fewer days than the number of days you are not in school! *365 − 180 = 185 days*

Shuffleboard

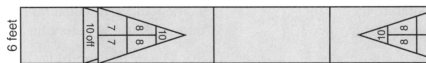

6 feet

52 feet

Shuffleboard is played on a court that is painted on the floor. Players use cues to push disks from one side of the court to the other. Points are awarded based on the position of the disk at the end of a player's turn.

You can play shuffleboard using a ruler as a cue and pennies as disks. You will need to draw the court shown above onto tagboard.

Write the score each player earned.

1.

2.
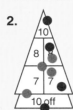

3.
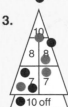

4.
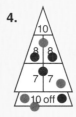

Keeping Score

7 points

are given for a disk shot to the **7** space.

8 points

are given for a disk shot to the **8** space.

10 points

are given for a disk in the **10** space.

0 points

are given for a disk **touching** a line.

⁻10 points

are deducted for a disk in the **10 off** space.

Cumulative Review

Write the letter of the correct answer.

1. $\frac{2}{3} + \frac{1}{10} =$

   a. $\frac{23}{30}$ c. $\frac{23}{10}$

   b. $\frac{3}{30}$ d. $\frac{3}{10}$

2. What is the volume of the three-dimensional figure?

   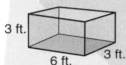
   3 ft.   6 ft.   3 ft.

   a. 18 ft.^{3} c. 54 ft.^{3}

   b. 21 ft.^{3} d. not given

3. Solve.

   $48.24 \div 16 =$

   a. 2.251
   b. 3.115
   c. 3.015
   d. not given

4. Solve.

   $\begin{array}{r} 3 \text{ pt. } 1 \text{ c.} \\ - \quad 2 \text{ c.} \\ \hline \end{array}$

   a. 3 pt. 1 c.
   b. 2 pt. 1 c.
   c. 2 pt. 3 c.
   d. not given

5. Solve.

   $2\frac{1}{4} \times 3\frac{1}{5} =$

   a. $6\frac{1}{20}$ c. $7\frac{1}{20}$

   b. $7\frac{1}{5}$ d. not given

October Utility Expenses

$\frac{1}{10}$ telephone

heating $\frac{3}{10}$

water $\frac{1}{5}$

electricity $\frac{2}{5}$

6. What part of the October utility expenses is the electricity?

   a. $\frac{1}{10}$ c. $\frac{3}{10}$

   b. $\frac{1}{5}$ d. $\frac{2}{5}$

7. Which category on the circle graph had the least expense?

   a. telephone   c. water
   b. electric   d. heating

8. What is 50% of 27?

   a. 2.7   c. 13.5
   b. 12.5   d. not given

9. Solve.

   $\begin{array}{r} 7 \text{ hr. } 19 \text{ min.} \\ + 4 \text{ hr. } 45 \text{ min.} \\ \hline \end{array}$

   a. 11 hr. 4 min.
   b. 12 hr. 4 min.
   c. 13 hr. 45 min.
   d. not given

10. Which sign will make the sentence true?

    $^-4$ $^-9$

    a. >   c. =
    b. <   d. not given

Glossary

A

acute angle   an angle that measures less than 90°

acute triangle   a triangle with three acute angles

A.D.   an abbreviation for the Latin words *anno Domini*, which mean "in the year of the Lord." A.D. is used in giving dates after the birth of Christ

addends   the numbers added to give a sum

A.M.   an abbreviation that indicates morning hours from 12:00 midnight to 12:00 noon

angle   the figure formed by two rays with a common endpoint

area   the number of square units within a region

Associative Property of Addition   The grouping of addends may be changed without changing the sum. (Grouping Principle of Addition)

Associative Property of Multiplication   The grouping of factors may be changed without changing the product. (Grouping Principle of Multiplication)

average   (1) a typical number in a set of numbers found by adding two or more quantities and dividing the total by the number of quantities; (2) the mean for a set of data

B

B.C.   the abbreviation for "before Christ." This abbreviation is used in giving dates before the birth of Christ

balance   the total amount of money in an account after all the transactions have been completed

bar graph   a picture that shows mathematical data by using bars

C

Celsius   a scale used to measure temperature in the metric system

center point of a circle   the point which is the same distance from every point on the circle

central angles   angles in a circle formed by the intersection of two or more radii; the sum of the measure of the central angles is 360°

chord   a line segment that connects any two points on a circle

circle   a closed curve of which each point on the curve is the same distance from the center point

circle graph   a graph that shows a whole divided into parts

circumference   the distance around a circle

common denominator   a common multiple of two or more denominators

common factor   a factor that is the same for two or more numbers

common multiple   a multiple that is the same for two or more numbers

Commutative Property of Addition   The order of addends can be changed without changing the sum. (Order Principle of Addition)

Commutative Property of Multiplication   The order of factors can be changed without changing the product. (Order Principle of Multiplication)

composite number   a number greater than 1 that has more than two factors

cone   a three-dimensional figure with one circular face, one curved surface, and one vertex

congruent figures   figures which are the same size and shape

coordinate graph   a graph that describes the location of objects using numbered rows and columns and a set of numbers called an ordered pair

cube   a three-dimensional figure with six faces that are squares

cubit   a unit of length used in the Bible; about eighteen inches

cylinder a three-dimensional figure with two circular faces separated by a curved surface

D

decimal fraction a number with one or more places to the right of the decimal point

denominator the digit(s) below the fraction bar in a common fraction; names the number of equal parts in all

deposit an amount of money added to a bank account

diameter a line segment that connects two points on a circle and passes through the center point

difference the answer in a subtraction problem

Distributive Property The product of two factors can be found by separating one factor into parts, multiplying each part by the other factor, and adding the partial products together. (Multiplication-Addition Principle)

dividend the number to be divided

divisible able to be divided with a remainder of 0

divisor the number by which another number is divided

E

edge the intersection of two faces in a three-dimensional figure

END a statement used to stop a computer program

equator the imaginary horizontal line circling the middle of the globe that is used as a reference for latitude

equilateral triangle a triangle with three sides the same length

equivalent fractions fractions that name the same part of a whole or part of a set

estimate *n.* an approximate answer; *v.* to give an approximate answer

expanded form a way to write a number that names the place value of each digit

F

face a flat surface of a three-dimensional figure

Faces

factor *n.* a number multiplied to find a product; *v.* to find the numbers which have been multiplied to give a product

factor tree a diagram used to find the prime factors of a number

$$\begin{array}{c} 24 \\ \diagup \ \diagdown \\ 4 \ \times \ 6 \\ \diagup\diagdown \ \diagup\diagdown \\ 2 \times 2 \times 2 \times 3 \end{array}$$

flow chart a diagram which shows a sequence of written directions; can be used to design (or plan) a computer program

FOR/NEXT a set of statements that tell the computer to repeat a series of commands

fraction a number that names part of a whole or part of a set

frequency the number of occurrences in a category

front-end estimation using the digits in the greatest place value to estimate the answer to a problem

G

GOTO a statement used to skip to a different line instead of continuing to the next line of a computer program

gram the basic unit of mass in the metric system

graph a picture of mathematical data

greatest common factor (GCF) the greatest factor that is the same for two or more numbers

H

heptagon a polygon with seven sides

hexagon a polygon with six sides

I

Identity Property of Addition When 0 is an addend, the sum is the other addend. (Zero Principle of Addition)

Identity Property of Multiplication When 1 is a factor, the product is the other factor. (One Principle of Multiplication)

IF/THEN a statement in a computer program that provides opportunity for choices. If a condition is true, the program will do one step; if it is not true, the program will do something else.

improper fraction   a fraction in which the numerator is equal to or greater than the denominator; its value is equal to or greater than 1

infinite   without end; e.g., the set of numbers is infinite

INPUT   a statement that tells the user to enter information into the computer

installment plan   a purchase plan in which a customer purchases an item by paying a down payment and agreeing to make monthly payments to the store until the bill has been paid in full (Interest is figured after the down payment is paid.)

interest   a percentage of an amount of money paid by the borrower to the lender for the privilege of using the money

intersecting lines   lines that have a common point

isosceles triangle   a triangle with at least two sides the same length

L

latitude   the distance north or south of the equator; measured in degrees

least common denominator   the least common multiple of two or more denominators

least common multiple (LCM)   the lowest multiple, other than 0, that is the same for two or more numbers

LET   a statement in a computer program that assigns a value to a variable, e.g., LET A=5; *A* is the variable

like fractions   fractions that have the same denominator

line   a straight path of points that goes on endlessly in both directions

line graph   a picture that shows mathematical data by connecting points on a grid

line of symmetry   a line along which a figure can be folded so that the halves match

line segment   a part of a line having two endpoints

longitude   the distance east or west of the prime meridian; measured in degrees

lowest terms   a fraction in which the greatest common factor of the numerator and denominator is 1

M

mean   (1) the average for a set of data; (2) a typical number in a set of numbers found by adding two or more quantities and dividing the total by the number of quantities

median   the middle number in a sequential set of data; e.g., for the set of numbers 76, 81, 84, 92, 95, the median is 84. If there is an even number of numbers, then the median is the average of the two middle numbers.

mileage scale   a scale on maps that helps to determine what the actual distance is on the map

minuend   the number from which another number (subtrahend) is subtracted

mixed number   a number that is the sum of a whole number and a fraction

mode   the number(s) or item(s) that occurs most frequently in a list of data

multiple   the product of two whole numbers; e.g., 0, 4, 8, 12, 16 are the first five multiples of 4

multiplicand   the number that is multiplied by another number; e.g., in the equation $5 \times 6 = 30$, 6 is the multiplicand

multiplier   the number that multiplies another number; e.g., in the equation $5 \times 6 = 30$, 5 is the multiplier

N

NEW   a command to clear the computer's working "memory"

numerator   the digit(s) above the fraction bar in a common fraction; names the number of parts being considered (that are special)

O

obtuse angle   an angle that measures more than 90° and less than 180°

obtuse triangle   a triangle with one obtuse angle

octagon   a polygon with eight sides

ordered pair   a set of numbers to correspond with numbered rows and columns on a coordinate graph; e.g., for the ordered pair (2, 3), 2 refers to a point on the horizontal axis and 3 refers to a point on the vertical axis

output   a solution to an equation or other information sent to the computer screen or printer

P

parallel lines   lines in the same plane that never intersect

parallelogram   a quadrilateral whose opposite sides are parallel

partial product   a product that is part of the total product

pentagon   a polygon with five sides

percent   per hundred; a ratio comparing a number to 100

perimeter   the distance around a figure

period   the divisions formed by each group of three digits, separated by commas

perpendicular lines   intersecting lines that form right angles

pictograph   a graph that shows numerical data by using pictures

plane   a set of points extending endlessly in all directions, forming a flat surface

P.M.   an abbreviation that indicates afternoon hours from 12:00 noon to 12:00 midnight

point   an exact location in space represented by a dot

polygon   a closed figure (flat shape) made of three or more line segments

polyhedron   a three-dimensional figure whose faces are polygons

prime meridian   the imaginary vertical line used as a reference for longitude; passes through Greenwich, England

prime number   a number with exactly two different factors; these factors are the number itself and 1

PRINT   a statement which sends information within quotation marks to the computer screen, e.g., PRINT "5 + 2 ="; also a command which calculates numbers to solve equations, e.g., PRINT 5 + 2 puts only the answer 7 on the screen

prism   a three-dimensional figure with parallel and congruent bases and parallelograms as sides

probability   the likelihood that an event will occur; the ratio between one result and the total number of possible outcomes

product   the answer in a multiplication problem

proper fraction   a fraction in which the numerator is less than the denominator; its value is less than 1

proportion   an equation stating that two ratios are equal

pyramid   a three-dimensional figure that has a polygon as its base and at least three triangular faces that meet at a common vertex

Q

quadrilateral   a polygon with four sides

quotient   the answer in a division problem

R

radius   a line segment whose endpoints are the center and any point on the circle

range   the difference between the largest and smallest numbers in a set of data

ratio   the comparison of two numbers; the comparison can be part-to-part, part-to-whole, or whole-to-part comparison

ray   a part of a line having one endpoint and extending endlessly in one direction

rectangle   a quadrilateral with opposite sides congruent and four right angles

rectangular prism   a three-dimensional figure with six faces that are rectangles

REM   the abbreviation for REMARK; allows the computer programmer to include comments in a program; does not affect the program; a useful tool to state the purpose of the computer program

repeating decimal a quotient in which one or more of the digits repeat an infinite number of times; a bar is written over the repeating digit(s) to indicate that it repeats

rhombus a parallelogram with all four sides congruent

right angle an angle that measures 90°; the shape of a square corner

right triangle a triangle with one right angle

rounding a way of estimating in which a number is expressed to the nearest ten, hundred, thousand, and so on

RUN a command used to start a computer program

S

sales tax tax paid by the customer when purchasing an item or a service. It is a percentage of the cost and is collected by the seller.

scale a ratio comparing the size of a map (or drawing) and the size of the actual object

scale drawing a representational drawing which can be larger or smaller than the actual object it represents

scalene triangle a triangle with no sides the same length

similar figures figures which are the same shape but not necessarily the same size

sphere a three-dimensional figure with one curved surface and no faces, edges, or vertices

square a quadrilateral with four congruent sides and four right angles

statistics the mathematical study of the collection, organization, analysis, and interpretation of data (information)

subtrahend the number that is subtracted from another number (minuend)

sum the answer in an addition problem

symmetrical figure a figure that, when folded along the line of symmetry, has halves that match

T

three-dimensional figure a figure with three dimensions: length, width, and height

time line a line that shows the sequence of historical events

trapezoid a quadrilateral that has one pair of opposite sides parallel

triangle a polygon with three sides

U

unlike fractions fractions that have different denominators

V

variable a memory location where a computer program stores a number; the value stored in that variable may change; variables with a $ store words instead of numbers

Venn diagram a diagram that uses circles or squares to show the relationship of sets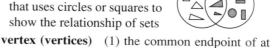

vertex (vertices) (1) the common endpoint of at least two rays that form an angle; (2) the point of intersection of two sides of a polygon; (3) the point of intersection of the edges of prisms and pyramids; (4) the most extreme point of a cone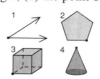

volume the number of cubic units within a closed three-dimensional figure

W

withdrawal an amount of money subtracted from a bank account

Z

Zero Property of Multiplication When 0 is a factor, the product is 0.

Zero Principle of Subtraction When 0 is subtracted from a number (the minuend), the answer is that number.

Index

Photograph Credits

The following agencies and individuals have furnished materials to meet the photographic needs of this textbook. We wish to express our gratitude to them for their important contribution.

Suzanne R. Altizer
Aramco
Boeing Commercial Aircraft
    Corporation
George R. Collins
COREL Corporation
Tim Davis
Delta Airlines
Peter French
Getty Images
Goodyear Tire & Rubber Company
Jim Hargis

Brian Johnson
John M. Kauffman
G. David Koonts
Library of Congress
National Aeronautics and Space
    Administration (NASA)
National Oceanic and Atmospheric
    Administration (NOAA)
National Park Service
PhotoDisc
Wade K. Ramsey
George Rogier

Doug RummingerCraig Schmitman
Schweizer Aircraft Corporation
The Wallace Smith family
Smithsonian Institution
United States Air Force (USAF)
United States Department of
    Agriculture (USDA)
Unusual Films
USAir
World Bank

Cover
COREL Corporation (airplane); PhotoDisc/Getty Images (top right); Unusual Films (bottom right)

Inside Front Cover
COREL Corporation

Chapter 1
Unusual Films 1 (both), 12, 13; Brian Johnson 3; NASA 8

Chapter 2
George R. Collins 17; John M. Kauffman 33; Peter French 38; Brian Johnson 40

Chapter 3
Schweizer Aircraft Corporation 43; George R. Collins 43 (inset); Unusual Films 56

Chapter 4
George R. Collins 69; Unusual Films 69 (inset); USAir 85

Chapter 5
Library of Congress 89; Smithsonian Institution 89 (inset); Unusual Films 96, 99, 106; USDA 101

Chapter 6
Library of Congress 111 (both); Unusual Films 128

Chapter 7
Unusual Films 133 (both), 137, 138, 147, 152

Chapter 8
Boeing Commercial Aircraft Corporation 157; National Park Service 169; Unusual Films 172

Chapter 9
Boeing Commercial Aircraft Corporation 177; U. S. Air Force 177 (inset); Unusual Films 188, 197; Brian Johnson 198

Chapter 10
George R. Collins 203; USAir 203, 221, 228; Suzanne R. Altizer 207; Delta Airlines 218

Chapter 11
U.S. Air Force 233; NASA 233 (inset); G. David Koonts 241; George Rogier 251

Chapter 12
NOAA 259; NASA 259 (inset); Unusual Films 279; Brian Johnson 280; Tim Davis 281

Chapter 13
George R. Collins 285; U. S. Air Force 285 (inset); Brian Johnson 298

Chapter 14
U. S. Air Force 303; Library of Congress 303 (inset); Unusual Films 315; Jim Hargis 320

Chapter 15
Aramco 325; Brian Johnson 336

Chapter 16
Unusual Films 341, 362; World Bank 341 (inset)

Chapter 17
Craig Schmitman 367; Unusual Films 378, 381, 382

Chapter 18
Goodyear Tire & Rubber Company 387; George R. Collins 387 (inset); Doug Rumminger 389, 398